# Captive Warriors

TEXAS A&M UNIVERSITY
MILITARY HISTORY SERIES
23

# CAPTIVE
# WARRIORS

A Vietnam POW's Story

SAM JOHNSON AND JAN WINEBRENNER

*Drawings by Rod Keitz*

TEXAS A&M
UNIVERSITY
PRESS
COLLEGE STATION

*Library of Congress Cataloging-in-Publication Data*

Johnson, Sam, 1930–
    Captive warriors : a Vietnam POW's story / by Sam
Johnson and Jan Winebrenner ; drawings by Rod Keitz.
    — 1st ed.
        p.    cm. — (Texas A&M University military history
series ; 23)
    ISBN 0-89096-496-3
    1. Johnson, Sam, 1930–    .  2. Vietnamese Conflict,
1961–1975 – Prisoners and prisons, North Vietnamese.
3. Vietnamese Conflict, 1961–1975 – Personal narratives,
American.    4. Prisoners of war – United States –
Biography.    5. Prisoners of war – Vietnam – Biography.
I. Winebrenner, Jan.   II. Title.   III. Series.
DS559.4.J64    1992
959.704'37 – dc20                              91-28247
                                                CIP

# CONTENTS

# ACKNOWLEDGMENTS

The strong support of my wife, Shirley, made the writing of this book possible. Her courage and dedication throughout the most difficult period of our lives continues to be an inspiration to me. She, along with our children, Bob, Gini, and Beverly, enabled me to relive the years of my imprisonment so that they could be captured in writing.

Without the persistent urging of my brother-in-law, Jim Melton, this book would never have been started. He continually encouraged and challenged me to put my experiences in writing. Finding the perfect co-author was a result of a conversation with Dr. Homer Adams, who said we should find a writer with high moral values and a strong belief in God. That person was Jan Winebrenner. Special thanks to Bill Mc-Kenzie and Billy Clayton, Texas A&M University Board of Regents, for their help and encouragement.

I truly thank my long-time friend Rod Keitz, whose extraordinary ability as an illustrator brought visual life to the words in this book.

I am forever thankful for the support and friendship of the Alcatraz Gang. We share a special bond; however, I am also indebted to all the POWs who endured North Vietnam's horrors and whose courage was often an inspiration to me. They are all great Americans, and I thank them for the privilege of serving with them in the protection of freedom.

— Sam Johnson

Ten thousand thanks to my family for sharing my enthusiasm for this project. Throughout many months of writing and research, my husband, Ken, and my children, Matt and Molly, expressed their support and encouragement in a myriad of practical ways. Their excitement for the story often energized me and enabled me to renew my commitment to the task.

My thanks to Jay Gaines for time and interest given to this project. His advice was invaluable.

My deepest thanks to Sam and Shirley Johnson for inviting me into their lives and for trusting me with their most personal and powerful story. They have honored me.

— Jan Winebrenner

# Captive Warriors

# PROLOGUE

# Frontier of Disorder

Lyndon Johnson once called Asia "the outer frontier of disorder."[1] The term offers a graphic picture of Vietnam. Its history is filled with disorder and destruction. By the seventeenth century, the tiny nation had earned a reputation among its neighbors for its fierce determination to achieve autonomy. Its early fall to French hands failed to quench the nationalistic zeal of its people.

It is ironic to me that, while I was a kid growing up in Texas, the United States was applauding the revolutionary efforts of a Vietnamese named Ho Chi Minh. Though he was known to be a communist — a devoted student of Lenin — American politicians praised him when he led his people in a war to oust the imperialist forces of Japan. It seems we were not yet ready to accept Japan as a capitalist competitor in French Indochina. It was Ho Chi Minh and his followers, called the Viet Minh, who, little more than a decade later, led the rebellion against French domination. United States applause waned.

The French, drained and weakened by World War II, floundered pitifully against the Vietnamese revolutionaries, and by 1952, the United States was financing forty percent of France's war costs.

In 1953, while American families were driving Studebakers and learning to adjust television sets, U.S. politicians and military leaders were working with the French to aid Vietnam in its quest for independence and sovereignty while allowing the French to salvage some of their investments in Indochina.

The Vietnamese siege at Dienbienphu that defeated the French in 1954 astounded the world. It also set in motion events that would divide the country and set the stage for the most complex, misunderstood conflict of the twentieth century.

The warring factions, Ho's communist troops and the French colonialists, were separated and the gunfire quieted by the Geneva Agreement which sent Ho to the North, above the seventeenth parallel, and the French to the South. Once a stable peace could be established, the people of Vietnam would vote and choose for themselves the kind of government they desired.

3

In the South, Ngo Dinh Diem was appointed prime minister and entrusted with the task of scheduling free elections. Well-educated and a devout Catholic, Diem had already earned a reputation as a passionate nationalist who was anxious to be rid of French domination. The task ahead of him—to restore some sort of political order so that the Vietnamese people above and below the seventeenth parallel could choose their leaders—was monumental. The logistics of national elections would require the best of even the most masterful political strategists.

In the North, Ho Chi Minh represented himself as a zealous nationalist who dreamed of a united Vietnam. But he contradicted such lofty ideals with his own words. In an essay for *L'Humanité*, the organ of the French Communist Party, he once declared unrestrained nationalism a "dangerous phenomenon" that was detrimental to the communist goal in colonial areas.

Ho feared the strong leadership of Diem. He recognized that the simple country people of Vietnam followed Diem without reservation. Among the Catholics and the refugees from the North, Diem was a hero. The assertion that Diem refused to schedule elections because he believed Ho would have defeated him is as false as Ho's claims of nationalistic fervor.

Wary officials in the South knew the scheming tactics of Ho Chi Minh. His plan for free elections was that, in the North where fifty-five percent of the population of Vietnam resided, there would be only one party on the ticket: the communist party. Regardless of who was on the ballot in the South, simple percentages would assure Ho's political victory.

From the U.S. point of view, Ngo Dinh Diem was the candidate of choice for leadership of a united Vietnam. Diem adamantly opposed communism and Ho Chi Minh. He set about building a system of government in a country that was already heavily infiltrated by communists intent on his defeat. Although we had agreed not to interfere with the terms of the Geneva Agreement—that is, free elections—by the early 1960s, U.S. armed forces were actively involved in assisting Ngo Dinh Diem in establishing his government.

In the early months after the signing of the Geneva Agreement, more than a million North Vietnamese fled to the South to escape Ho's brutal communist regime. Many thousands more left the North not as refugees, but as Ho's henchmen, sent to build an intricate infrastructure in the South: the National Liberation Front (NLF).

The NLF has often been identified as simply a group of South Vietnamese who grew dissatisfied with Diem's methods and motives in governing, but the evidence and the testimony of the Vietnamese themselves tell a different story. The core of the NLF was made up of North

Vietnamese sent down by Ho Chi Minh for the express purpose of disrupting Diem's government and destroying all possibilities for a government other than Ho's communism in the South. Le Duan, North Vietnam's leader at the war's end in 1975, proudly claimed credit for leadership of the struggle in both North and South Vietnam since the earliest days of revolution. He boasted of the North's control over the final outcome of the war, stating often that the entire revolution was orchestrated by the ruling party in Hanoi.

During the early 1960s, the struggle in Vietnam began to dominate national newscasts in the United States. American families watched in horror as the miracle of television, now perfected and in color, brought into our homes the images of Buddhist monks drenched in gasoline and set on fire to become burning torches of protest against Diem's rule—at least, that was what the viewing audience was supposed to believe. But the evidence is that these religious conflicts that so plagued Diem's regime were carefully orchestrated media events, under the direction of the North, to destroy western support for the South's popular leader. Eyewitnesses report of Buddhist monks being "recruited" for suicide missions to stoke the fires of fury against the Catholic "despot," Diem, and to create the illusion of a religious fanatic relentlessly working to rid his country of peaceable, pious monks.

More accurately, President Diem was involved in a furious struggle for the political life of South Vietnam. In the twelve Buddhist pagodas he ordered seized, his military leaders found Soviet weapons and materials for building bombs—odd utensils for worship by a religion that expounds peace. Other convincing evidence proved him correct in his belief that the pagodas were being operated as command posts for the NLF. Diem's armies never harmed a brick or tile on the other five thousand Buddhist pagodas in the country.

Nevertheless, opposition against Diem grew. Large numbers of South Vietnamese aligned themselves with the National Liberation Front. Many had grown disillusioned with Diem's efforts and turned to embrace communist ideology. But there were many more who joined the NLF because they were afraid *not* to. In most villages, it was the communists, the members of the NLF, who had the guns. It was they who told the others which side to fight for. It was they who terrorized and murdered any who resisted.

Little by little, the NLF undercut Diem's regime by systematically murdering his government officials, and by 1963, U.S. support for him had nearly dried up. He was no longer seen as the leader who could guarantee democracy in Vietnam. The CIA backed a military coup to unseat him and replace him with a leader more compatible with American thinking. Diem and much of his family were murdered. Though some in the U.S. government argue it, the facts point overwhelmingly to our active participation in that bloody event.[2]

While U.S. intelligence was applauding itself for aiding in Diem's removal, Ho Chi Minh was also clapping his hands – delighted by the fact that his old nemesis was out of the way. He predicted clear sailing into South Vietnam now. Over the next two years, South Vietnam's constitution was dissolved, and ten different leaders came and went. When the dust finally settled, power was in the hands of Nguyen Van Thieu.

The chaos in South Vietnam continued. John F. Kennedy, then U.S. president, was deluged by South Vietnam's repeated requests for more aid and more American troops. He had already sent sixteen thousand troops to South Vietnam: the famed Green Berets, a counterinsurgency force, and marines whose primary purpose was to defend U.S. bases. He was reluctant to involve the United States further in this Southeast Asian conflict and repeatedly declined. After his assassination on November 22, 1963, his successor, Lyndon Baines Johnson, changed that answer to yes.

As he stepped into the oval office to pick up the power of the presidency, Johnson took hold of Vietnam and said, "I am not going to be the president who saw Southeast Asia go the way China went."[3] The famed phrase, "the domino theory," entered newspapers and textbooks, stating succinctly that if South Vietnam fell to communism, all Southeast Asia would fall too. It was a theory that would be violently tested over the next decade.

Johnson decided that the only way to end the conflict and guarantee free elections for South Vietnam was to escalate the war. He determined to increase the number of U.S. troops and assign them a more offensive role. But he needed justification for such a move. The Tonkin Gulf incident provided it.

In August, 1964, the news reached Congress that on two separate occasions, North Vietnamese patrol boats had fired on an American destroyer in international waters in the Tonkin Gulf. Though he was unable to persuade Congress to declare war, LBJ was able to wrestle from legislators the Tonkin Gulf Resolution, which gave him what he so desperately wanted: a reason to increase involvement in the war. He now had authority to use "all necessary measures to repel any armed attack against the United States and to prevent further aggression."

It would be years before it was revealed that the events in the Tonkin Gulf may have been carefully contrived. It may have been an elaborate facade, using some actual and fabricated events to justify increased military involvement in Vietnam.[4] Evidence indicates that the first attack may have occurred while the American destroyer was in North Vietnamese territorial waters, and the second reported attack may not have occurred at all.

In 1965, the United States launched the first television satellite into orbit. Now armed with the capacity to receive and relay instant reports to and from the war zone, the president began fighting the war like an armchair quarterback. LBJ usurped the military command, and dictated final target selection on the battlefield. Military strategists, the Strategic Air Command, began calling plays and making strategic calls from Omaha, Nebraska, twelve thousand miles away. The navy and air force in Vietnam began taking orders directly from the Pentagon in Washington, D.C., rather than from the field command in Saigon. The organization and military structure taught in the war college were cast aside; military authority in the theater of war was handed off to political and military leaders far removed from the scene of battle. Confusion and chaos soon characterized the war strategy.

From the earliest days of U.S. involvement, warfare methodology was a constant source of conflict. Should the U.S. military employ conventional methods or the newly touted unconventional warfare, counterinsurgency—the strategy Kennedy had so heartily endorsed for fighting this jungle war? The new warfare called for guerrilla operations. The tactical pattern implemented night ambushes and patrols, commando raids, and movement deep into enemy territory to fire on enemy supplies and equipment with little or no artillery and almost no combat air support.[5] At odds with this methodology were the traditionalists who wanted to rely on the principles of conventional warfare which requires roads for the transportation of troops, supplies, and artillery, and heavy use of air support against strategic targets.[6]

The objectives of war began to be in conflict, too. The military traditionally rewards its members for success—the number of sorties flown, amount of land taken, number of bridges claimed. Statistics such as these are vital to the consideration of a soldier's rank and promotion. In the new warfare, such measurements of success are vague. A quadrangle of land claimed in a midnight raid may be vacated in a few days and regained by the enemy before the jungle dew dries the next morning. To the traditionalists, the entire exercise is futile and foolish, but to the advocates of unconventional warfare, such action is considered an effective measure for countering the efforts of enemy guerrillas.

Further complicating matters were the arbitrary dicta coming out of the White House regarding which munitions and weapons could be used. LBJ's advisers convinced him that if the United States employed limited nuclear warfare, China would retaliate. Despite the fact that China had no such weaponry or capability for retaliation, LBJ announced to the world that the United States would not employ limited nuclear weapons. Having made that declaration, the world's strongest military power was then forced to fight the war with one hand tied behind its back. The watching world called us a paper tiger.

Extremely conscious of public opinion, LBJ grew uncomfortable with the increasing numbers of cameras in the war zone. Full-color horrors of the war played daily on U.S. newscasts. The president's goals for a "Great Society" seemed contradictory when uttered against a television background noisy with gunfire and the whirring engine sounds of helicopters hovering over tall jungle grass while the dead and wounded were lifted aboard. He worked to soften the visual effects of the war by limiting or prohibiting the use of the weaponry necessary to end it.

America became, in Lyndon Johnson's phrase, a "frontier of disorder." While military leaders and politicians in Washington, D.C., argued and struggled over warfare methodology and munitions, racial tensions between blacks and whites grew to violent proportions. Antiwar sentiment mushroomed and tens of thousands of people began gathering across the country to protest American involvement in what they considered Vietnam's own private revolution.

Meanwhile, communist troops in the South swelled to more than three hundred thousand. Ho's forces moved steadily forward, fueled and supplied by the Soviets and Chinese, intent on the goal of grabbing South Vietnam and establishing a communist state with no dividing lines.

On April 16, 1966, there were two hundred thousand Americans involved in the fight for South Vietnam. In a sense, we all unwittingly became puppets, dangling from the strings of American politicians intent on their own opportunism in a country torn by dissent. We were also puppets of the military strategists, who were themselves puppets of those making decisions far beyond the war zone.

But Ho's troops were puppets as well, manipulated by the Hanoi regime that dictated their every action and their every thought. And, perhaps most insidious of all, we, the American prisoners of war, became his puppets too. In his obsession to win international approval of his war of aggression against South Vietnam, he applied his most creative energies to employing unwilling and injured American POWs to tell his story. He danced us across the stage of world opinion and presented the world with the best orchestrated propaganda show this century has beheld.

## Notes

1. William Appleman Williams, Thomas McCormick, Lloyd Gardner, and Walter LaFeber, eds., *America In Vietnam* (Garden City: Anchor Press/Doubleday, 1985) p. 216.

2. Ibid.

3. Ibid.

4. Jim and Sybil Stockdale, *In Love and War* (New York: Harper & Row, 1984).

5. Richard Alan White, *The Morass* (New York: Harper and Row, 1984).

6. Ibid.

# ONE

# Modern Air Warriors

I opened my eyes to see thin shafts of light that seeped in through cracked window shutters and then bled quickly into the gray dimness. The torture room was empty now, except for my mangled form lying in a corner like a tossed-out carcass. The concrete floor was mottled with splotches of dried blood mixed with layers of grime. Peeling paint hung from stark white walls like limp streamers left over from a party in a shop of horrors.

I tried to sit up. *Oh, God, it hurts to breathe, to move . . .* Dizziness swamped me. I closed my eyes until it passed and then, with careful movements, inched myself upright until I could lean against a wall.

*Okay,* I told myself. *You're okay so far. Now try and stand.* Bracing my back against the wall, I used my legs to push myself to my feet.

I could stand, even walk. And my thoughts were clear.

*I'm not spitting blood. No internal injuries. I'm okay.*

I peered out at the courtyard through a crack in the shutter. There was little to see: an occasional Vietnamese walking by, and the dingy, once-white buildings I had seen before. I sank back down on the floor and returned my attention to the torture room.

The desk and chair that the interrogator had used during the hours of questioning the night before had left with him. The guards had carried them in when he entered and carried them out again as he left, leaving the room with a single adornment: a large steel hook which hung from the ceiling like a meat hook in a butcher shop.

My gut tightened. My imagination went crazy. I closed my eyes tightly against a picture of limp and bleeding men, their bodies slung over the point of the hook like slabs of beef. But the images entered unbidden and stayed, like torture scenes from an old horror movie frozen on screen. I could not close them out. I could not wipe them away. My dislocated shoulder and shattered arm hung from me, useless appendages.

I shook my head to try to clear away the haunting picture. Hours later, I learned that nothing I imagined equaled the sadistic realities the communist North Vietnamese practiced on their prisoners of war.

---

Thailand in April is hot and muggy, like a Texas summer. But my Texas home was far from my thoughts that afternoon in 1966 as I strode down the flight line on the air base in Ubon, Thailand, toward the F-4 Phantom I was to fly into North Vietnam. This was to be my twenty-fifth night mission with the 433rd Fighter Squadron, Satan's Angels. There was nothing to indicate it would be my last. No gut feelings, no premonitions.

I had always believed such feelings should not be allowed a space in the mind of a professional. And I was, of all things, a professional: a member in good standing of the brotherhood of fighter pilots who lived for fast, hot planes and the challenge of battle. I had neither the time nor the patience to consider omens. I did, however, wage a daily war with frustration.

I was operations officer of the 433rd. As my expertise was in weapons and weapons training and delivery, I knew the munitions and weaponry necessary to carry out our missions, yet we seldom had them. Added to that frustration was the fact that the objectives of this war were often unclear, and the conditions for carrying them out were implausible.

Consider the air base we used at Ubon. It was operated and controlled by the Royal Thai Air Force. The space allotted to the U.S. military was far from adequate. Our F-4 Phantoms were squeezed onto a small ramp that offered no revetments, no protection. A too-narrow taxiway led to a short runway that made every pilot gasp at the thought of having to abort on takeoff. A barrier that could stop a plane at 190 miles per hour stretched across the runway at all times, but few pilots relished the idea of being yanked to a stop in a plane loaded with bombs.

Walking toward my plane, I was halted by a shout from squadron operations.

"Major, we've got a communication link to the States. You want to talk to your wife?"

The room was noisy with the sound of the air conditioner, and the phone connection was poor. Communications had patched us from Thailand to the Philippines to Hawaii and San Francisco before finally connecting with Shirley's voice in Texas. It was good to hear her, but she sounded upset. She was worried about me because of a recent letter I had sent, telling her about a mission I had flown over Dienbienphu, and how I'd gotten into an air-to-ground shootout with the North Vietnamese and their heavy guns. I had told her I was unhappy with the way the war was being run, that I disliked the air-to-ground combat stuff I was having to do.

My real love was air-to-air combat: dogfighting. As director of the Air Force Fighter Weapons School, the equivalent of the navy's Top

Gun, I had spent hundreds of hours teaching and practicing the tactics of dogfighting. It was what I did best. I liked seeing the enemy—battling against another pilot eye to eye. I was trained to pit my skill against the skill of another fighter pilot rather than avoid impartial and impersonal ground fire from unknown sources.

But regardless of the manner of fighting, I was confident in my abilities as a pilot, and I tried to communicate that confidence to Shirley.

"As long as you can see the shells coming at you there's nothing to worry about," I told her.

She was neither reassured nor amused.

We talked about our three children, Bobby, who had just turned fifteen; Gini, twelve; and Beverly, nine. Shirley filled me in on what had gone on in their lives since her last letter, and we talked about what they would be doing over the next few weeks. We had agreed to make tape recordings for each other. It seemed like a good way to stay close. Perhaps hearing each other's voices would shrink the size of the oceans that lay between us. I had just made my first tape for her, and I told her I would send it as soon as I returned from this mission.

If I'd had any premonitions that this would be my last conversation with her for nearly seven years I would have said many other things. I would have tried to prepare her somehow for the separation that lay ahead for us. I would have given her some suggestions and instructions about the many practical matters of family life she had always left to me. But I had no way of knowing. And so we said the things husbands and wives in love say to each other long distance, said good-bye, and hung up the phone.

I joined Lieutenant Larry Chesley, my backseater for the mission, and we walked together down the ramp toward the F-4 Phantom parked in its slot on the flight line.

Larry was a great backseater, or "whizzo," as they were sometimes called. He was a veteran of over ninety missions, and I was glad to have him behind me. I knew he chafed at having to accommodate the Pentagon's idea of pilot training by riding in the back seat. He was more than ready to move up front to the controls—was even thinking of extending for an extra fifty missions to fly front seat.

The Phantom was really a navy aircraft designed for fleet defense, for firing missiles at distant air targets, such as enemy aircraft. Under Robert McNamara's consolidation practices in the Defense Department, the air force was ordered to use it too—never mind that it had no bombing system for air-to-ground combat, which the air force needed for ground support. Never mind that it had neither gun nor sight system for both bomb targeting and dogfighting. And most objectionable, it departed from the air force philosophy of a single-seat fighter.

Millions of dollars later, the Pentagon presented the air force with an ungainly specimen hastily fitted with bombing and gun systems, its gun sights little more than chewing gum stuck on the windshield. Its back-seat system of radar was to be manned by air force–trained pilots who, unlike the navy's radar operators, had little expertise in radar and weapons systems and whose hearts were in the front seat.

Irony hit me as I approached the plane. We were preparing to engage an elusive enemy in a war with no real defined goals. We were using an F-4 Phantom equipped with a makeshift bomb and gun sight and an added-on gun pod. We were carrying partial loads of munitions and often had only minimal radar and weapons systems operational. It took the entire length of the war to improve these deficiencies in the F-4.

I shook my head to clear away the troubling thoughts that had been with me for days. Chesley and I were modern air warriors. We would fly whatever we were commanded to fly.

I wiped drops of perspiration from my forehead. The afternoon heat was intense through the dark, olive-drab flight suit I wore. My survival vest, loaded with gun, radio, and other miscellaneous essentials, hung heavy on my shoulders. The tropical air was thick with moisture that rose from a river flowing near the base. The sight of dark-skinned natives riding the river on narrow, flimsy boats to hunt for tigers along the bank reminded me again how far I was from Texas.

Larry and I reviewed the afternoon's briefings. We had studied maps, photos, bomb and weather charts, and been assigned call names and frequencies; Chesley and I in the lead plane would be Panther One, our wingman Panther Two. I had plotted our strategy and tactics: we would fly in low, evading radar detection, and attempt to use the element of surprise in our attack.

When the paperwork was completed, the briefings over, April 16, 1966, was history—on paper. Only its execution remained.

Our mission was simple. Reconnaissance photos showed new enemy road construction, believed to be a branch of an already extensive supply system which delivered Soviet and Chinese weapons from North Vietnam to the National Liberation Front (South Vietnamese communists) in the south.

On the map, the road through the jungle was a thin, wiggly line drawn across markings that indicated mountains and passes. It ended at an open clearing on the river bank where a truck park and a ferry transport system had been built. The ferry, a primitive rope and pulley system, with barge-like rafts consisting of logs tied together, seemed hardly adequate for the trucks it carried, but it provided another link in the supply chain to the communists in South Vietnam.

Often, night missions did little more than harass the enemy, but I expected tonight's to be different. The road was new, only recently discovered by intelligence, so the North probably felt fairly safe in using it. And we were coming in over it before dark. It was likely we would be able to catch supply trucks en route to the South.

Larry and I, in formation with the second plane, were to complete armed reconnaissance along the road—attack anything that moved on the road. Since only the military owned and operated vehicles, we knew we could shoot without fear of harming civilians. We would be looking for targets of opportunity: convoys, and any other military vehicles and equipment. We would report all sightings back to intelligence.

Aerial photos, brought back by photo reconnaissance planes and interpreted by experts, revealed dozens of supply trucks camouflaged among the heavily forested areas surrounding the clearing. This truck park, hidden from view, was to be our secondary target, if we didn't unload all our fire power on the road.

The mission was routine. We expected very little air defense from the ground. We had reviewed an in-depth intelligence analysis of the target area defenses—an analysis that included information about anti-aircraft as well as enemy fighter interceptor threats, such as Russian-built fighter planes (MiGs). The report showed no serious threats, no surface-to-air missiles (SAMs) in that region of North Vietnam.

Nothing had been overlooked. We were confident.

We reached the plane, stowed our gear in the cockpit, and began the walk around the plane to inspect it before takeoff.

"Napalm!" I exclaimed, seeing the canisters fitted on my plane. "We really do have napalm!"

I shook my head and grumbled as I returned the salute of the half-naked crew chief who leaned against the body of the plane.

"What'd ya expect, Major? Miracles?" he answered as he wiped his hands on an oil-blackened rag.

"For once it would be nice to come out here and have the right stuff hanging from my bird."

"Yeah, and I'd like a case of Scotch, but I ain't complaining. Saigon's got the one-thirties being stingy all over. We barely got enough to give everyone a load."

"Typical," I replied.

The situation should not have surprised me. Air force headquarters in Saigon issued "fragmentation orders" (frag orders) stating what munitions were to be used for each mission. A rail system from a Thai seaport delivered most of our munitions from the navy; but when they ran out, deliveries had to be flown in from all over the world. Even NATO stockpiles in Europe were being steadily depleted. On those occasions,

Sam, far right, in flight school, 1951

Sam, Shirley, and Bob, celebrating a joint Thanksgiving and Christmas, November, 1952, before Sam left for Korea. *Dallas Morning News* staff photo

Sam in Korea, 1953, on wing of F-86 named "Shirley's Texas Tornado"

Sam as first lieutenant, 1957, solo pilot on Thunderbirds. U.S. Air Force photo

Sam (seated, with sunglasses) with Thunderbirds and crew chiefs, 1957

Thunderbirds in front of North American F-100 Super Sabre at Nellis Air Force Base, Nevada, 1957. *From left:* Capt. William H. Scott, Jr., narrator; Capt. Robert H. McIntosh, spare pilot; Capt. Douglas D. Brenner, right wing; Maj. J. A. Robinson, leader; Capt. J. M. Bartley, left wing; Capt. Sam Johnson, solo pilot, and 1st lt. W. R. Pogue, slot man. U.S. Air Force photo

Sam with Shirley, 1958

Sam and children, 1958

huge C-130 Hercules transports delivered weaponry and supplies to the various air bases.

The demands of the war zone often meant that we at the Eighth Tactical Fighter Wing received only minimal supplies and sometimes none of the weaponry listed on the frag orders. And, as on this particular day, individual squadrons scrambled for whatever munitions were delivered. I seldom knew what I would be outfitted with.

I was astounded to find my plane loaded with the gasoline-based jelly. This was the first time I had seen it on the base; it was also the first time I would carry it into battle. I had flown practice flights dropping napalm, and I understood its function as a weapon of war. Because of its unique properties as a jelly-gas, it spills out in a straight line and can stop an advancing army. It is best suited to close air support of ground troops, as it had been used in previous wars, such as World War II.

The spreading explosion of fiery napalm can suck all the oxygen out of the air up to one hundred yards away, creating a vacuum and a twenty-mile-per-hour fire storm that can suffocate people without ever touching them. Many an American ground soldier in Europe during World War II owes his life to the air force's proper use of napalm against an advancing enemy troop.

My training as a soldier and fighter pilot preempted any feelings of revulsion at the thought of dropping napalm on an enemy target. I believed napalm to be no more horrible than fragmentary bombs, which explode and send their steel fragments bone-deep into their victims. What I did feel, again, was frustration: napalm was not suited to the objectives of this mission. But it seemed Washington was not concerned with suitability, nor with consistency or rationality. The U.S. rules of war prohibited us from taking napalm into North Vietnam—but made no such prohibition regarding South Vietnam.

It was a state department restriction on the Pentagon because of ongoing negotiations between the United States and North Vietnam. Someone, somewhere in a war policy meeting in the White House decided that prohibiting the use of napalm in Ho Chi Minh's backyard would mean the peacemaking efforts could proceed without propaganda interference.

It was a public relations thing. Vietnam was the first war of its kind —the first war ever fought on television. For the first time the visual horrors of war, previously seen only by those in combat or shown frozen in magazine photos, were able to penetrate the family rooms of America via the television camera and satellite.

Vietnam was a first for America in other ways too. It was the first time we sent in our air force to fight without any intention of following up with ground forces. And, as the war stretched out over the years, it would also become the first war Americans fought on foreign soil without the support of European allies. Even the weak bond of the Southeast Asia Treaty Organization (SEATO) disintegrated as the war intensified.

I thought again, *It's a dumb way to run a war, Mr. President.*

There was no doubt that LBJ was a major player in this public relations game. Concern for U.S. interests and the protection of U.S. fighting men hung low on his priority ladder. Again and again the military objectives of the war had been sacrificed for the sake of public opinion. He refused to rebuild weapon supplies in the States, while draining dry the European stockpiles. He was trying to run a war, maintain a peaceful environment in the United States, and be true to the country's NATO commitment. It seemed to me he was failing in all three objectives.

"We don't even have a full load." Chesley stared at the four 150-gallon napalm canisters suspended below the Phantom. It could carry three times that number of incendiaries. And we had only two of a possible four air-to-air missiles.

"Hope we don't meet any MiGs," he said shaking his head.

"Yeah, I know," I answered.

The crew chief wiped a black smear across his face with his greasy rag and tried to laugh. "It's been a slow week."

The dangers of this mission began pressing in on me. Inside my flight suit, sweat trickled down my body in little streams. I knew the hot, damp air was only partially to blame. But there was no point in fuming about the munitions problem. Our supply source was a long way from Ubon, and we had no options but to execute our mission with what was sent us.

"Well, let's get on with it, Larry. Start engines is seventeen-thirty."

We continued visual inspection of our plane.

"How's the cannon?" Chesley asksed the crew chief. As backseater he was responsible for the munitions preflight check.

"It's perfect, Lieutenant," was the answer. "I had the maintenance chief tear the gun completely apart and rebuild it a piece at a time."

"What's the problem?" I didn't like the sound of that conversation, or the possibility of yet another hindrance to the success of this mission.

"I flew this plane on a mission last night, and the gun jammed," Chesley answered.

"What happened?"

"The usual. We pulled the trigger and . . ." he shook his head. "Nothing. Not a sound."

I walked over to look closely at the plane's belly where the 20 mm gun was bolted. I was disturbed but not surprised. No air force pilot would have been. The Phantom was navy. It didn't need a gun. But the air force adaptation in the early 1960s had fitted it with the M-61A1 gun pod which, when it worked, was a fine weapon, an excellent ground support gun that doubled as a MiG destroyer. But it had a success rate of about fifty percent. There was always a gamble: which half of your mission would fail?

"Well, Sergeant?" I put it to the crew chief.

"She's good, Major. Supervised her strip-down myself. All circuits checked okay. We'll still have to check her upstairs, see what the switches say."

Even after a cockpit check, green lights didn't guarantee success; I knew that. But we had to trust them. We had no choice.

At thirty-five years old, I was a veteran fighter pilot. I knew about risks and gambles. I had learned to fly at the controls of an early World War II fighter-turned-trainer, the T-6, or the "Terrible Texan," as we sometimes called it. I had earned a high class standing and had been given my choice of flying vocations. There was no hesitation: I loved fighters.

The T-33 and the P-80 initiated me into the jets. By the time I reached Nellis Air Force Base in Las Vegas, I was ready to begin training in air-to-air warfare.

I never really thought of myself as highly competitive. But dogfighting over Korea in F-86s and sharing air space with pilots like Buzz Aldrin and John Glenn revealed a part of myself I hadn't known before. I was an only child—no siblings to stimulate and hone that competitive edge. My middle-class home life in Dallas, Texas, led me toward interests in business, insurance, real estate, and law. I had never flown a plane—never even flown *in* a plane—until the Korean conflict interrupted my life.

At Southern Methodist University in Dallas, I was a member of the first ROTC graduating class, and in 1951, at the end of summer camp in Colorado, my class was activated. I applied for flight school and was accepted.

Sixty-two combat missions over North Korea with the 16th Fighter Squadron, 51st Fighter Wing, made me confident. I had been credited with one kill, one probable kill, and a damage in air-to-air combat. Another twenty-four combat missions over North Vietnam only increased that confidence; however, I wasn't foolish enough to believe I had made my own success. I knew I was part of a team of specialists, and each member was essential to the whole. I understood the principle of interdependence. But I had no idea of the limits to which that principle would be tested in the months and years ahead.

When the final review of the mission was complete, we climbed into the plane's cockpit and rechecked all switches. I glanced at my watch. Five seconds to start engines.

"Fire engines!" I commanded, and I flipped the switch to left and right for start. Two ear-splitting blasts of power answered as both engines started instantly. I pushed the throttles forward.

"You're clean, Major. She's looking good," the sergeant's voice crackled to me through the intercom.

"Thanks for the help. See you in a couple of hours."

"Roger, good luck."

The chief gave Panther One a thumbs-up signal as he disconnected his intercom jack. Chesley and I returned the signal. Panther One began to roll forward. A hundred feet down the line, Panther Two slid from its parking place. It, too, carried limited ordnance, and was riding lighter than usual. Tower instructions directed the planes to the runway.

"Good evening, Panther. You're cleared for takeoff."

# TWO

# Captured!

It was dusk when we left Thailand and entered Laotian airspace. Thai authorities objected to fully armed planes flying in their jurisdiction, so we waited until clear of her borders to run a systems check.

Chesley scanned the switches on the console and reported, "All ordnance shows armed. Radar clear."

A short while later we flew low and fast over the border into North Vietnam. Beneath us in the gathering darkness, the supply road lay empty. No trucks moved, no troops scrambled for cover along the shoulder.

We completed our reconnaissance of the road, flying a standard weave pattern, with our wingman in a loose formation on the inside of Panther One's next maneuver. If we rolled left, Panther Two stayed thirty to fifty degrees behind and to the left. This was a common procedure that provided more effective visual "recce" (reconnaissance) of the road. It also provided a base for "jinking," should the need arise.

Jinking is the execution of quick aerial movements in any direction every few moments, making a plane look like a mosquito darting about in no predictable pattern. It also makes it difficult for an enemy to lock gun sights on you for more than a couple of seconds. Never far from my mind was the knowledge that if we gave them three seconds of steady flight the chances were good that they could shoot us down.

Gunfire erupted below us as we neared our target area in the southeast corner of the Quang Binh province.

"Nice little reception," Larry commented.

"Well, the local militia's got to get out and feel useful every now and then." I grinned beneath my oxygen mask. "The fresh air's good for them. Besides, the people think they're doing something important when their army makes 'em line up and shoot at the great big bad airplane."

It always struck me as funny to think of people firing bullets up into the sky at American bombers. From our low altitude we could see them gathered outside their huts and lined up to fire rifles at us. The curtain of bullets they sent up toward us was not harmless. Their weapons had a range and accuracy distance of two to three thousand feet, while our altitude was usually only about two hundred feet to avoid enemy radar.

Though their rifles could not be called toys, the people seemed to me like children playing at war. I wondered, as I had often wondered when flying into North Vietnam, how the villagers always seemed to know the exact time we would arrive overhead. It was too neat, too well planned to be a sudden, spontaneous response to the sound of our engines.

"Two minutes to target," Chesley said into the intercom.

"Systems check?"

"Affirmative. Bombs set. Gun's ready."

Chesley scanned the switches before him on the console and reported Panther Two in position forty-five degrees behind and slightly above us.

"Altitude steady on five hundred," Chesley reported from the back seat. "Speed's four-hundred fifty knots.

"Altitude's two hundred, speed's at four-fifty," Chesley's voice continued the call-outs.

"Roger," I answered. I scanned the land below, hunting for the horizon that seemed to blend with the darkness and create a shapeless void.

"Visual contact should be imminent. Thirty seconds to target."

Off to our right, a vague outline of a mountain rose up out of the jungle, telling us we were nearing our target. The maps showed a river flowing just beyond the mountain's base and the road we were following should show the ferry transport where road met river. As we readied for contact, I knew Chesley shared the tension I felt.

"Altitude's one-fifty. Speed's up to four-seventy."

Before I could respond, lights burst from the ground and exploded in the air around us. These were no farmers' rifles shooting into the air. A North Vietnamese army division fired tracer bullets at us from heavy antiaircraft guns. I had no thoughts of children's games now.

The radio silence we had maintained since takeoff at Ubon was no longer necessary. I flicked a radio switch and activated the mission's frequency to command, "Two, go right!"

Panther Two rolled hard into a right turn. I rolled Panther One to the left and began climbing. By splitting our formation, we could force the antiaircraft gun crew to choose between targets. If they hesitated, even slightly, I could use that split second to get a fix on the gun's location.

"We're at three-hundred. Speed, four-thirty."

I didn't like being that high. Survival in this situation meant flying low, "on deck," skimming treetops at altitudes no greater than fifty feet, where you weren't exposed to random shots from any direction. But if we were to knock out that gun, we had to find its exact location, and that meant gaining some altitude for observation.

Tracers revealed the position of the gun at the end of the road, across the river. Even in the darkness I could easily see them. I turned eastward to see two guns firing from the opposite bank. I guessed them to be Russian; the smaller looked to be a 12.5 mm, the other a rotating quad 50 mm. There were no doubt several more I couldn't see. It was more than adequate protection for an average-looking parking lot. No pilot would want to linger for long.

I memorized the specifics of the guns and the truck park and began a quick descent, easing down to fifty feet. In a few scant moments, we altered course, radioed Panther Two, and rendezvoused near the mountain.

"Guns are directly across the river from the end of the road," I informed Panther Two. "We'll circle around the hill, kick in the burners, and take 'em from the west. Over."

"Roger, One. Will be waiting for you. Over."

"On the deck, flat out at six-fifty," Chesley reported.

"Right, backseat. We're checking upstairs."

I pulled back on the stick and felt the plane lurch upward a hundred feet, to give us a last look at the target area. Enemy shots from below flew up toward us, but detonated harmlessly.

"Back to fifty," Chesley called out, as I brought the plane back down. "Speed's six-seventy."

Panther Two answered with, "Take 'em, Cowboy!"

The plan was simple. We would neutralize the antiaircraft gun with bursts from the 20 mm, then eliminate the truck park with the two loads of napalm.

We were a mile out and closing fast. The guns slid into place across my viewing screen and I positioned my hands on the controls. As the sights lined up, I squeezed the trigger, my ears ready for the familiar rattle of gunfire from the Phantom's underbelly.

Nothing happened. No sounds. No tracers' path in the darkness.

"Gun's not firing!" I shouted.

Instinctively I ducked my head down to look at the switches. My attention was dangerously divided between rechecking the gun switches and executing jinking maneuvers to avoid the explosive debris flying around us.

Green lights showed operational, all switches on.

"Gun shows armed," Chesley answered as he rapidly reviewed all the switches.

I kept my finger on the trigger, hoping the gun would activate. I tried jiggling the trigger and cycled the switches. But nothing worked. The gun was dead.

"We'll have to burn 'em, Larry," I said, referring to the gallons of napalm. Without a gun, we would have to go in low and fast and unprotected and drop the canisters on the target.

Chesley answered quickly, "Speed at six-sixty, and we're still on deck."

The next instant gunfire hit us.

Chesley felt it first — an increasing steady shake. But before he could alert me, the plane began a porpoising motion, leaping up and down. I had never felt anything like that, at that speed, in a plane before.

Pilots commonly call that out-of-control sensation a "J. C." maneuver, a nickname bred from the kind of terror that makes one scream, "Jesus Christ!" In those moments, as my plane dove and leaped as if with a mind of its own, that name was on my lips as a desperate prayer for help.

"Must be in the tail!" Chesley shouted.

"I know it," I called back. "It's the stab-aug — the warning light is on!"

The plane's stability augmentation provides smooth flight at high speeds. With its capabilities damaged, the only way to stabilize was to nose the plane up and reduce speed. But the higher altitude exposed us to greater risk from flak. We could stay on deck and continue jinking, but that was dangerous, too. I didn't like the idea of flying low over the trees without complete control of the plane.

There really was no choice at all. I tilted Panther One up thirty degrees.

"Five hundred feet, speed six-even," Chesley called out.

In the next instant, another shell exploded against the plane and rocked us hard against our seats.

"Hit again!" yelled Chesley.

"Yeah, I felt it!" I looked down. All emergency lights on the panels had lit up. Another boom shook us.

"And again!" Chesley shouted.

"The right engine's on fire," I called out as a fire warning lit up on the panel.

Instinct took over. I shut down the right engine and threw the left engine into afterburner to maintain our speed. Our survival depended on that extra thrust.

I remember my fingers closing around the throttle, and feeling the stick yanked forward out of my hand. At that moment, the Phantom nosed down and sped toward the ground. The negative gravity of the sudden rapid descent lifted me from my seat, and the intense pressure slammed me against the plane's glass canopy, even though my seatbelt was cinched tight. I struggled to reach out with my right arm toward the control stick. When I finally wrapped both hands around it, it wouldn't budge.

Every ounce of strength I could gather fought against the frozen stick; first pushing, then pulling, to try to break the fatal plunge of the Phantom.

"Larry, get out!" I shouted. "Repeating — get out!"

No response. Vital seconds passed. I checked the intercom. It was still working, though most of the other equipment no longer functioned.

"Larry, get out!" I called again.

Still no answer. I grabbed the yellow and black striped ring beneath my seat and yanked it to activate the ejection system.

The canopy jettisoned. A small pilot chute flew up and filled with air. A second later the seat ejected, slamming into my backbone.

The main chute trailed out into the sky, and its silk folds filled the air around me with the sound of hundreds of birds flying over. As it opened, I could feel my body snap straight and my arms and legs flail wildly.

Jump school had taught me that the first action upon ejection is to examine the panels of the opened chute. I considered it nothing short of a miracle that I had them all. I remember being impressed that anything could stay intact after a sudden deceleration from six hundred miles per hour to near nothing. It had all happened in four short seconds.

Below me, the plane continued to hurtle toward the ground. *Get out, Larry,* I begged silently.

Panther One rolled toward the ground in a ball of red and orange. I estimated its altitude and began counting, knowing in another second Chesley's survival would be impossible. Just when I was sure he would be lost, a tiny speck of white pricked the darkness; then the spreading light of a main chute told me he was out of the plane. Then, from my seat in the sky, I watched Panther One hit the ground and explode.

I had never imagined this could happen to me. I was too good to get shot down! But after sixty-two missions over Korea and twenty-five over Vietnam, I had been betrayed by my own weapon. I hung helplessly in the air over enemy territory, moving closer every second to possible capture and/or death. The irony was bitter. But there was no time to mourn—either for myself or for the plane. I had to think about surviving. I felt grateful to be alive, and I determined to stay that way.

Below me another explosion erupted, sending bright red and orange flames into the sky. *Maybe the mission wasn't a complete failure after all,* I thought, as Panther One's limited load of napalm torched a nearby building. And there was satisfaction in knowing I'd been able to radio the gun positions to my wingman, Panther Two, before ejection.

The ground was coming at me quickly. I figured I must have been about eight hundred feet above the ground at the time I ejected. I tried to remember the training I'd gotten at Fort Bragg. I was supposed to be equipped for just such a crisis. I had to take stock of myself.

*My gloves,* I thought, *I've lost my gloves . . . my watch! And my helmet and mask!* Then, *My arm. It's twisting! Oh, God, it's broken completely off!*

I watched my right arm windmill for a second or two and then tried to reach out with my left to pull it close against my body.

*Whoa, something's wrong with the left one too,* I thought, as the shoulder snapped loudly. *It's not working, but got to get that other arm in before landing . . .*

I don't know how, but I managed to use my left arm to place my right arm close to my chest. But then I had no arms to adjust the chute's risers and direct my landing. I'd have to take whatever the ground offered me.

*Got to find the top of the trees, keep legs bent . . . Be ready for landing roll . . .*

I couldn't make the trees. A dry rice paddy rose up to meet me. It was the softest landing I'd ever made. I landed standing up between the plow rows, but downward momentum quickly pulled me into a sitting position on the soft ground. *What to do now?* I thought.

I knew I was in the middle of a North Vietnamese army division. I had to find a place to hide, quickly. The survival vest I wore held a .38 pistol and a radio—but with my useless arms hanging at my sides, how would I get them out? I looked around helplessly. Parachute paraphernalia draped from me like strings from a broken marionette. I had to figure out some way to disentangle myself without the use of my arms. Suddenly, two Vietnamese in loose, black pajama-like garb appeared and raced toward me, one waving a machete and the other a pistol.

*I'm dead,* I thought. But my despair quickly turned to astonishment as the two cut the risers on my chute to release me and motioned to me to get up. I struggled to try and rise out of the soft dirt of the rice paddy, but my legs were suddenly limp and shaking. The two Vietnamese reached toward me, and with gentle hands, pulled me to my feet. In hushed voices, they whispered to each other and pushed me forward toward the jungle that surrounded us and spread up the nearby mountain.

It didn't make sense, but these men were trying to rescue me. I held my broken right arm with the injured left one and began stumbling with them toward the jungle. In only a few moments, I was running almost easily toward what I hoped would be safety from the scores of North Vietnamese soldiers who were probably already scouring the jungle for me.

By the time we had crossed three rice paddies and reached the edge of the jungle, the adrenaline that had been aiding my escape was depleted. We met with a steep climb into the rough mountains that bordered the entire western edge of the country, and my legs resisted every step. Though there was a full moon, the dense trees cut off all light, and thick jungle forced us into single file on a narrow trail.

We ran on in total darkness, one Vietnamese in front of me and another behind. Strong hands pushed against my back when I lagged, or pulled me forward by my survival jacket when I slowed down or stumbled. Their voices chattered softly back and forth, in turn scolding me and then encouraging me, as if assuming I could understand their un-intelligible words.

I was constantly aware of the radio and gun in my pockets, but my arms wouldn't work. They seemed unable to respond to any of the commands my brain sent them. So I just kept running, my body slumped forward at a sharp angle toward the ground and my arms folded helplessly at my torso.

At a fork in the path, my rescuers seemed to hesitate just a moment before turning quickly to the right to continue into higher terrain. A sudden loud shout coursed through the jungle, and the Vietnamese stopped as if frozen. They answered back in Vietnamese and then, changing sides suddenly, they shoved me to the ground. They fumbled with the survival vest I was wearing and stripped me of the pistol and radio I had been unable to handle for myself.

A Vietnamese officer stepped into view and shone a flashlight down into my face. He leaned over me and yanked the vest off me. Then, with harsh commands and rifle gestures, he sent my rescuers running off into the jungle darkness. They ran back down the mountain trail without daring a backward look at me. I knew, without doubt, that if they had resisted the officer's orders and attempted to show me further compassion, at least a dozen rifles would have filled them with bullets. I could not blame them for running back into the safe cover of the mountain's darkness.

The jungle was suddenly filled with North Vietnamese soldiers. Within moments, I was surrounded by soldiers dressed in dirty khaki uniforms and caps adorned with a single, bright red star.

Their hatred of me was an almost palpable thing hanging in the night air. They shouted obscenities and jabbed and struck me with their rifles. At a terse command, two soldiers took hold of me and pushed me roughly ahead of them toward the mountain trail I had just climbed. My legs crumpled, but the soldiers pulled me upright and pushed me on. I moved slowly and awkwardly, prodded constantly, my mind deluged with thoughts I had not had time to consider until this moment.

*Just how bad off am I?* I wondered. *Can I escape?*

I knew that most successful escapes occur almost immediately after capture. It had to be now. But how? Without the use of my arms I had little chance. I couldn't fight my way out, or swim or climb or even drive — should I be so lucky as to get a chance at a truck. And I could see dozens of them, camouflaged among the trees, as we passed down the trail and approached the river area that had been cleared for the ferry transport system. But a truck was no good to me if I had no arms to drive it.

Then, before my discouraging thoughts could paralyze me, I heard the sound of aircraft overhead. Low over the treetops zoomed two navy fighters, A-1s. I watched them drop their bombs and score a direct hit on the larger antiaircraft gun—the position of which I had radioed to Panther Two before bail-out. I learned later that my wingman had radioed our situation to the navy who were flying a mission nearby. They diverted from their target with the hope of rescuing us.

The explosion sent the gun and its crew catapulting into the air. Shouts and screams erupted all around me. Before I could wonder if this might be my chance to escape, one of my guards struck me with the butt of his rifle and shoved me into a slit trench.

I remember thinking, *I've never seen a direct hit on a gun before . . . the gun barrel split from its base!* And then, almost laughing, *Ha, the planes are already gone and the Vietnamese have just now started firing their flak—good job, Navy!*

And then shock set in and I blacked out.

I don't know how long I lay there, but it seemed like hours. The two soldiers eventually returned and brought along what I guessed was a medic. He looked at me and ordered a stretcher. My guards resented the task of carrying me, their enemy, and used the act of placing me on the stretcher as an opportunity for torture, pushing and pulling me roughly onto the canvas litter. They picked up the ends of the stretcher and began carrying me through the truck park.

Even in the darkness I could see that this place was not just a primitive clearing in the jungle to park a few trucks. It was a large settlement, and there were more trucks than I had at first thought. It seemed as though there was a well-camouflaged truck behind every tree—at least three times more than we had figured when we had planned our bombing mission. They were full of supplies, and all were using the ferry boat to cross the river. No lights shone anywhere, but all movement and activity had resumed, as if the navy bombers had never flown over.

Even though I was badly hurt, my military instincts were still intact. I remember thinking, *I need to remember all this for intelligence.* I twisted my body on the stretcher, trying to get a good look at everything we passed: vehicles, manpower, buildings. I was determined to count, to memorize, and analyze, as if I was scheduled for a routine debriefing session in the morning.

We passed a few empty trucks, and I wondered if my guards might put me into one and drive off, but they continued walking through the truck park and out into the jungle. After a while, I let my body sink back against the taut fabric of the stretcher, and I eventually drifted off into a restless shallow sleep.

It was hours later when we stopped at a tiny thatched shack. A family of at least ten sat inside eating together. The soldiers entered the hut, pushed them aside, and commandeered the shelter for their own use. The hard dirt floor slammed into my injured back as my guards dropped the stretcher in a corner of the hut. They took up positions on either side of the tiny room and sat down. The family quickly offered their meager supply of food to the soldiers.

The tiny, dark room bulged with small people dressed in dark, baggy clothes. They bustled about here and there, speaking in sometimes shrill, sometimes whispered, sing-song tones. The soldiers barked out terse commands that sounded too loud in the confines of the little grass and reed shack.

An old man, curious and perhaps somewhat compassionate, came over to me and tried to spoon something like soup into my mouth. I shook my head and turned away from the stench in the bowl, but the old man persisted. He chattered something I couldn't understand and pushed the spoon toward my mouth again. My survival instincts told me to try, just try and eat, if only for the strength it might provide. The old man seemed to read my mind. He nodded at me, spoke again and, seeming pleased with himself, dipped the spoon back into the foul-smelling broth.

I remember being struck with the incongruity of the setting in that small hut: the soldiers in one corner, glaring at me across the narrow room, perhaps hoping for a reason to shoot me; and the peasant family fussing over me, as if anxious for the comfort of a houseguest.

Vague thoughts of courtesy came into my mind. My southern upbringing was too strong to be forgotten, even in this Southeast Asian jungle where I lay surrounded by Vietnamese farmers and enemy soldiers. It seemed unthinkable to me to offend this small, wrinkled-faced man who hovered over me with the bowl and spoon. When he brought the spoon to my lips again, I swallowed a small sip of awful-tasting stuff. My whole body revolted. I vomited and passed out again.

# THREE

# No Little Enemies

Hunger and pain are unfriendly companions. They joined forces to taunt me throughout the long hours of that first night in North Vietnam. I fell into a fitful sleep but was awakened often by the sound of my own groaning. The pain in my arm and shoulder was so bad that I was only vaguely aware of a dull, throbbing ache in my back. I learned later that I had sustained a painful but not paralyzing compression fracture in a vertebra in the lower spine.

I had no pillow. No blanket. The bare dirt floor I lay on had hardened under the constant pounding of feet across it, and it offered no comfort for my injuries. Neither did my captors.

It was still dark the next morning when they shook me awake, gave me back the boots they had removed the night before, blindfolded me, and pushed me out of the door of the hut toward a waiting truck. I sensed the presence of the old man in the doorway, watching my departure. The deep jab of a rifle in my back hurried me forward.

I twisted the the muscles of my face just enough to be able to peek under the dirty cloth tied over my eyes and see Larry Chesley, my backseater, stripped to his underwear, already seated in the back of the truck. I stopped, stunned at his appearance. Guards pushed me forward roughly and commanded, "Get in."

I raised one leg toward the truckbed, but without my arms to pull me up I could only stand there helplessly. Three soldiers grabbed hold of me and threw me in. Then one of them climbed in to sit between Chesley and me.

"No talk," he ordered us in clipped English. Then again loudly, "No talk!"

We managed to exchange a few grunts, just to offer each other some small reassurance, and then our journey began. Every bump on those rough country roads reverberated through my injured arm and shoulder. We finally reached the two-lane concrete smoothness of Vietnam's main north-south highway, built by the French and labeled Highway 1. I was more worried than relieved. We were now a target of opportunity for any U.S. plane flying armed reconnaissance over that major north-

36

south supply artery. We could easily be killed by one of our own planes sent out to strafe the highway. I sat in the truck, tense and sweating, straining to hear the sounds of distant planes.

I had it all figured out: at the first sound of plane engines, I would hurl my body toward the side and roll out of the truck bed. Once on the ground, I would wave at the low-flying fighters who would recognize my flight suit and identify me as a captured U.S. pilot. It could work— I could still be rescued. I just didn't know how I was going to wave my arms.

The air grew warmer as daybreak approached. The tangy moisture of the ocean filled my nostrils. We were headed north, I knew that. I speculated on my fate as the miles sped by. Maybe it was too late to hope for escape. No, I couldn't let myself believe that. Did Shirley know by now that I had been shot down? I was tired and hurting, but thoughts continued to hurtle through my brain.

Suddenly the truck engine began to cough and sputter. It gave a final bark before it died and coasted toward the side of the road. The driver climbed out and looked under the hood. It was obvious to me, even with my limited vision, that he didn't have a clue as to the workings of an engine. He peered at it, then quickly looked around him, then up at the sky, as if expecting to see enemy aircraft overhead at any moment. I shared his anxiety—we were an easy target.

He tinkered with the wires for a moment while his eyes darted back and forth from the engine to the skyline. After a few moments, he climbed back into the truck, pumped the gas pedal, and the engine sparked into life. I was surprised that the rusting, dented piece of junk had even a labored breath left in it. The dashboard looked as if it had been vandalized—except for the speedometer, there were gaping holes where the gauges should have been. If the truck was low on fuel there was no way to know it.

We returned to the road and were soon wheezing along at close to sixty miles per hour. We had gone only a short distance when again the engine coughed, gasped, and died. This time the guard and driver were both nervous. They knew the bombing schedule of the Americans. If my friends in the air were on time, they would soon be sighting their guns on the camouflage-colored truck and strafing what looked to them like just one more enemy supply truck.

I tried to control the sense of panic that threatened me. I had to stay calm and think of my options. I had to be ready. My life depended on clear thinking. Once the firing began there would be no time for foolish acts. I moved over closer to the side of the truck.

The guard and driver had the same thoughts. They too wanted to avoid being fireworks. They pulled Chesley and me from the truck and led us a few yards from the road to hide us among clumps of small trees growing in the soft, marshy soil. One soldier stood close to us, his rifle held ready; the other hurried back to the truck and began fidgeting under the hood with wires and valves.

*This is it,* I thought. *If we're going to escape, the time is now.* I tried to send my thoughts to Chesley — we still were not allowed to talk with each other. We would have to work together, but I thought we could overpower the two guards. First, the one closest. With my injured arms I would be little help, and the risk was great. At the first sound of a skirmish, the other guard had only to turn around and shoot at us, and it would be all over. Could we take that chance?

The land around us was much like the outer banks of North Carolina. We had to be only a mile or so from the gulf — I could feel the ocean. If we could get across the broad, sandy marshland to the coast, commandeer a boat, and head out to sea, our chances of rescue by the navy were good.

Suddenly we heard the engine spark to life. We turned to see the truck speeding away, leaving the guard, Chesley, and me standing by ourselves alongside the road. A spate of vehement Vietnamese words filled the air as the guard left behind stomped and swore at his cowardly comrade. He was furious. He yanked our blindfolds off us and pushed us ahead of him to resume the journey on foot.

For hours we walked in front of the angry guard, prodded and pushed by his rifle butt. For miles we followed the road, staying just off the shoulder in case of low-flying American fighters, before we turned and headed out across country to follow a railroad running east-northeast. It was desolate land, empty of people and vegetation except for clumps of stunted trees that grew here and there in the soggy soil. Then suddenly, as if out of nowhere, a small band of villagers appeared on the railroad track ahead.

At first sight, they might have been just a party of travelers, but as they neared us, their angry voices grew louder and more distinct. We knew they had come to meet us. Their fury exploded.

"American imperialists!" someone shouted in a shrill, nasal voice. More voices joined the noise. Small, dark, pajama-clad people shook their fists in our faces and yelled angrily. Children jumped and hollered and pointed at us. An ancient man holding a baby pushed his way through the crowd. His strident voice reached us before he did.

"American imperialists!" he shouted. His small dark body shook with the intensity of his hatred. His angry black eyes were nearly buried in the myriad of wrinkles that creased his face. He thrust the child up close to us. "American imperialists!" he screamed again. Where the child's arm should have been there was a scarred and ugly stump.

It was a staged demonstration. No doubt our truck driver had alerted the villages ahead that captured Americans would be coming through. The village leaders stirred the peasants into a noisy, agitated band to taunt us. Their intent was to convince us that this war was immoral and illegal; to rend from us admissions that we were, indeed, war criminals. I knew it was a propaganda ploy.

I made myself keep walking and steeled my face to appear unmoved lest my captors see the battle of emotions that raged inside me. I was hardened, somewhat, by one war already. In Korea, I had seen what our weapons could do. I had seen the victims of war. But I was not so hard that I could not feel revulsion at the sight of the maimed child and pity for his pain.

The villagers continued to walk along with us. I knew this was only the first of many such scenes planned for the American captives. Communist party members in each village would be planning others for us, all for the purpose of convincing us of our "crimes against humanity." Of course, any such admission by an American military man would then be transmitted to the United States, where it was believed public opinion would influence our leaders to stop the war. To gain an American's admission of guilt as a war criminal was, to the North Vietnamese, almost as good as a coup. Over the course of my imprisonment in Hanoi, my captors said many times, "We will win this war in the streets of America."

The demonstration followed us for miles. The villagers stayed bunched up around us as we walked, jeering and shouting all the while. I tried to close my ears to the sounds of their voices.

I was so hot, so desperately hot and thirsty. Finally, I couldn't make my legs take another step. The guard dug his rifle into my sides to force me on, but I couldn't move. We had had no food or water all day, and my strength was gone. The sight of a lake only a few yards away, and down a slight incline, was more temptation than I could resist. I tucked my arms close to my body, ducked my head down, dove toward the ground, and rolled into the water. Angry voices shouted at me to get up, but I just lay there and felt the coolness of the water lap against me. A dozen voices yelled at me, but I didn't even try to get up. Nothing mattered, nothing frightened me.

I could feel several hands pulling and pushing to lift me up, but my limp body was too heavy for them. At six feet, two inches, and 190 pounds, I was like Gulliver to the tiny Vietnamese people. After several tries to drag me to my feet, they gave up. The guard muttered and poked his rifle into Chesley's ribs, and the two of them walked on, leaving me behind. The villagers stared at my sprawled body resting in the shallows at the lake edge like a huge, beached sea creature.

The water felt cool and soothing to my aching body. I started to lap at it, like an animal, but even in my state of near delirium I saw its filth and spat it out quickly. Algae and scum floated on its surface, and odd debris bobbed here and there around me in the shallow water. I lifted my head just enough to speak to the little crowd that stood watching me.

"Water," I asked weakly.

No response.

*Please understand,* I begged silently, but no one moved.

"L'eau," I muttered, trying some of my limited French vocabulary on the staring crowd. Still no response.

I closed my eyes and sank deeper into the soft, muddy bank. A hand touched my shoulder, and I looked up into the wrinkled brown face of an old woman. She knelt beside me and put a canteen to my lips. I sipped the lukewarm water greedily and thought I had never tasted anything so sweet.

It was evening before two soldiers returned for me. Some tiny residue of strength fed me and I was able to raise myself and help as they pulled me to my feet. They placed themselves on either side of me and half-carried, half-dragged me down the path to the village of Dong Hoi where they dropped me onto the dirt floor of a tiny room. Moments later, a screened door opened and a guard, speaking heavily accented English, ordered, "Stand up for the captain."

"I don't see any captain," I answered. The thought of having to stand up made me ill. Every movement, every breath was painful.

The guard pointed to a young woman standing in the doorway. She stepped into the room and stared at me while the guards punched and prodded me with their guns until I stood. She never said a word. She just stood there about three feet in front of me and stared at my slumped and filthy figure. I stared back.

She was one of the most sophisticated of all the women I saw in that country. Her black hair was clean and neatly tied back under her khaki hat. Her pressed uniform clung to a curvaceous figure, and she was clean and well groomed. She studied me intently, taking careful note of my muddy, light brown hair, my blue eyes, and everything from there down, including my muddy boots. I doubt she had ever seen an American pilot before, and she was certainly the first Vietnamese woman officer I had seen. For ten minutes we stood silently staring at each other. And then she walked out of the hut.

As the second night closed in around me, I battled hopelessness. Thoughts of escape still hung around the edges of my mind, but I needed food and medical attention desperately, and my captors still offered neither. I fell into an exhausted sleep only to be roused around midnight, blindfolded, and dragged to a clearing outside the village.

I managed to peek out enough to see about twenty soldiers, but there was no sign of Chesley. For hours we waited in that clearing for a truck that never came. It was nearly dawn when they dragged me back to the village where they dropped me onto the dirt floor of another tiny dark room. Exhausted and hungry, I passed out.

I awoke to bright sunlight and the sight of dozens of brown faces peering in the windows and doorway of what I now saw was a two-room house. I must have been a strange sight in my olive flight suit, now brown with dirt. My boots had been taken away—to discourage me from trying to escape—and every inch of my body was muddy. All day small, dark, almond-eyed people pushed into the room and peeked in the windows to see the big, strange-looking man with round blue eyes and fair hair.

There was no such thing as privacy. No toilet, no curtain, no door. I was worried about my body's failure to perform the most basic bowel functions during those days, but I was also a little relieved at not having to worry about where or how I would manage without toilet facilities. For thirty days my system was in shutdown due to stress, injury, and malnutrition.

I was in the home of one of the more influential families of the village. They kept me in one room of their two-room structure while they occupied the other room which boasted a primitive cooking apparatus. As in many homes in North Vietnam, a radio speaker dangled from a wire in the ceiling and transmitted propaganda programs from the state-controlled radio in Hanoi. The poorly relayed, static-filled messages played hour after hour in every home. I learned later Chesley was being held in a similar house only a few yards away.

It was obvious that we were in an "upper income" area on the outskirts of the village. The widely spaced, thatched houses had a sort of primitive plantation look to them. Each was met with a narrow dirt driveway lined with banana trees and other jungle foliage. Vegetable gardens and brightly colored flowers grew in the yards. A few utility poles stood around the village like skinny sentries connected by a single loosely draped electric wire.

Pigs ran here and there, and water buffalo stood tethered in grassy patches. There were no dogs in the village—at least not for pets, I learned. Dog meat, when available, is a delicacy on the Vietnamese menu. Cats were strangely absent too—the villagers killed them—which may have accounted for the many huge rats that ran across my legs and around my head as I lay on the dirt floor of the hut.

The man of the house where I was kept appeared to be something like a village elder. He wore a gun tucked in the waist of his loose-fitting clothes and carried himself with an air of importance. His son, about seven, was already well indoctrinated in communist thinking. He spouted all the anger and rhetoric of one who had learned his propaganda lessons thoroughly. He poked at me, jeered and yelled, and brought his friends around to share his fun. Benjamin Franklin must have had him in mind when he wrote, "There is no little enemy."

The girl in the family looked to be about twelve, the same age as my daughter, Gini. She was quiet and watchful, and graceful, I thought, as she walked across the floor to bring a bowl of rice—the first food I had been given since my shootdown and capture three days earlier. She set the bowl down next to me, glanced about her, and then silently took my hand and slid a dozen or so peanuts into it. I hoped she understood when I whispered, "Thank you."

Early the next morning I awakened to the sound of cans banging and voices shouting. It was a bombing raid. I saw a primitive alert system in action, as word passed from one village to another via clanging cans and shouts that the Americans were flying a bombing mission.

My guards dragged me outside and pushed me into a slit trench. I moved as quickly as I could to keep up with them as they directed me to a remote area about a football field's length away from the house. The entire village was connected by slit trenches and they quickly filled with villagers, all armed with rifles. In a few moments planes came into view. On a signal, the villagers fired up into the air at the Americans flying overhead toward their target.

Everyone had a rifle for the bombing raids. Men, women, and children all participated. They loaded their Soviet- or Chinese-made weapons and fired a curtain of bullets into the air. I'd flown through that kind of barrage only days earlier, but at that moment it seemed like a century ago. Now it was my turn to watch a bombing raid from the ground. Air force F-105s and A-1s roared overhead. From my position in the slit trench I was only about a hundred yards from the target: a truck park much like the ones I had been sent out to destroy. I watched the planes release their bombs and saw the explosions that followed.

*This is crazy,* I thought. *These people were ready for us before the planes ever came into sight. They know when we're coming!*

I was struck again by the illogical way this war was being run. Commands came out of Saigon. The raids were scheduled in waves: 8:00 A.M. to 10:00 A.M., then 3:00 P.M. to 4:00 P.M., then the night missions, every half-hour all night long. It never varied. No wonder the enemy always knew when to expect us. No wonder they were always ready and in place with their weapons.

There was some logic to the plan. Each mission required about two and a half hours, then the planes had to be turned around and used again. Logistics and timing had to be considered. But surely intelligence knew about the Vietnamese siesta period in the afternoon. Why didn't we schedule some raids then? Bombings never occurred at that time of day when the element of surprise might have shielded our pilots, to some degree, from ground fire.

It also puzzled me that on those rare occasions when we did vary our bombing schedule, the North Vietnamese knew it, and we arrived on target to find them waiting for us. Again, having twenty-four years of historical data to draw from, it seems espionage is the likely explanation. Perhaps we will never know for certain, but I will always believe we were betrayed.

As I watched the American bombers flying low overhead, I wanted to jump out of the trench and scream at them, "Go back! The truck park is empty."

I had discovered something my friends in the sky were ignorant of: the truck parks emptied during the day. Photo reconnaissance planes, flying at night, reported back on the locations of trucks parked in the jungle, but at daylight those trucks were moved. North Vietnamese drove the trucks to other locations and camouflaged them during daylight hours, leaving most of our assigned targets empty. Most daylight interdiction missions were thus futile; their risks senseless.

The village functioned on a rigid schedule which operated around the bombing raids. Every day the children rose early to work in the rice paddies. Then around 9:00 A.M. they went to school. Political indoctrination classes filled the afternoon, often running for as long as two to three hours. Later, in the prison camp in Hanoi, I saw this practice continue. Guards sat through communist indoctrination classes, often bored and half-asleep, much like adolescents forced to sit through a long Sunday sermon. The only difference was that the indoctrination classes were held daily, not just once a week.

It was soon obvious to me that my captors in Dong Hoi had learned their lessons well.

On the second night, soldiers came for me shortly before midnight and led me out of the house and down the road. *We're moving out again,* I thought. But instead they walked me to another house and into a tiny dark room where black-out blankets hung at the windows. The only light radiated from a single naked bulb that dangled from the ceiling and cast bizarre shadows against the thatched walls. An imposing-looking Vietnamese sat at the only table in the room. He motioned for me to be seated at a stool opposite him. Twelve more Vietnamese crowded together in a tight semicircle. The room was quiet. The man across the table from me began to speak in Vietnamese. A man standing near his side interpreted.

"You are not entitled to military treatment. You will be tried by the Vietnamese people as a war criminal."

I assumed the man at the table was supposed to be the presiding judge. The other twelve were supposed to simulate the American system of trial by a jury of peers. It was all a sham, of course—a kangaroo court, and I suddenly felt like laughing. Could they really believe I would accept this as a facsimile of the U.S. justice system? Did they actually believe this charade would give them credibility in my eyes? That I would submit to their authority and accept their judgment meekly?

"You are a pirate!" the interpreter shouted at me. "You are imperialist criminal! You must repent!"

Repent. This, I learned quickly, was a favorite word in the communist rhetoric. It would be used often during the interrogations I would endure later while in prison in Hanoi. "Repent of your crimes against the Vietnamese people," they told me, and I would receive as my reward the empty promise of "lenient and humane treatment by the Vietnamese people."

I sat on the stool in the middle of the room and listened to the anger and venom of the men on the "jury." The judge, through the interpreter, asked questions about the plane I flew for the U.S. Air Force.

"I don't know," I answered to every question. My pain was so intense that I could hardly sit up on the stool. I slumped forward and nearly fell to the floor several times. Each time, a soldier from the "jury" hit me with his rifle and forced me back into an upright position.

After more than an hour of questions I could no longer hold onto consciousness. I slid off the stool and hit the ground with a grinding thud. The pain of the fall was almost as bad as that from the rifle butts that pounded my shoulders and neck.

Rough hands pulled me back up and onto the stool. The judge shrieked and the interpreter echoed, "You are guilty! You have been sentenced to die!"

Pain and exhaustion created insulation from the terror I should have felt when my captors announced their "verdict." Fear and shock hit me moments later when my jury marched me to a clearing and stood me up against a tree to face three soldiers armed with rifles. An execution squad.

Each soldier, with studied movements, reached into his back pocket and pulled out a clip. Then, almost in unison, they jammed the clips into the rifles. The familiar click-click sound of an automatic rifle being loaded echoed in my ears. On a signal from the ranking officer, each soldier put his gun to his shoulder and sighted in on me.

I remember feeling as if I was suspended in time, as if I was standing outside my body and watching some macabre play. It wasn't happening! It couldn't be happening! Everything inside me rejected the hideous scene that played in front of me. Then through the fog of disbelief, a tiny piece of my brain skidded toward reality, and I said silently, "Jesus, I love you."

In the next instant the officer signaled, and each soldier squeezed his trigger.

Click, click, click . . .

The sound of the hammers hitting the empty chambers cracked the silence. I felt all the breath in my body expelled as my chest sank and my body sagged against the tree. In a moment the soldiers grabbed hold of me and trekked me back to the house in the village.

They had had their fun for the night. The next time the commander might order them to load bullets into their rifles, and the victim would face loaded rifles instead of empty ones. One never knew. That was the trick.

Now that it was over, I knew I had just lived through a terror tactic in common use by communist forces in Korea a decade earlier.

The prisoners of war who had returned from Korea revealed the communist concept of treatment of POWs. The term "brainwashing" emerged as they told of being subjected to torture and cruel treatment for the purpose of drawing from them admissions that the communist cause was "just" and American interference "immoral." As the U.S. military learned of POW experiences in Korea, survival school was modified and updated to include training in the terror tactics utilized by communist captors.

We were taught to expect to be used for propaganda purposes, to expect brainwashing tactics to be used on us because the survival of communism depends on world opinion. Communist aggressors must saturate the world with their side of the story. The more voices they employ, the more credible their witnesses, the more believable their case. The irony is obvious, of course: who could believe in the just and equitable principles of communism when these were spouted by captives, testimonials wrung from unwilling speakers, after hours of unspeakable torture?

Such treatment of prisoners of war is forbidden by the Geneva Conventions, of course, but as I would soon understand more fully, the North Vietnamese had no regard for the principles that governed treatment of military men captured during armed conflict. They had their own interpretation of the carefully drawn up articles of the Geneva Conventions. They refused to be monitored by, or regulated by, any but their own edicts.

Survival school was supposed to have prepared me for all this. I was supposed to know what to expect at the hands of this people. But nothing can adequately prepare a man to draw his last breath under an enemy's gun sight.

Nearly every night a terror tactic was employed in the hope that I would submit and say something that would be useful for propaganda. If, as an American, I would denounce my country's involvement in Vietnam's struggle for unity under communism, they would splash the message across the world, hoping to influence policy makers in the United States to get out of the war; hoping to feed American displeasure with the war effort.

"See," they would declare proudly, "your own fighting men denounce what you are doing here. They have admitted that they are criminals, engaged in illegal acts against humanity." And to the rest of the world they would say, "American soldiers, highly trained and intelligent military men, believe in the just cause of the Vietnamese people. They support our right to a united Vietnam. They have denounced the actions of their own nation as piracy and imperialist aggression."

The morning after the mock execution, a military man wearing a Red Cross emblem approached me as I sat in a trench watching a bombing raid. He handed me a pencil and paper and, in poor English, commanded, "Write a letter."

*This is it,* I thought. *Things are going to get better. If the Red Cross has found me I should be able to get some attention for my arms,* I thought. Then, looking at my numb and mangled right hand hanging limply at the end of my broken arm, I wondered, *How am I going to write?*

"Tell how good your treatment is," he told me. "Write about how you've been fed and cared for by the humanitarian policy of the Vietnamese people."

I recognized the rhetoric, but I wanted so badly to believe that the Red Cross was still the *Red Cross*—the compassionate extension of a compassionate people, ready to minister and intercede for the injured and helpless. My fantasy was shattered. His urging to describe my "good treatment" told me what I should have known.

As an arm of a communist government, the Red Cross in North Vietnam was operated by the military, and it responded to prisoners of war under the direction of the military. But more importantly, it operated under the direction of the communist party. What I had yet to learn was that there was no freedom within the ranks to think or respond with compassion. Communist doctrine permeates every military organization, down to the lowest level, and controls all the actions of the military, including the Red Cross. Later I would see that a party member actually held more power than a high-ranking military commander. Party position always took priority over military rank.

The letter I wrote to Shirley was barely legible—I had to write with my left hand. I told her of my injuries, said I'd had no medication, but that I was okay. I learned years later that they never sent the letter. Although I addressed an envelope, it was never mailed to Shirley. It would be two years before she knew for certain whether I was alive or dead.

Still, I hoped naively. I wanted to believe that because the Red Cross had taken account of me, things might get better. I waited for medical aid, but none came. I was fed rice twice a day and continued sleep on the dirt floor. I hurt so badly that I tried using a crumbling brick for a pillow — anything that would offer some little comfort — and I was in such bad shape it actually felt good.

Yet I still refused to give up the idea of escape. A military rescue was not a possibility while in this village, that I knew. But if I could just get away, get to the coast. . . . I cursed my useless arms. While I towered over nearly every guard assigned to watch me, and was certain I could have overpowered any one of them, without my arms, I couldn't even try.

On the seventh night in Dong Hoi, my captors took me through the village to a little hut, about eight feet by eight feet, the size of a small gardening hut back home. They pushed me down onto a wood-frame bed covered in a dirty, army green blanket.

In lousy English, one of them said, "This doctor's house. Sit. You wait."

In a few moments, a Vietnamese wearing a white coat entered the room. The "doctor" opened a shabby-looking case and pulled out a long hypodermic needle that looked as if it belonged in a veterinarian's bag. He proceeded to fill the syringe with a clear liquid. I could feel my body tense. I hugged my broken right arm close to me. The doctor spoke no English, but he pointed to my arm, and as I drew back from him, three guards took hold of me. They gripped my aching shoulders while he picked up my arm and turned it to study it. He mumbled something and then stuck the needle into my shoulder. The guards held me as the needle jabbed deep into my flesh. In minutes, numbness began to travel down the length of my arm.

*They're going to cut off my arm!*

I closed my eyes against the thought. Real fear, deep and pulsing, throbbed in my chest. I was helpless.

The arm hung grotesquely from my sloping shoulder. It was a double break above the elbow — I could feel the spaces where the bones were separated. The doctor spoke to the guards, and one of them lifted the arm and held it out from my body while the doctor pushed and pulled, pressing against muscle and bone with not unfriendly hands.

I sensed that the doctor was trying to do *something* for me, but I was sure he had no idea what he should do. I wondered if a white coat was the only requirement for wearing the title "doctor" in this country. My contact with other doctors over the next seven years confirmed my suspicions: knowledge of medical science in North Vietnam was scarce, and practice of legitimate healing almost nonexistent.

The quiet of the doctor's house was suddenly shattered by sounds of clanging cans and shouting voices. Villagers scrambled into the slit trenches that ran along the side of the house, and in moments rifles were firing, and shells were exploding and pounding away at the truck park only a few hundred yards away.

A guard quickly turned off the light in the doctor's house. The heavy blankets at the windows cut out all light, and the room was black-dark. A guard lit a skinny, short candle and the doctor returned to his work. He busied himself with something in his grubby medical box, then he motioned to the guard holding the candle. The guard stepped up and held the candle so close that I could feel the heat of the flimsy flame. I wondered if he might set fire to the hair in my armpit.

The doctor manipulated the bones in my arm for what seemed like hours. Finally he appeared satisfied. He bent my arm at the elbow and cast it from fingers to shoulder. The local anesthetic had begun to wear off, and the pain was excruciating, but the awful business wasn't over yet. There was still my left shoulder to be tended. The guards stood me up and turned me around. The three of them grabbed my left arm and, on a signal from the doctor, they all pulled. I heard a swooshing sound as the shoulder slid back toward the socket, but it didn't quite reenter as it should.

I couldn't stand any more. I was limp from exhaustion and pain. I sat back down on the dirty bed and felt myself almost relax as I slumped over. Instantly the guards were on me.

"Sit up! No lie down! Sit up!"

At that moment I thought that, of all the cruelty I had experienced at the hands of this enemy, this was by far the worst. Here was a bed, albeit a dirty one, and they would not let me lie down on it.

Days later, I was again blindfolded and marched through the village. I could squint under the cloth and see that Chesley walked next to me but, as before, we were forbidden to talk. Villagers came out en masse to shout and poke at us as we stumbled through the streets.

It was almost humorous. Squinting under my blindfold, I could see the Vietnamese chasing and carrying on as they had been commanded — it was another ordered demonstration — but their thoughts appeared to be elsewhere. They laughed with each other, and then, as if suddenly recalling their orders, they began shouting furiously at us again. Then a second later they returned to other conversations. They scratched where they itched, giggled and whispered, and then jumped back into character to slug us, screech at us, and demonstrate their anger at the American aggressors. It was an oddly imposed scene, just for the sake of impressing us with the "unity of the people" and their support of their cause for a sovereign and independent Vietnam. It seemed any event could be used to rally the people.

In a nearby clearing, soldiers thrust us into the back of a truck that joined a convoy hauling troops north to Hanoi. It was dark by the time we started the trip out over the rough, bumpy back roads. The trucks used only slit lights to avoid detection by the U.S. reconnaissance planes flying low overhead.

I leaned back in the truck bed and rested my head against the dark green canvas canopy that enclosed me. There was nothing I could do for myself. I fell asleep thinking about my family.

# FOUR

# Missing in Action

I always believed I was indestructible. I knew my abilities as a pilot — I had worked and studied hard to be the best. While serving as weapons officer and tactics instructor at an air base in England, I issued a standing challenge to the other squadron pilots: a case of beer to any pilot who could outmaneuver me. I never had to pay up.

There was little I did not know about flying. When I was chosen to fly with the Thunderbirds, the air force's high-precision aerial acrobatics team, I was thrilled. In the early 1960s, while at Nellis Air Force Base in Las Vegas, I collaborated with John Boyd, one of the premier fighter technicians in the armed forces, to write the first air force tactics manual for fighter pilots. Fighter ace Fred Blesse's *No Guts, No Glory* explained maneuvers and tactics, but the air force had no formal instruction manual for training. Ours was the first to teach and explain the use of the plane on all three of its axes, instead of on two, like an automobile. Energy maneuverability theories for air combat later evolved from these technical studies.

Throughout my childhood, my parents took me to church and Sunday school. Looking back, I can see that, while I was listening to the stories about God, I was also learning the character of God. I am sure that knowledge was a key to my survival many years later. God was more than mere religion to me, and His son Jesus more than a good teacher. My faith was deeply personal. The event of my baptism was a significant moment of commitment in my life, and I can still remember the emotions of that day.

My father was a quiet man who believed children needed discipline. I remember when I was about ten years old, I refused to do a chore he had given me. I ran out of the house, hoping to escape across the creek out back before he caught up with me, taunting him as I ran, "You can't catch me!" How wrong I was!

Mom was a working mother in an era when most mothers stayed at home. I had no brothers or sisters to take my side in schoolyard or neighborhood skirmishes, and so I learned early to take care of myself and fight my own battles. Perhaps those factors account for some of my stubborn independence.

I lived the first six years of my life in San Antonio, Texas, until the insurance company my father represented transferred us to Georgia. Over the next six years we lived in the Decatur and Atlanta areas. The year World War II broke out, we moved to Dallas.

Sunday, December 7, 1941, is one of the most vivid memories of my childhood. I was out hiking with a Boy Scout troop when the news of Pearl Harbor reached our town. Mom and Dad were sitting quietly at the kitchen table when I walked into the house. The somber looks on their faces told me that something serious had occurred, but the magnitude of that something far exceeded anything a little boy's imagination could conjure.

I remember sitting close to the radio later that night and listening with Mom and Dad to President Roosevelt's "chat" with America. We had been caught by surprise, he said.

In those days, I would never have questioned the honesty and integrity of our commander in chief. It was a time of innocence and national pride; a time of ration cards and radio chats. As an eleven-year-old boy, I pinned a map to the wall above my bed and followed the victories of our armies across Africa, Europe, and the Pacific. Billboards and war bonds reminded every American family that this was *our* war – Congress had declared it! And we could all find ways to help fight it. What a contrast that was to the war I fought later in Southeast Asia.

As a teenager, I exhibited many of the typical swashbuckling tendencies that would later carve out a comfortable niche for me in the fighter society in the air force. Although I had established a spiritual base early in my life, by the time I reached my teens, I was far from what could be described as devout. I didn't reject God or stop believing in Him, but as many youngsters do, I allowed His relevance to recede into the background. My appetite for adventure overruled my appetite for spiritual things.

During my years at Woodrow Wilson High School in Dallas, I lived on the edge of mischief. I drank beer and drag raced at midnight down Central Expressway. Once I spent half the night in jail after shooting out street lights with a gang of kids who called themselves the Lakewood Rats.

The summer I was fifteen, my mother's position with Western Union helped me get a job on a road crew. The only kid in a crew of a dozen men, I lived in a railroad car and ate my meals in the dining car. Every day we dug holes, set poles, and hung wire across the northern-most region of the Texas Panhandle. At night, I followed the men into the bars in nearby towns to wash down the Panhandle dust. I learned, at fifteen, how to hold my own in a Texas barroom brawl. John Wayne would have been proud.

Maybe it was that summer of sweating under the hot Texas sun that swayed me toward a business career. More likely it was my parents' careers in business and finance that influenced me to apply to Southern Methodist University's six-year business and law program in 1947. I hadn't been a serious student, but I managed to graduate in the upper one-fourth of my class, so my acceptance to SMU was automatic. I pledged Delta Chi fraternity and entered the college scene with gusto.

In 1947, Louanne's was a popular teen night club on Dallas's famed Greenville Avenue. It was always crowded with students, underage teens refused admittance to the other Greenville clubs where liquor was served. The music blared, and the dance floor was always a blur of swirling color. I saw Shirley Melton there one night, and although I had known her in high school, that night I felt as if I was seeing her for the first time.

I had long before noticed she was a cute brunette, but that night I found her completely irresistible. She was vibrant and alive, radiating a teasing, competitive spirit that was utterly compelling. I was helpless. Though we were both there with other dates, neither of us seemed to care. We danced with each other the entire evening, and from that night on we were inseparable. We were married September 1, 1950, just before the start of my senior year.

Shirley had grown up in the Methodist church, and I soon saw that her spiritual roots went deep. Early in our marriage we had minor skirmishes over some of the distinct differences between Wesley's Methodism and the doctrines with which I had grown up, but most of them we were able to resolve. On others we agreed to disagree.

As newlyweds, we thought we were headed up the corporate ladder. We were prepared to climb to the top, one rung at a time, but the Korean conflict erupted and our plans were irrevocably altered. Dreams of pinstriped suits, a leather briefcase, and a house in the suburbs quickly dissolved into the reality of flight suits, pilot training, and air force housing. By the end of 1951, we were members of a tight society of air force pilots, and the parents of a healthy son, Bobby.

Ours was a typical air force marriage. We crisscrossed the country, living at various bases: from Bartow, Florida, to Bryan, Texas; then to Nellis, Nevada, and from there to Montgomery, Alabama; overseas to Europe, back to Nellis, and then to Norfolk, Virginia. Our two daughters, Gini and Beverly, were born at intervals along the way.

Our separations were painful, but a normal and necessary part of the life of an air force pilot. There were the months I spent fighting in Korea, special schools I had to attend, and the two-year stint with the Thunderbirds. But wherever and whenever it was possible, we packed up the family and went together. While I was stationed at Chaumont, France, we saw Europe together, living for months in tiny rented rooms in a crumbling old castle in Bar-sur-Aube.

After attending the Fighter Weapons School, I joined Shirley and the children at Lakenheath Air Base in England, where we lived in a typical English home, The Gables. Our years there stand out in my memory as idyllic.

I will always be glad we made the decision to settle in Plano, Texas, in 1965, shortly before I left for my first assignment in Vietnam, where I joined General Westmoreland's staff in the Emergency Action Center in Saigon.

Plano in 1965 was a small town of about ten thousand people with a main street laid in bricks. Located twenty miles north of Dallas, it was far enough away from the big city to have a quaint identity all its own, and close enough to Carswell Air Force Base to be a reasonable commute. It had not yet begun to bustle, as had some of the Dallas suburbs, but it promised a future of growth. Shirley's dad had done business there for years, and we believed it offered opportunity and a sense of community for our family. As an air force wife, Shirley had become adept at the job of moving. In only a few days she had unpacked all the boxes, hung pictures on the walls of our new home, and enrolled the children in schools. I flew to Southeast Asia.

As part of the Military Assistance Command Vietnam (MACV), I participated in monitoring and directing the entire war and all its players: army, navy, air force, marines, the paratroops, and South Vietnamese troops as well. We were set up to take care of problems as they came up, to "put out the fires" when needed. We initiated and directed the first series of B-52 bombings during my stay in Saigon.

Vietnam's heat and humidity were unlike any I had ever known. The air was like a damp blanket too heavy to shed. Any physical exertion produced sweat that ran in rivulets down one's body. Even indoors there was little relief. Few places were air-conditioned, and ceiling fans accomplished little more than to stir the moisture and serve it back steamed.

I remember stepping out onto the balcony of MACV headquarters at night, hoping for a hint of breeze to dry the sticky sweat on my neck. I remember standing there and marveling at the incongruity of life in Saigon. All around me the city's neon lights flashed, advertising restaurants and hotels too expensive for most American soldiers' pay, while just a short distance down the road, along the banks of the Saigon River, I could see bursts of fire from the guns of battling Vietcong and South Vietnamese troops. I knew that in the morning, from the same vantage point on the balcony, I would see American GIs waterskiing behind power boats speeding down that same river.

A few miles outside town, the horses ran every day at the Vietcong-controlled Cholon Racetrack. The Vietcong also controlled the road that led to Vung Tau, an exclusive beach resort; but for a price, they would allow U.S. servicemen to pass through, unharmed, for a romp in the surf.

Many of the men assigned to Saigon spent their off-duty hours in officers' clubs where they drank until they could forget where they were and why they were there. Others lounged on the long verandas of French-built hotels and nursed tepid drinks while they ogled Vietnamese women who walked by. Unlike the pajama-clad peasant girls of the farming villages, many of the women of Saigon had a look of European sophistication about them. Hollywood's depiction of them as slim, curvaceous, and clad in tight-fitting sheaths is an accurate one. They paraded past the Continental Hotel and toward an adjacent street where bars outnumbered all other businesses. Tiny, dark, poorly built structures, the bars stood bunched up against each other, crowded into small, smelly spaces, offering forgetfulness for the price of a drink.

After a few months in Saigon, I found myself sitting on the same barstools, hanging out on the same verandas as the other servicemen, drinking to assuage my loneliness and the frustration I often felt at having to sit at a desk instead of in a cockpit.

The officer's club on the ninth floor of a large, modern building was my favorite place of refuge. From there, I could look out at the lights and imagine I was thousands of miles away, in any other city in the world. I could divorce myself from thoughts of strategy and weaponry; I could forget about the confusing and contradictory orders coming out of the White House. For a while, with a drink in my hand, I could almost forget about the heat and the boredom. But there were times when, even on the top floor of a modern building, the war intruded.

One night, I was leaning against the gleaming bar, clinking ice in my tall glass, when an army lieutenant walked in and stood beside me. I smelled him before I saw him. His torn uniform reeked of sweat and muddy, jungle streams. He was young, no more than about twenty-one. He gripped the edge of the bar with hands that were scratched and bleeding. His whole body was trembling.

"You need a drink?" I asked him.

He looked at me with eyes that didn't really see.

"Bourbon or Scotch?" I asked him.

He shook his head as if unable to speak.

"Bartender, bring a Scotch, will you?"

The lieutenant swallowed it in one gulp, and then in a terrified whisper, he said, "We were on patrol . . . only ten miles east of the city when the VC ambushed us. There were ten of us. . . ." His hands shook as he cradled his glass, and he nodded when the bartender offered a refill.

"All my buddies were killed—every one of them. I don't know why I'm not dead . . . they just missed me, I guess. I ran back here, firing behind my back, hiding in the brush til I got into the city."

He raised his head and looked out of the windows at the city lights burning below. Where the lights ended, the jungle began. He shook himself, as if to shake off the horror of the last hour, and turned and walked out of the bar. I ordered another Scotch.

I spent a lot of time in that tall building. *Too much* time, with *too many* drinks. In a perverse sort of way, the flights of stairs to the bar on the ninth floor helped to save me from alcoholic stupor. Frequent power outages rendered the building's elevators useless, so I had to climb nine flights of stairs if I really wanted a drink. After hundreds of climbs on a previously injured knee, I became almost crippled with stiffness and pain. The air force sent me home for rehabilitation just in time for the Christmas holidays in 1965.

It was good to be home, but I knew I couldn't stay. For the sake of my career, I had to go back to Vietnam. My advancement in the air force would be hindered if I didn't reenter the war. This time I asked to be sent back—it was the only way I was going to get the assignment of my choice: flying. I was a pilot, and I had had enough of the desk and office kind of stuff. Officer Personnel found openings at the Eighth Fighter Wing in Ubon, Thailand.

I was home long enough to see that Shirley and the children had settled easily into Plano. They had joined a church and begun to feel part of the school and neighborhood activities. They had made new friends, and Shirley was enjoying living only a half-hour's drive from her mother and brother in Dallas. I felt peaceful about them when I left for my second tour of duty in Vietnam. They seemed comfortable and secure. Three months later, on a Sunday afternoon in April, that security was shattered.

It was a sunny spring day. Shirley and the children had attended church services earlier that morning and had come home for an afternoon of gardening. Shirley was on her knees in topsoil, readying a flower garden for bedding plants, when she heard a car pull into the driveway. She wiped her hands on her jeans and hurried into the house to answer the doorbell. Three air force officers stood at her front door. She had been an air force wife too long not to recognize the somber entourage: a notifying officer from personnel, a doctor, and a chaplain. Before they spoke, she knew.

The conversation was conducted in soft tones, official jargon mixed with offers of assistance and consolation, but no promises – probably because the air force knew very little at that time. The report from Ubon was that Chesley and I had both been equipped with beepers that were supposed to direct rescue teams to us, but they had received transmissions from only one beeper. No one knew which of us had activated the beeper. And our wingman, Panther Two, had reported seeing only one chute open after we'd been hit. Since the backseater is typically the first to parachute out, the assumption was made that only Chesley had escaped, but the air force had no certainty of that yet.

The report of the surrounding enemy troops and deep jungle in the area of our shootdown complicated air force hopes for our rescue. Even with navy search assistance they were not optimistic. They gave Shirley little hope as they left her that afternoon.

"This is classified information at this time, you understand," the personnel officer told her. "I have to ask you not to tell anyone about this. We've sent officers to notify Sam's parents, of course, and they are waiting to hear from you. But we don't want you discussing the shootdown with anyone else."

The ridiculousness of this edict hit Shirley within minutes after the trio drove away. How could she possibly not tell her friends and her family? Did the air force really believe she could keep quiet and behave as though nothing in her life had changed? The children would have to be told, of course. Did they believe the children would keep it a secret? She decided to ignore the command.

As the news of my shootdown slowly sank in, something inside Shirley refused to let her accept the possibility that I could be dead. Although more than two years passed before she received tangible evidence that I was alive, she never did believe I'd been killed. In fact, in order to make herself take charge of the family and do the tasks she normally left for me, she tried to force herself to think of me as dead. Even that was almost impossible, but it helped her make herself go ahead with the essentials that couldn't be left undone indefinitely.

Shirley's next days were almost unbearable. She possessed courage and faith in large quantities, but virtues cannot be depended upon as insulation from pain. She prayed and cried and washed her face a dozen times while trying to muster her strength and make plans. What should she do? For the children's sake, routine must be maintained. She went through the motions of meals and baths and bedtime, all the while wondering: Is he injured and suffering? Has he been captured by the Vietnamese? She felt helpless, but she would not give up hope. Nor would she rob our children of the order and continuity their lives needed.

The Monday morning after learning of my shootdown, she roused the children for school. After they had dressed and eaten, she drove them to school that morning as if it were a day like any other day. All went well for the first few hours until, after school in the hallway, she ran into the principal.

"How are you, Mrs. Johnson?"

It was a simple inquiry, but it opened the floodgates. Shirley's control broke and the tears returned. The principal stammered and stuttered, trying feebly to comfort her when she told him, almost unintelligibly through her tears, that her air force husband had been shot down and was missing somewhere in North Vietnam.

"I'm sure he will be found," she said confidently, once her tears subsided. "Even if he is captured he will be okay."

She believed that with all her heart.

The air force assured her that they would continue to fly over the area of our shootdown, but days passed and they had nothing new to report. She had no certainty but her feelings – she would not even consider that I might be dead. She prayed constantly for me and read and reread familiar promises in her Bible, grasping for comfort and reassurance. The pastor of her church called on her a few times, thinking he could comfort her, but his solace consisted of such comments as, "He'll probably never come home, you know . . ." and, "You should accept the fact that he is dead." She soon found ways to avoid his duty calls.

My parents, too, seemed unable even to hope that I might be alive. They wanted to believe it, but the chances of my survival seemed too remote. Maybe it was just too hard for them to hope against such odds. In some way, Shirley stood alone in her certainty that I was still alive.

The following Sunday, one week after my shootdown, our home was filled with well-meaning friends, determined Shirley should not be alone on this family day. They brought casseroles and desserts and words of encouragement, but to Shirley, it was like a wake – dozens of people sitting in the home of the deceased, talking and whispering and saying things that sounded like condolences. She would not let them act as if I were dead. She moved about the house and kitchen as if in charge of a party and determined that, in the future, she would be too busy for guests on Sunday afternoons.

Over the next couple of weeks, Shirley's best source of information was my squadron commander and roommate at Ubon, Lt. Col. Bob Crouch. His letters gave her a few more details and helped direct her hopes toward realistic possibilities:

[April 18, 1966] . . . As of this letter full scale search and rescue operations have been suspended because there has been no contact with Sam or Larry [Chesley] for an extended period of time. I'm afraid we cannot interpret why with any accuracy. . . . I am confident their ejections were successful because they were both seen to eject and the chutes did open properly. Their landing spots were also observed and it seems [unlikely] that they were harmed either by the enemy fire or the ejection.

Even though Sam may have so far evaded capture, the longer we go the less likely it becomes that we will be able to rescue him. While it would not be impossible for him to walk out I must honestly say that the hostile nature of the terrain and the countries involved make it unlikely at best. I also think that the worst that could have happened is that he has been taken prisoner.

I will be hopeful about his recovery for the next couple of days, but I'm not really optimistic. All of us are still looking and listening for signals and we will continue to do so.

I know I don't have to tell you how strong, imaginative, resourceful, and courageous Sam is. He will bear what must be borne and come out on top. . . . I will take care of his things. . . .

It was a difficult letter for Bob to write, as we had become good friends. For Shirley, however, the letter brought encouragement since two parachutes had been sighted; this was reason for hope. Still, the letter also told her that it was unreasonable to hope the ordeal would be over quickly and easily. But the next letter, while it did not feed her hopes of a speedy return, did bring her encouragement and support.

[May 7, 1966] . . . I know what you mean when you talk of your helplessness in wanting to do something for him now. But I honestly don't know of any help for it. When we lost him that nite I called all our people together and told them that no matter how hard I'd worked before and no matter how good I'd tried to do things before, I was going to work harder and do better in every way that I could to make this squadron and our work a testimonial to Sam's courage and his honor. He means an awful lot to us and we are all doing our very best for him to end it and get him home to you. . . . Unofficially the guns that hit Sam are gone because we went over and got them. And we go there every chance we get and those people must surely be wondering what they ever did to deserve what has happened to them. We will never allow those people to shoot again at that place. At least not for long. That may not mean much to you, but it's been the best we could do.

In June he wrote again to say that two more crews had gone down, and these would not be coming back. Again, it was "unofficial," but he wanted Shirley to know everything that concerned my squadron. He was reluctant to send my things to Shirley: "I know in my heart that he won't be back for a while but I guess I'm fighting it. I'm not going to do anything until I have to."

In the beginning, Shirley felt certain the ordeal could not last longer than a few months, at most. Already the war had been a long one, but it must be nearing an end. World War II had not lasted this long. It would be over soon. She would make it through. When friends from the air force told her I could be gone for as long as three years she refused to believe it. She could not let herself believe it. She would go on with the routine of family life. She really had no other options.

I too, had no options. Half a world away, every moment of my every day was controlled by khaki-clad men whose sole objective, it seemed, was to hurt me as much as possible. The memory of my transport from Dong Hoi to the prison in Hanoi is one of pure agony. A few details are slightly obscured, no doubt by the indescribable pain of my injuries.

I remember speeding along at sixty miles per hour over crater-ridden roads that tortured with each bump. Convoys, solid lines of traffic hauling equipment, materiel, and men filled the two-lane concrete road going in both directions. Photo recce planes flew low overhead but gained scarcely a glance from the Vietnamese. They recognized that the planes were equipped with nothing more than cameras.

The presence of American bombers prompted quick detours into the bush where the trucks paused just long enough for the planes to pass over and out of sight. Then, just as quickly, we drove back onto the road again and continued on our way. It was like a closely timed production, with every player directed and cued for action. Checkpoints all along the way guided drivers on how to go on through, where and when to pull off. When the bomb-damaged road narrowed to one lane, checkpoint officials controlled traffic to be sure munitions going south had priority.

U.S. bombers had effectively destroyed the bridges at nearly every river crossing on our route. And at every river, traffic bottlenecked like that at an exit ramp on a Los Angeles freeway during rush hour. Some crossings were made on hastily built, flimsy pontoon bridges that looked scarcely able to support the weight of one truck, much less an entire convoy. At other rivers, small barges functioned as ferries but were able to carry only one or two rows of trucks on each crossing. Either way, it was a slow process, made interminable by heat heavy with humidity.

Our first night out, as we approached a bridge that had so far escaped destruction by U.S. bombs, the navy flew in low and unexpectedly to remedy that oversight. By now, Chesley and I had become adept at using the muscles of our faces to shift our blindfolds, and we watched the aircraft come in low, then pull up and maneuver into position. It was a maneuver I had done a thousand times. I imagined myself in the cockpit, my hands on the throttle. I was the pilot punching that button on the stick to release the bombs.

It was a perfect trajectory and a perfect hit. We watched our captors' faces register first surprise, then terror, as the bombs exploded and the bridge collapsed. Unable to applaud, I exclaimed under my breath, "Yea, Navy!"

Our driver hunched over the wheel, pushed his rusting, coughing truck to its limit and steered toward a ditch on the side of the road. We hit the embankment with a jolt that threw Chesley and me into the air and then dumped us back onto the hard steel of the truck bed. The truck tottered precariously as though about to overturn, then settled quietly in a whirl of dust as the driver and guards jumped out to hide in the bushes. Chesley and I struggled to right ourselves in the back of the truck, and then we watched, straining our eyes against the darkness, until the night skies swallowed the planes.

The guards eyed us from the bushes, and as soon as the dust and debris from the explosion settled, they pulled us from the truck and began walking us through fields and rice paddies. With the bridge out, the destination plans changed. They had to find a place to spend the night. The Buddhist pagoda up ahead would serve nicely. It was isolated – I had the feeling our guards wanted to avoid the masses that night – and it was easily commandeered. The guards threw the resident monk out, threw Chesley and me inside, and ordered us tersely, "No talk!"

The stone pagoda was small, only about ten feet by twelve, but a cool paradise after hours of travel in the tropical humidity. Windows placed high in the walls prevented us from being able to see out, but they offered ventilation for the hot air that would otherwise have been stifling. Candlelight within revealed stone and wooden carved artifacts placed all around the room. Two waist-high interior walls separated the room into three small compartments where, for centuries, Buddhists had knelt and chanted their prayers.

A guard motioned to Chesley and me to sit down in the compartments farthest from each other, then positioned himself between us in the center compartment, no doubt to prevent us from trying to talk to each other. The other two guards stomped out into the darkness.

The guard seated between us could just barely see over the walls that separated us. His eyes darted back and forth between Chesley and me. It was obvious he was nervous. I don't know what he thought we would do to him – we were unarmed – but he got up and walked outside to join his buddies, leaving us alone together for the first time.

Finally, we could talk to each other. Like schoolboys in detention hall, we sneaked as close to each other as we could and whispered softly, hoping we would not be discovered by the guards. At this point we didn't know what they would do to us—we weren't certain of anything. All we really knew was that they were not going to adhere to the Geneva Conventions. For all we knew, they could decide to shoot us for talking to each other. We talked quickly and quietly, keeping an alert ear to the sounds from outside the pagoda.

"What took you so long to get out of the plane?" I whispered, mentally seeing again Panther One's deadly plunge toward the ground and the vibrant orange and red explosion.

"I didn't think I was going to be able to get out," Chesley whispered back. "I pulled the ejection handle between my legs and nothing happened. I guess I just sat there staring at it, mesmerized for a second. Then I had to fight the negative Gs to get my hands on the other handle when the plane went nose over. It was close."

The Vietnamese had stripped him of his flight suit upon capture and left him in his underwear. This was to discourage him from attempting to escape, I'm sure, but I wondered if it might also have served to make him feel more vulnerable. I suppose they hadn't expected me to be capable of much trouble because of my useless arms, and they hadn't bothered to strip me; although they had, at different times, taken away my boots or just the shoelaces. It all seemed so childish.

I think, at that moment, I felt that Chesley needed me. It may have been only my imagination, but it gave me a reason to keep going. I was the senior ranking officer (SRO) in this little military setting, and I had a charge to keep.

We were able to talk for hours. We relived the shootdown from every possible angle, each adding details to the other's impressions. Chesley had also sustained a compression fracture at the time of ejection. We commiserated with each other's pain. We almost managed to laugh at the memory of the navy's quick destruction of the enemy guns that had disabled the Phantom.

It was a night of revelations—not just about our experiences, but about ourselves. We were hungry, thirsty, and covered in filth that, in that confined space, began to offend our own noses. A stray mongrel on any American street would have been treated with more care and humanity than we had received from the "lenient and humanitarian Vietnamese people." In that setting, the defenses that guard deep personal privacy came down. Chesley began to share his thoughts and his second thoughts about flying.

"I wasn't sure I wanted to be a pilot in the first place," he said in a low voice. "I'm not sure I want to continue when we get out of this."

"You'll do just fine, buddy," I answered, looking at his dirt-smudged face. He looked young and scared and exhausted. "A lot of men feel that way in a crisis, but they come out of it even better pilots than before."

It was true. I knew a dozen stories about good pilots who had thought they could never climb into a cockpit again after experiencing what we had just been through in the air. Like them, Chesley would be okay with a little encouragement.

My own feelings surprised me a little. I looked down at my mangled hand, and in spite of the pain that was pulsing throughout my whole body, I was lusting for a mission to carry out. Since my first time in the cockpit of a fighter, I had known that I was made to sit in a pilot's seat. The mixture of speed and precision and the element of danger created a powerful draft that I couldn't resist. I was drawn into it as if I had no other will or options for my life.

It never occurred to me, even in that desolate setting in North Vietnam, that there was anything else I would ever want to do. It was inconceivable that I would ever willingly sever myself from that unique, tight, if sometimes raucous band of fighter pilots who teased death in the air at speeds that often exceeded a thousand miles per hour.

Air-to-air combat, plane against plane at those unimaginable speeds, was my dearest love. But Chesley's love lay elsewhere. He had been trained as a radar systems operator. His education had made him one of the best backseaters I ever flew with. I knew I could feel confident with his operation of the complex equipment found in the navy-turned-air-force Phantoms. He was among the best technical men the air force could produce, but technical expertise did not always equip a man for the traumatic experience of warfare. It seemed that air force personnel policy seldom strove to match the man with the mission.

I had always been fascinated with the way the Israeli Air Force recognizes the subtle shades in the term "fighter pilot." It takes careful note of each pilot's personality type: is he suited to a particular niche in the air force? After identifying the aggressive, danger-loving pilots who thrive on competition and risks, it directs its best toward air-to-air combat; the next-best are steered to air-to-ground attack; and the final category of pilots fly transport and support. Each man is assigned where his unique personality will best aid his effectiveness and survival.

Chesley was a fine pilot. He had all the skill needed to move up front, and until our shootdown, he had been itching to do so. But with the image of the fiery F-4 Phantom vivid in his mind, he was suddenly unsure of himself. I knew he was asking if perhaps the air force demanded of him something that did not exist naturally within him. He began to question if he possessed the nature of a true fighter pilot.

I had answered that question for myself over Korea more than a decade earlier. Dogfighting and other combat experiences had given me a sense of that fighter substance inside me and had begun the first efforts at shaping it into a usable form, but the experiences that lay ahead for me in North Vietnam would mold it further and test it to its furthest limits.

Chesley and I knew that, sooner or later, we would face military interrogation. They would pressure us for information, and we decided to use this time alone in the pagoda to get ourselves ready for our enemy. Between us, we concocted a story that we hoped would satisfy them. It would go like this:

> It was my first mission into North Vietnam; I had just arrived in Thailand. (The part about flying out of Thailand was supposed to be secret, but everyone knew we were doing it. Washington denied it, but flights took off from Ubon on schedule all day every day. It was just one more tile in the elaborately built facade that U.S. politicians erected throughout the Vietnam war.)

> I picked up the plane in Thailand and brought it to Danang. I landed but never left the plane while it was being loaded with bombs. Of course, I didn't know what kind of bombs they were loading because I never left the plane. I didn't know much about the plane because I hadn't flown it much. I didn't know about radar or weapons. All I knew was that I should get over the target and push the button on the stick and the bombs would drop off.

> Chesley had just arrived in Vietnam on the day of our shootdown. It was his first mission. I didn't know him and he didn't know me. He just climbed in the back seat at Danang. Of course, he didn't know this plane either—it was brand new to him. If they asked about Danang we would have to say neither of us had been there long enough to learn anything. We just sat in the plane while it was loaded and fueled, then flew up to North Vietnam to drop our bombs.

It was the kind of story that would be unbelievable to any informed U.S. military person, but just possibly the Vietnamese would believe it. It was deliberately intended to make us appear ignorant, but perhaps that "ignorance" would save our lives, or at the least spare us some measure of agony under interrogation. It was vital that we both tell the same story. We would be questioned separately, and our stories must jibe so that there would be no reason for them to disbelieve us.

While General Eisenhower was president, the air force had altered the "name, rank, and serial number only" rule for captured military. The entrance of communism into the arena of war made it unfeasible to obey it. We learned in Korea that communist captors will not respect the warrior of an antagonistic country. They will torture a captive until they achieve the desired result, whether that be information, material for propaganda, or admission of "guilt."

The air force survival school taught us to give name, rank, and serial number in the beginning. But if torture intensified, if permanent maiming, death, or insanity seemed likely, we were to give the enemy something, anything that would not harm U.S. interests. Be creative, but keep it simple. You could expect to have to tell your story over and over again, and under great pressure. You had to be sure you told it the same way every time. Placate with misinformation, preserve your life and limbs if possible.

The next night, as darkness fell, we left the pagoda and resumed our journey. We passed through an angry mob held at bay by the guards — another of the many staged demonstrations I had already learned to expect. Villagers lined up like spectators at a parade and wielded sticks and clubs, landing their blows on our backs and shoulders and faces. Even the very young and the very old took part, picking up stones and hurling them at us, bouncing them off our already bruised and stinging bodies. Shrieking and shouting, the younger ones in the crowd followed us the farthest. They dropped back in the distance as we started out across the soft soil of the levees outlining the flooded rice paddies that covered the land like a huge patchwork quilt. We boarded a truck and continued our trek along the worst of the roads we had encountered so far.

The journey was rough. We moved slowly over miserable, deeply rutted paths that scored the inland territory. The truck rose and descended with bone-rattling force as it crept across the bomb-pitted terrain. As before, we were blindfolded, but I could see well enough to compare the devastated countryside with pictures I had seen of the cratered and desolate surface of the moon.

Our guards were distinctly more hateful toward us that morning. We could feel their increased animosity. They were probably more than a little irritated about the bombing by U.S. planes the night before, while I was delighted by it. Perhaps they sensed my peasure at their losses. Maybe that was why they became excessively abusive that day. At our first attempt to communicate with each other they slammed their rifles against our heads and shoulders and pounded their fists into our faces until we were bloody and limp.

"No talk! Shut mouth!" They hissed the few English words they knew. "Be quiet! No talk!"

They were definitely not in a mood to be trifled with, but oddly, I was not afraid of them at that time. They must have sensed that, and that, too, angered them. They turned on me with the kind of fury you've seen in a man who kicks a dog, and then kicks it again because it will not cower.

At one point on that horrible journey, a guard grabbed me and threw me against the cab of the truck. I was too weak and injured to protect myself and, as my body crashed against steel, I heard a sickening sound. The cast on my arm cracked and the broken bone that had begun to heal separated again. I slid down into the truckbed like a rag doll and slipped in and out of consciousness for what seemed like hours. The broken plaster hanging heavily on my arm was agony. Every part of my body throbbed as we bumped and jolted across what was left of the rotten Vietnamese road system. We finally stopped at what I believed to be a medical clinic in a small town.

It was a typical French-built structure, resembling a large house with a long porch across the front. Its stone construction and tile roof made it cooler than the tiny wood and thatch huts I had stayed in in other villages, and it was cleaner than the other facilities we had seen. We could see a few uniformed women who may have been nurses and some primitive medical paraphernalia, such as hypodermic needles, gauze, and tongue depressors. But nothing about it resembled even a poorly equipped U.S. hospital.

For one short night and a day we received something resembling compassion. Although they did not treat our injuries, they did try to make us a little more comfortable. They put us together in a small room and gave us bamboo mats to lie on. We were both too exhausted to talk. Despite my pain and the hardness of the concrete floor, I slept all night and most of the next day. I awakened only once—when groups of twenty to thirty people at a time were being led into the tiny room to view the captured American pilots. The small, dark-eyed people studied me, from the top of my mud-caked head to the bottom of my size twelve feet, as if they were viewing a freak in a circus sideshow. I stared back at them and wondered, with a hint of perverse humor, if some industrious soul had set up a booth outside the clinic and was charging admission to see the big, bad American pilots.

As soon as it was dark the next evening, we were again blindfolded and led out. Another staged demonstration gathered in the street, but this time we were not among disinterested peasants. I could feel the insanity of a mob that was out of control. They would kill us if they could, and the guards knew it.

It was an ironic scene. The guards who had beaten and abused us twenty-four hours earlier were now trying to protect us from the vicious blows of stones and clubs. They tried to force the crowd to clear in front of them as they steered us toward waiting trucks, but finally gave up and ordered the trucks to drive into the crowd. They threw us into the truck bed and drove, honking and shouting, through the unruly mob and back onto the torturous road.

We drove all night. In places, the truck nosed down at a sixty-degree descent as it crept through bomb craters in the roads. Again, there was a steady flow of traffic going both north and south. Just before dawn, the truck stopped and dumped us off in the middle of a rice paddy. Our guards walked us, one at a time, down a tiny path that was little more than a dike between paddies, and into a small enclave where three bamboo houses sat. They put me in one and Chesley in another.

We had arrived in the village of Vinh, a sort of holding place for military prisoners. Interrogation began in earnest here. I had the feeling our captors were trying to determine which of the prisoners would be useful, which ones would give information. They didn't play all the same propaganda games that we had seen in the other villages, but they spouted the same rhetoric, the same jargon.

"Imperialist yankees!" and "Criminals!" cropped up often during the interrogation sessions, but the intent of the interrogator was distinctly different.

"Why did the United States attack Vietnam?"

"Do you know the history of Vietnam, that the French came in and mistreated the Vietnamese people?"

They never used rough physical force to press me into telling them anything at this point, only lightweight attempts. They never asked us a question that prompted us to tell them the story we had concocted that night in the pagoda. It would be useful later, however.

In Vinh, I had a chance to observe the workings of village life under communism. Although equality is an often touted claim, its practical implementation in North Vietnam was a farce. The women worked very hard and received no respect or help of any kind from the men. I watched them kneel in the dirt to serve meals to the soldiers.

Every morning, work began at around five, with youngsters and adults alike in the rice fields. Young boys rode water buffaloes through the irrigated paddies, and the girls worked ankle- or knee-deep in the water. Their backs were stooped and bent under the weight of a yoke-type bar laid across their shoulders. Baskets heavy with pickings hung from each end of the bar.

As elsewhere, school for the children began at about nine, and indoctrination classes started in the early afternoon. While the children were away at school, the parents continued to work the paddies, always the men on the oxen or buffalo, and the women walking along in the water.

At the close of the French-Indochina war, Ho Chi Minh had confiscated land held by the wealthy and divided it into equal shares for everyone: a hectare (a little more than two acres) for every man. Each man thus had a spot to grow his own food, though he could scarcely support himself, much less a family on such a tiny piece of land. All proceeds of the land went into a commune at harvest and were divided up among the villagers as needed. Though very proud of "owning" their own land,

North Vietnamese farmers had no authority over it. They could neither sell it nor travel freely from it—nor could they enter the commune and take from their own harvest what they desired.

While in Vinh, I began to think again about trying to escape. My injuries were no better, but I knew once we arrived in Hanoi my chances for escape would be even more remote. It was worth a try.

I began gnawing through the wire that bound the straw to form the walls of the hut. *If I could make a hole large enough to climb through, I might be able to get out of the village in the darkness . . . I could hide out until I could decide what to do next . . . maybe get a truck and head for the coast. . . . But could I drive?*

For the next couple of days, I gnawed on the wire every time I was sure a guard was not close by. At one point, I heard a sickening crunch. A front tooth had broken off in my mouth. It seemed a negligible price to pay for a chance at freedom. The other front tooth already had a porcelain cap on it—I'd just have to get another when I got out of this mess. I spat the gritty crumbles out of my mouth and kept on chewing on the wire.

In the middle of the night, when the hole was just big enough for me to step through, A very large guard walked by and peered in.

"What this? What doing?" he grunted.

"Just lookin' around," I answered, hoping I sounded nonchalant. Moments later, a guard was ensconced inside the hut with me. I consoled myself by thinking I probably wouldn't have gotten far without being noticed by someone in the heavily populated area around Vinh. No doubt I would have been discovered quickly.

Chesley and I were moved in together into another house a few days later as more prisoners arrived in the village. Guards walked us outside, handed us a bucket of water, and told us to bathe. With my broken right arm and dislocated left shoulder, I felt helpless as a baby. Chesley had to pour the water over my head. It was our first opportunity to wash since our shootdown fifteen days earlier, and one bucketful of water wasn't going to be enough. We smelled and looked rank.

My body was still in shutdown, and now after two weeks I was really troubled about it. Later, I learned from other POWs that most of them had experienced the same condition. Many, like me, went more than a month without a bowel movement. And all of us had felt the same fears.

The rains came while we were in Vinh. Every day Chesley and I sat and watched the roads and paths turn into rivers that washed away all our hopes of escape. We had started to work on another escape plan, but now there would be no chance. Between the sparse bowls of rice and the meager tea twice a day, we tried not to let ourselves give up.

Early one evening, guards blindfolded us again and led us out to board a truck. It was a familiar routine by now, but we were surprised to find two other U.S. prisoners in the truck.

"No talk!" the guards ordered. Chesley and I ignored them. They slammed their rifles and their fists against us when we tried to whisper to the newcomers, but it didn't matter to us. It was so good to see another American! We were starved for information. But the newcomers were too frightened of the guards to talk to us. They shook their heads and turned their backs to us, facing away, so that the guards couldn't accuse them of communicating. After several hours of trying to get them to tell us what was happening in the war, we finally gave up. They were just too frightened of the guards to risk it. We never saw them again.

All night and half of the next day we traveled toward Hanoi at a furious speed. As we neared the city, I could see railroads and stockpiles of rail supplies ready in case of bombings. Workmen were busy repairing bomb damage even as we drove by. Camouflage nets lay everywhere—over railroad cars and engines, over bridges and supplies. Some bridges were half-buried in debris and netting to make them appear as though they had already been a bomber's target.

Hanoi bustled like every other oriental city I'd seen. A passenger train sped past, streetcars ran, bicycles rolled by, and crowds moved in every direction past shopkeepers and shouting street vendors, as if oblivious to the fact that a war was in progress.

Our arrival at Hanoi's Hoa Lo Prison was an event I will never forget. Adept as I was at peering under the blindfold, not a detail of North Vietnam's penitentiary escaped me. We turned down Hoa Lo Street and approached a tall, grimy, yellowish wall of concrete. Crossing a wide cobblestoned alley that encircled the prison like a moat, we entered through a gate and a tunnel-like pass cut in the wall.

I shuddered as a set of iron gates clanked shut behind me. The truck drove forward, taking us into the middle of a large courtyard flanked by dirty, once-white buildings. Another gate slammed shut behind me, closing the door on all hope of freedom. A sense of finality fell on me, as though dirt were being sprinkled on my coffin.

Rough hands pulled me from the truck and prodded me toward a building and into a room that held a single desk.

A guard ordered, "Sit on floor," and then he walked out, leaving me alone with no food or water.

At about dusk, an officer and two guards entered the room. The guards pulled me to my feet, and as soon as the officer had seated himself at the desk, they pushed me down onto a small, four-legged stool that wobbled under my weight. The officer opened the desk, pulled out a recent issue of *Time* magazine, and slapped it down in front of him. He stared at me for a moment, and then, drawing himself up as tall as he could, he began speaking in perfect English.

"We know all about your military organization," he said. "Specifically the air force."

He raised his eyebrows and peered down at me, waiting, watching for some reaction. I stared back at him. He was small and wiry-looking, with a thin, whisker-like mustache. His pointy face had a sort of rodent look about it, and I sensed he had a similar nature, as well. I learned later that the POWs here had nicknamed this official military interrogator the Rat. The name fit him well.

"We are not here to make you tell us anything," he continued in a sinister-smooth voice. "We just want to know how you lived, and a few things about your life on the base."

I figured he had intended to gain credibility with me by displaying the *Time* magazine, as if I would respect his knowledge of the world and see that he was able to discuss large and important matters. He kept waiting for me to look impressed.

"We know everything about your airplane, you know," he said. And to emphasize his words, he pulled out an air force magazine and plopped it down on the desk.

I suddenly felt like laughing. He wanted me to believe that he was highly informed on American military data because he had read a commercial magazine to which all the world had access. I knew immediately, if that were his source, he had no specifics of weapons or anything else of vital military importance. It was a facade, a front to make me think he understood the intricate workings of our military; it was an attempt to draw me into a discussion that would reveal classified military information. To me it was laughable. And ineffective.

"I am going to ask you some questions now." Rat straightened his shoulders and again pulled himself up to his full height. "You will answer them."

"I need some food," I answered. It was a stall, but it was also true I hadn't eaten all day.

"No!" he replied.

"I need water."

Again he answered, "No!"

A change had taken place, and I could feel it as clearly as one can feel the change in temperature when the summer sun sinks behind a mountain. I sensed that it was now time to begin taking things very seriously.

All that I had endured during that long and painful journey since shootdown nearly twenty-one days earlier was nothing compared to what I was about to experience. If I had thought I was at war before, I was about to learn that, until now, I had fought only minor skirmishes. The real war was about to begin.

The blows from the guards' rifles, the staged demonstrations en route to Hanoi, the efforts to separate Chesley and me, the poor care and lack of medical treatment – these had been only a sampling of what I would be treated to in Hoa Lo Prison. I knew I was about to begin fighting as I had never fought before, but without the benefit of the conventional weapons of war. It was psychological warfare. The only offense I had was my stubborn will to resist; my only defense, my wits. Yet I believed I was better equipped to win than were my opponents.

"Where are the air bases?"

"How many airplanes?"

It was time for the story Chesley and I had cooked up between us. It didn't seem to satisfy him.

"You think about it," he said, and strode out of the room.

I lay down on the concrete floor, finally yielding to the exhaustion that had been threatening to overwhelm me. Immediately a guard stepped into the room and ordered, "Sit up!" For hours I sat there, unable to lie down or even lean back against a wall.

"I need a bathroom," I said. My body ached all over. I had sat still for so long that I knew I had to move or fall over.

The guard scowled fiercely, walked out, and returned in a moment with a paint can so rusted that it crumbled when my hand touched it. It was to be the only toilet facility I would have for the next five years. It would become a trusted aid in the constant effort to communicate with fellow prisoners. It would hide messages and be a reason for leaving the cell and walking to the place where we emptied our refuse, offering one more opportunity for some means of communication with another POW.

Midnight came. The interrogation room was dimly lit by one bald light bulb that dangled from the ceiling. It seemed such a small light in such darkness.

More questions. More commands to "Sit up!" I refused to answer. I wondered if they might leave me alone because I looked so beaten, so pitifully ill. I had no strength and felt at times as though I were only half-conscious. What could they expect to gain from me?

Two guards studied me. "We will talk about it," they said and walked outside. Before I could even begin to hope for rest, another guard entered the room and pulled me to my feet. I was heavy for him, but he shoved me against the wall and pelted me with his fists. He landed his punches against my injured shoulder and arm with the precision of a gunner sighting in on a target. Though he wasn't a big man, he threw all his weight into each blow, and I was powerless to protect myself. I had never felt such pain. I slumped to the floor and lay there while he leaned over me and continued to pound on me until I was delirious. It suddenly didn't really matter any more what they did to me. I was beyond caring.

The two guards returned to the room. The "enforcer" yanked me into a sitting position on the floor, stepped back, and the questioning resumed.

"Tell us about your plane."

I was too groggy with pain to answer.

"What was your mission?"

Could they really expect me to be able to speak? I struggled to find the story I had prepared for them. It was somewhere in my brain. I found pieces of it floating in my delirium, but when I tried to tell it, it sounded unintelligible.

The interrogator nodded to the brute standing by, and he stepped back into action. Taking hold of my broken arm, he pulled it behind my back, straining it as far as it would go, and then he twisted it until the pain robbed me of consciousness. I don't know how long I was out, but when I came to, the room was empty, and I was lying on the floor.

The next day I waited, often in a stupor, for something to happen, but for hours I sat alone in that room. At the sound of every footstep and every voice I wondered what would happen to me next. I still hadn't eaten, and the mixture of pain and hunger produced an awful nausea. I was thirsty, tired, and in severe pain, but no one entered that room all day.

When the oppressing darkness of night settled in around me, the three men returned. Again, the two asked questions, and again I answered with the same answers. Again, the third guard, on command, grabbed my broken arm housed in its cracked cast, twisted it, and pulled it behind my back. When he was sure he had squeezed every ounce of pain out of that endeavor, he yanked my left arm behind my back, wrenching the dislocated shoulder. I could not believe a body could endure such excruciating pain and remain conscious. While I was gasping for breath and praying for oblivion, he reached for the right arm again and pulled both arms together behind my back, stretching them beyond the normal limits of their injured sockets. Nothing in my life had ever produced such pain.

Mercifully, blackness came over me, and the pain retreated to a distant place I wouldn't find again until consciousness returned sometime later that night.

# FIVE

# Devil's Island

If hell is here on earth, it is located on an oddly shaped city block in downtown Hanoi, North Vietnam, and goes by the name of Hoa Lo. It is the North's main penitentiary system, and its name means "hellhole." To the American military men who waited out the interminable years of the Vietnam War within that dingy fortress, it is aptly named. But some POWs, holding tightly to their humor and a sense of the ironic, renamed it "the Hanoi Hilton."

A concrete wall, just under twenty feet high and about two feet wide, surrounds the prison grounds. In a layer of concrete at the top of the wall, large, sharp splinters of glass are embedded. It is a burial ground for fragments of fancy French champagne bottles, smashed and discarded like the haughty French colonialists who once reigned there.

Hoa Lo Prison is said to be inescapable. Armed guards stand in each of the four corner guard towers, keeping careful watch on the prison grounds. More armed guards pace the courtyards, alert to every movement, every sound of the prisoners. Of course, only after he has escaped the stocks or leg irons must a prisoner worry about detection by one of the prison's sentries.

The noises of the city travel over the wall—the shrill voices of shopkeepers, the ringing bells of the trolleys, the wheezing of an occasional motor engine—to tease prisoners with the sounds of freedom. But on the other side of the wall, with its electrified strands of wire, lie narrow streets that wind through the city like a confusing maze. The city is a teeming mass of tiny Vietnamese people among whom American soldiers would stand out like Gulliver in Lilliput. We quickly understood that an escape over Hoa Lo's prison wall was not an escape into immediate safety. A journey to freedom would be a long and dangerous one.

In earlier decades, Hoa Lo Prison was used to house Vietnamese: rebels who resisted the controlling and condescending imperialism of the French. The French imprisoned and executed thousands within those walls. Ho Chi Minh himself, a zealous revolutionary, had once been a prisoner there because of his actions against the French. Many of the guards who walked up and down in front of the tiny tomb-like cells had,

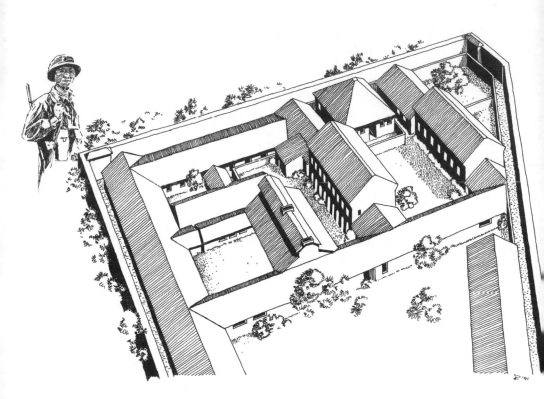

themselves, worn the same stocks and leg irons that now held other prisoners' legs. They knew every cell, every line and mark scratched in the
walls, every cobblestone in the courtyard. They had memorized the inside of every torture room.

The first American POW imprisoned in Hoa Lo was Navy Lieutenant (j.g.) Everett Alvarez. His incarceration began on August 11, 1964.
He was the first of what eventually became a steady flow of American
fighter pilots into the infamous Hanoi Hilton over the next three years,
until a bombing halt slowed the flow to a trickle.

Hoa Lo held others besides the American pilots unfortunate enough
to have been shot down. North Vietnamese civilians, political prisoners
– those who disagreed with Ho Chi Minh, and others who had simply
known someone who disagreed loudly – also lived behind those walls.
Purges intended to cleanse the country of dissidents and troublemakers
often resulted in the imprisonment of not only the dissenter, but family
members and friends as well.

South Vietnamese soldiers taken prisoner by the Viet Minh were also
deposited in Hoa Lo. Unlike the American POWs, the South Vietnamese were used as slave labor during their incarceration. They worked
on road gangs outside the prison alongside several thousand Chinese
laborers sent down by Mao to help repair the roads and fill in the craters
left by American bombs.

The South Vietnamese prisoners who spoke English told us that the
South Vietnamese prisoners' quarters were tiny facilities designed to accommodate half their number. As many as forty or more were confined
to each tiny room that could barely house thirty people tightly. They
slept and worked in eight-hour shifts because there wasn't room even
to stand if all were present in the room at the same time. As one shift
would leave for work, another would return, people falling exhausted
into beds still warm, vacated only moments earlier by those now trudg-
ing toward trucks that would carry them to the roads that must be re-
paired and the craters that must be filled so that supplies could be transported and the war could continue. Their health and safety was of no
interest to their captors. They lived and died without much notice.

Such treatment of prisoners offends and appalls civilized men and
women. Civilization has traveled a long and bloody road through the
centuries to reach the stage where international laws govern the humane
treatment of captives taken in the act of armed conflict. Codes, written
and unwritten and agreed upon by the world's noble and prominent nations, stand as powerful guards against the mistreatment of prisoners
of war, outlining policies of humanity, outlawing the use of force or
duress to obtain military information from a prisoner, guaranteeing medi-

cal care and treatment, and defining a reasonable program of exchange and release.

Refined, rewritten, amended, and adjusted, the codes found their best expression in the twentieth century with the Geneva Conventions and the administration and supervision of such compassionate organizations as the International Committee of the Red Cross. But the twentieth century also gave expression to the most blatant violations of those carefully constructed codes. World Wars I and II saw inhumanity and mass annihilation that rivaled and even surpassed the bloody practices of the Dark Ages. The Soviet massacre of Polish POWs, Germany's attempt at genocide of the Jews—it was as if the world had lost its footing and was sliding back into the days of barbarism.

Nazism, fascism, socialism, and communism gave birth to psychological and political warfare. Mind games became a principal part of the strategy of war and prisoners of war the primary game pieces. No more was it sufficient to capture a man and detain him to diminish the might of the enemy. The captive became an important weapon in the hands of his captor. The objective: destroy the captive's will to fight; manipulate his thinking; rehabilitate him; use him to influence his countrymen to end their aggression; or destroy him.

In 1949, with the horrors of World War II still fresh in all minds, the Geneva Conventions sought to articulate the honorable and humane treatment of prisoners of war and attempted to call all nations to accountability. But inevitably, nations operating from a totalitarian premise refused to agree. Their success can only be ensured if all opposition is eliminated. They are obsessive about gaining the support of world opinion. Prisoners of war can help accomplish that goal. They can be tortured and abused until they are willing to tell the world how just and worthy and honorable the totalitarian state is. Any articles or codes that interfere with this use of prisoners of war are simply ignored.

As a young pilot dogfighting in the air above Korea, I saw graphic examples of total communist disregard for the articles of the Geneva Conventions. Brutality and unnecessary cruelty were common both in the sky and on the ground.

From forty thousand feet in the air, the ground seems a long way down, but a spiraling plane shot by an enemy MiG loses altitude quickly. I watched once as a plane left a smoking trail in the sky and nosed toward impact. My wingman and I circled and watched to see if the pilot was able to bail out. We held our breath until we saw the white of his chute spill into the sky. We flew in close, alert for more MiGs, and radioed his position for rescue. Our voices were still crackling on the radio lines when enemy planes flew in beneath us and made a firing pass at the pilot as he dangled helplessly in the air. We turned our guns on them immediately, hoping to draw them off, but there were enough of them to keep us busy while others fired at the pilot. There was nothing we could do to save him.

I remember attempting to rescue a pilot who had landed in the water after parachuting out of his burning plane. We could see him below us, floating on a raft. As we circled overhead, readying for the rescue attempt, a North Korean boat approached him. He raised his hands in the air with the gesture of surrender, but they leveled their rifles and filled him with bullets. I can still feel the shudders of fury and revulsion that hit me as I watched helplessly from my seat in the sky. We fired on the boat and watched it begin to sink as we flew off, but we had been too late to save the pilot.

I grew up in the skies over Korea. Until then, I had been like a kid playing in the air with big, expensive toys. The air force had taught me to fly, but Korea taught me to kill. It wasn't something I could learn from a lecture or a textbook, nor could I learn it from the aces with whom I flew. I had to see it for myself, and then I understood: war means killing.

At that point a change came over me. I no longer shot at machines; I shot at men. I knew it was their lives or mine. If they shot my plane out from under me they would murder me on the ground or on the way down. It was a danger every American pilot faced with every mission.

North Vietnam and its military forces in the Vietcong followed the example of Korea. Laos made it very clear that prisoners of war would be shot at the time of capture. For that reason, most pilots avoided Laotian airspace if at all possible.

Although civilized nations had for centuries been refining the international codes, forming conventions, and establishing organizations to govern and ensure the honorable treatment of captives taken during armed conflict, Ho Chi Minh's government consistently violated those codes and conventions. He refused to recognize certain articles of the conventions as binding if they in any way hindered the speedy and effective accomplishment of his goals. He placed himself and his government on a plateau above international law. The unification of Vietnam under communism was his primary objective. Whatever practices would advance that cause were acceptable.

But the concern of communism to garner positive world opinion creates a perverse irony: while violating international law established through the centuries by honorable nations, the communist nation must actively persuade the world that it, too, is honorable. Hence the use of the POW as a spokesperson for that cause.

And what is it that prisoners must say? That the government that is starving and torturing them is a lenient government, and all in the world should be so fortunate as to live under such a regime; that the country that murders or disposes of citizens who disagree with its politics is truly a virtuous nation where humanitarianism and leniency are practiced.

So it was for us at Hoa Lo. Although most of the world's nations adhered to policies that would have protected us from abuse and torture, North Vietnam was a world unto itself. Constant and creative cruelty was employed to try to solicit from us statements justifying the aggression of North Vietnam against South Vietnam, and declaring the just cause of communism.

Intelligent, educated American military men were not easy to convince. We could see — even laugh at — the ridiculousness of it all, but we still suffered because of it. Most of us made only feeble, incoherent statements, intended to be misleading to the Vietnamese and foolish-sounding to the ears of Americans back home; foolish enough to clue them to the fact that we were speaking or writing under duress; that the things we wrote were not the things we believed in or espoused. Even so, we sometimes suffered intense feelings of guilt and regret for having given our captors anything at all. Our only solace was in knowing we had resisted until, as Eisenhower allowed, we faced the loss of our sanity, our limbs, or our lives to the so-called lenient and humanitarian treatment of our captors.

# SIX

# Animal House

Survival school must create its curriculum from the accounts of survivors of past wars. I could recall nothing in survival school that explained the use of the meat hook suspended from the ceiling of the torture room. It hung above me like a sadistic tease, suggesting bloody, trussed-up bodies hung like something butchered and bleeding. I could not drag my gaze from it.

My vision was blurry, my eyes mere slits in the puffy, swollen tissue of my face; but the sinister outline of the hook was unmistakable. I soon learned that it was a favorite instrument of torture. I believe I was spared its use only because I was already so injured as to provide my captors with ample opportunity to inflict pain.

In a routine torture session, the Vietnamese tied a prisoner's hands and feet, then bound the hands to the ankles, sometimes behind his back, sometimes in front. If tied at the back, the ropes were then tightened, straining his shoulders and arms toward his feet until his back was bowed and his ribs pulled so tight against his lungs that he could only draw tiny gasps of air. If his hands and feet were tied together in front, the guards tightened the ropes until he was folded in half at the waist and unable to breathe. Then bowed, or bent in half, he was hoisted up onto the hook to hang by the ropes, letting the weight of his body pull the ropes even tighter, cutting off circulation to his limbs.

Guards returned at intervals to tighten the ropes until all feeling was gone and the prisoner's limbs turned purple and swelled to twice their normal size. There he would hang for hours, even days until, crazy with pain, he would agree to write something, anything that would appease them so they would let him down. Sometimes weeks passed before a man could feel or use his arms and legs after a session with the ropes and hook. Many suffered permanent nerve damage.

I forced myself to look away from the hook. I could not afford maudlin musings. I had to ready myself for whatever lay ahead for me.

In only a few hours, the ordeal of the night before was reenacted. Interrogation, beatings, isolation. And for four days more it continued, each day like the one before. Rat asked the same questions.

"How many animals do you have on your bases?"

"I don't know what you're talking about," I answered. I was genuinely puzzled the first time he asked the question. "Do you mean pets?"

"What are pets?" he asked. I explained, and he then shook his head. "No, how many sheep and hogs and cattle on your air bases?"

Then I understood. He wanted to know about our food supplies. The Vietnamese had no concept of a sophisticated system of food delivery such as the U.S. military employed. Their meals were on the hoof. Every company carried its own cattle and sheep and slaughtered them as needed. They were scrawny, skinny yearlings, killed before they were fattened.

Later, while held at a POW camp we called the "Zoo" during one of the more lenient treatment periods, I watched out of my window as an untrained Vietnamese guard became butcher to a skinny, undersized calf. He cut its throat, carved out the sparse bits of meat and tossed them on the dirt. It was close to Thanksgiving, and camp officials felt generous when they ordered a thumbnail-sized piece of beef for every prisoner's plate. Such was the means of food supply for the Vietnamese military.

Out of his lack of knowledge of the world, Rat assumed the American system of food supply was similar to his country's, where the amount of livestock represented prosperity, or lack of it. He was asking for a measure of our wealth and strength.

"How many animals?" he asked again.

"We probably have about twenty sheep," I told him. I really wasn't lying. The Thais did keep some animals, and we were on a Thai air force base.

"How many chickens?"

"Maybe twenty," I answered. "I don't know, I never counted."

Then came the questions about my mission, my plane, the munitions in use, and the bases from which our missions originated. Always I gave him the same answers. Always he was dissatisfied. The torture guard pounded on me until I passed into oblivion, and the next day it all began again—until day five. Then a change occurred. The backdrop was the same, the setting unchanged, but the plot seemed subtly altered. Act One, military interrogation, had ended; political interrogation, Act Two, was about to begin.

Just after daylight, a different group of officers and guards entered the torture room carrying the familiar desk and chair. It was an odd entourage. A very young-looking second lieutenant, about thirty years old, sat down in the place of authority. His flat face and big jug ears had earned him the nickname "Rabbit" from the other POWs. His English was poor, as was his interrogator's, but I understood them well enough to know that the questioning had taken a distinctly different turn. He was not interested in the mission I had been flying when I was shot down. He didn't care about animals on the bases, my orders, my airplane, or anything that related to military matters. He wanted to know my feelings about this war.

"Do you believe it is right for your country to bomb our people and our land?" he asked. His back was straight against the chair. His slit eyes were not much more than a crease in his tense face. He waited for me to answer.

"Yes, I do," I said.

Rabbit's shrill voice ricocheted off the dirty concrete walls.

"You are a criminal! We will try you as a war criminal! You will see how the Vietnamese people feel about your bombs and your planes! You are no different than Nazi Germany's war criminals! There is no protection for you. The Geneva Conventions do not apply to you."

While I was trying to figure out what kind of distorted logic would equate American intervention in Southeast Asia with Hitler's maniacal practice of genocide, Rabbit continued his tirade.

"Your government has no authority over you. The people of Vietnam will try you for your crimes," he hissed.

It was more of the same rhetoric I had heard before. I would hear it again and again until I would want to vomit. It was the political indoctrination and propaganda story the communists never tired of spouting. I would hear it every day of every week and month and year of my captivity. Rabbit would make sure of that. He was the communist party official at Hoa Lo, though I didn't know it at the time. The camp commander was a major, but this funny-looking second lieutenant actually wielded the power. Regardless of military arnk, all the other camp personnel were little more than flunkies. As the officer in charge of political interrogation, he would be responsible for much of the misery and torture that American POWs would experience in that hellhole we called the Hilton.

"We can do whatever we like with you," he told me with a slight smile of superiority.

Rabbit's words were typical communist rhetoric, carefully chosen, rehearsed, and deliberately spoken to discourage me, to maneuver me into a position of submission. They landed on my already weakened spirits with the power of a physical blow.

I had never felt so weary. My arms and shoulders hurt so badly that even the muscle movement needed to breathe was a sacrifice. I had had only a few spoonfuls of water since being put in this room five days before. I was desperately hungry, but all my requests for food had been denied.

"We probably would allow you to eat if you would just write a letter saying you are dissatisfied with the war and that you would like it to stop," he said, watching me closely as he articulated each word. His eyes seemed to penetrate my skin to see the churning in my empty stomach.

"What's the purpose?" I asked, trying not to let myself think about the possibility of food.

"That is not your concern. You write it, and we will address it to your president and your congress. You will ask them to stop this inhumane and illegal war."

"That isn't what I believe, and I can't write that," I answered.

Rabbit stood up, placed his fingertips on the desk, stared hard at me, and then walked out of the room. The guards picked up the desk and chair and followed him out, leaving me alone with the hook in the ceiling and my rusty paint bucket.

I waited, unsure of what would happen next. They had left too easily. No pressure, no pain this time. And no one returned to beat me into unconsciousness, or worse yet, submission. Perhaps it was over. Would the rest of the battles be psychological? I felt confident I could win in that arena, but I wasn't sure to what extremes they would go to try to defeat me. It wasn't long before I found out.

The entire entourage returned in the evening and issued the same command.

"Write to your president. This war must be stopped. You must tell him to stop the killing and misery on both sides."

I gave them the same answer as before.

"There will be no food for you and no more water," Rabbit said tersely, and his desk and chair followed him out of the room.

I slept very little that night. The hardness of the concrete floor and the pain of my shoulders kept me awake, and probably served to distract me somewhat from thoughts of food. But in the morning hunger overwhelmed me. Weakness pressed down on me, and I could not even sit up.

During the first three weeks after my shootdown, I had been fed only meager bowls of rice twice a day, each serving no more than a half cup, and an occasional dish of insipid gruel or pumpkin soup. Now, another six days had passed with no food at all and only an occasional sip of water. I was growing thinner by the day. My bones seemed to be poking through my skin. For the first time since my capture, I wondered if I might actually die of starvation. But delirium would come before death. And that frightened me almost as much as thoughts of dying.

*I will not lose control of my thinking,* I vowed to myself.

All that day I lay on the floor, too weak to get up. In the evening, Rabbit and his guards returned to the room.

"Get up!" a guard ordered.

It was a futile command. Surely they could see that I was too weak to stand. A heavy boot landed in my gut, and I doubled over in pain. The torture guard dug his rifle into my ribs and yanked hard on my shoulders. He pulled me to my knees and then slid me up onto the small, four-legged stool.

"Here is a pencil and paper. You can write whatever you want to," Rabbit said.

"You write it and I'll sign it," I mumbled, gasping and trying to stay upright on the ridiculous stool. I was trying to stay ahead of my captors too, and for a moment I thought I was pretty smart. Anything they wrote would be communist garbage.

"I can't write anyway. My arms won't work." I nodded at my right hand in its cracked and crumbling cast.

I was surprised at how lucid my thoughts were. I was hurting, but I was able to think and plan. If I let them write it, I figured, it wouldn't be my statement. Even if it bore my signature anyone reading it would recognize it as propaganda. Let Rabbit write some nonsense, I'd sign it – unintelligibly, of course – and they would bring me something to eat. I figured I had just scored the first point in this mind game. I was doing all right.

"Write with your left hand," Rabbit commanded.

"I've never written anything with my left hand," I lied.

"Well, today you will try."

"I can't think of anything to say," I countered. "If you want something in writing, you are going to have to write it."

Rabbit and his desk and chair exited the room, and I let myself slide to the floor and into oblivion. Some time later he returned with his flunky. The guards dragged me back up onto the stool, and Rabbit thrust a form letter at me across the desk.

"Write this," he ordered.

It was a poorly constructed statement that reflected his limited use of English, and it didn't sound at all like something I would say. The gist of it was this: "The capitalist, monopolist leaders in the United States have started this illegal war, and they must stop it. In the name of all the citizens of the United States and the soldiers fighting in Vietnam, I ask you to stop this war now."

I knew no one back in the United States would believe such a statement from me, so I answered, "I guess I could write something like that, but my arms . . . I can't write."

"You try!"

I took the pencil in my left hand, but I couldn't make my fingers close around it. I tried to move it across the page, but it produced nothing more than a scribbled mess. Rabbit looked at it and decided that was the best he was going to get from me, for now. He left with his desk and his flunkies. Later that night he returned to say, "You will go to a cell now."

It was over. Six days in the torture room. I had undergone both military and political interrogation, but I had given them nothing. They were giving up for now. For just a moment I felt a tiny sense of triumph. In this game, points were given for resistance, and I figured I was ahead, one to nothing.

The torture guard pulled me up to my feet and prodded me down a hallway and into another cellblock. A heavy door slammed shut behind us. Dust stirred, and my nose stung with the ammonia smell of urine and sewage. The hallway was lined with doors, four on each side, and in the dimness I could see that each door had a small window covered by a hinged shutter that could only be opened from the hall. The guard stopped in front of the third door on the left side of the hallway, opened it, and pushed me into a concrete cell, about seven feet square. It looked just about like what I would have expected in a place called "Heartbreak Hotel."

I stood still for a moment and tried to shut out the sound of the thick door scraping shut behind me. With my back to the door, I faced a wall with a large, high window striped with steel bars an inch thick. Each side wall held a narrow cement bunk which jutted out into the room, taking up more than half of the meager width of the cell and leaving about two feet of standing space in the middle. Affixed to the foot of each bunk were wooden leg stocks secured with a steel bar and large, rusty lock.

Suddenly I remembered the hunger gnawing at my insides. Desperation made me strong enough to turn quickly and call to the guard.

"Wait! Where is my food?"

He only grunted and continued locking the door before he trudged down the hall.

*Help me, Lord,* I prayed, and I realized, not for the first time since this nightmare had begun, that I hadn't prayed this much since junior high. I wondered if I could expect Him to answer.

The tiny cell was not much bigger than a tomb. One quick glance should have been able to take in everything there was to see in that space, but somehow I had not noticed the enamel dishes placed on one of the bunks. There was a green metal cup with Vietnamese words painted on the sides, a bowl of rice, another dish of something I couldn't identify, and sitting beside it all, munching contentedly, was a rat the size of a house cat.

"Get outa here!" I shouted. I couldn't wave my arms to frighten it away, but I stepped toward it and tried to appear menacing. It seemed more irritated than frightened, but it jumped off the bunk and ran outside through a drain hole in the floor between the two bunks.

For a minute I thought I was going to throw up. I sat down on the bunk and looked at the stuff. There was a small scoop of rice, some pumpkin soup, and floating in the soup was a piece of pigfat with the skin and hair still clinging to it. Bile rose into my throat. An oddly shaped spoon lay in the rice. I grabbed it with my good hand and flung the pigfat toward the drain hole where the rat had exited. My stomach revolted at the thought of sharing dishes with a sewer rat, but I was too near starvation to pass up the rice and soup. I made myself eat a few bites.

The tiny feeling of triumph I had felt upon leaving the torture room was gone. I felt suddenly like a weary traveler who, after reaching an almost impossible plateau, discovers that the destination is still unimaginably far away, obscured by endless miles of rugged mountain range no one has ever been able to climb.

At that moment, the sound of a voice traveled through the cement walls of the cell.

"Who's there?" someone asked in a whisper. "Come to the door."

I moved to the door and put my face up to the tiny, barred window. "I'm Sam Johnson, Air Force."

"Jerry Denton here."

He had waited until the cellblock was empty of guards before calling to me through the little window in his door.

Another voice traveled the length of the hall. "Jim Stockdale down here."

Commander Jeremiah Denton, U.S. Navy, was my first next door neighbor in Heartbreak Hotel. He had been shot down ten months earlier while flying a mission from the carrier *Independence*. Down the hall, in the first cell next to the cellblock entrance, was Jim Stockdale, commander of Carrier Air Group 16, from the carrier *Oriskany;* he had been a prisoner since September, 1965. I was in good company.

Jerry's voice was the closest, and I leaned hard against the door to hear his every word. His voice was soft but strong, a whisper that he hoped wouldn't be heard by a guard, but it transmitted confidence and assurance to me. He was accustomed to leading men. His voice gave me an immediate feeling of courage. Nothing in his tone suggested that he had just come off a torture session with the ropes and hook. Rabbit and the torture guard had sent him back to his cell with his arms purple and swollen and without feeling, but he made no reference to his own condition. He only asked how I was.

Stockdale's voice sent authority and strength down those dismal hallways. He was a born commander. I sensed his intelligence and leadership immediately, and a bond of trust and friendship was forged between us right away. He, too, had experienced severe torture because of his "bad attitude." His leg had been broken at the time of his shootdown, and inadequate medical care had left it deformed and stiff at the knee. He was in excruciating pain most of the time.

I sensed the courage and integrity of both Stockdale and Denton in the first moments of our meeting. A special kinship began to grow among us that first night.

"There's a code you need to learn," Denton told me as I pressed my face to the door. "I'll tell it to you and then we'll lie down on our bunks and practice it."

Denton had only one concern at that time: to get me into the communication system as quickly as possible. He knew the desolation of Heartbreak Hotel would overwhelm me unless he could distract me with something constructive. And he proceeded to teach me the tap code.

The letters of the alphabet are placed in five rows of five letters each; eliminate the K, which is in on the third row, and use the C for a K. The first taps correspond to the placement of the letter in the horizontal row, then a pause; the second series of taps correspond to the position of the letter in the vertical row. Using the metal spoon, I scratched a grid into the concrete wall and put the letters in the proper spaces, not knowing the guards would punish me if they found it.

The code was simple in theory, but it would take practice to become adept at using it. Having to use my left hand made me feel like a kid in a remedial class, but I thought in time I would get the hang of it. Just then I heard a door slam and a voice command, "No talk!"

More banging noises I didn't recognize. Then the sound of heavy boots on the concrete floor, a door dragged shut again, and then silence. I strained to hear something that would let me know what was happening outside my cell. The sounds were too unfamiliar, and I felt ignorant and helpless. They were foreign feelings to me, and I hated them.

The silence continued. I sat down on one of the concrete bunks and tried to put up the mosquito net the guards had tossed in before locking me in the cell. Until now, my flesh had been fair game for the myriad of droning mosquitoes in North Vietnam. At first I had tried swatting at them with my left arm, but it was a painful and futile use of the little energy I had, and I soon gave up.

Assembling that net should have been a simple task. It needed to be secured at four corners of the bunk with four string ties. I fumbled with the ties, cursed my limp right hand, but finally affixed the net and lay down under it.

In the quietness, I heard soft, muffled tapping. I listened for a moment and tried to decipher the code. Jerry was telling me to move to the bunk closest to the wall that separated our cells. We could tap softly to one another and look as if we were sleeping if the guards checked on us. At night it was difficult for them to see us through the mosquito nets. Already Jerry was paying for having talked to me earlier. The noises I had heard were the sounds of the leg stocks and the steel bar being slammed and locked against his legs. He couldn't get to the window on the door to talk to me, but the punishment of the leg stocks didn't stop him from tapping. All night we "talked" on the wall.

I was slow, but after a few hours I began to pick up speed with the code. Most of the tapping that went on in Heartbreak was between Jerry and me. Stockdale was too far away, and the empty cells between us interfered with transmission. We had to communicate with him in whispers when the guards were out. At those times, he was our clearance man. He lay on the floor in his cell and watched for the crack of light when the main door opened. Then he banged loudly, a signal for us to stop talking quickly.

That first night in Heartbreak Jerry pumped me for news about the war. He had been locked up for nearly a year, and he wanted to know how it was going. I can almost laugh now when I think back to my answer. I was optimistic then. In spite of the munitions problems and the other frustrations inherent in this undeclared war, I believed we were winning it.

"I think we'll be out of here in a year," I tapped on the wall.

As he asked me more questions about world events, the 1965 and '66 baseball World Series, college and professional football teams, I realized how news-starved he was. Soon everything I knew would be yesterday's headlines, and I too, would be desperate for information about the world outside the concrete walls of Hoa Lo. Our captors would make sure we heard only what they wanted us to know. Any accurate news about the war and world events would come to us as bits and pieces brought in by the new shootdowns and tapped on the walls at risk of beatings or a week in leg stocks or, in later years, a stint in leg irons.

It was still dark the next morning when I awoke to the guards' harsh, animal-like grunts as they trudged through Heartbreak's corridor. In a few moments, a guard opened my door. He grunted and motioned for me to pick up my bucket and walk down the hall. Directly across from Stockdale's cell he stopped and shoved me into a cell converted into a makeshift washroom.

Gray patches of mildew grew on the cement walls. The air was heavy with the smell of open sewage. A thin stream of water dribbled onto the floor from a pipe running up the far wall. With no faucets to shut it off, the "shower" ran continually and flowed into a sewage drain hole in the floor. Using gestures and grunts again, the guard made me understand I was supposed to shower and rinse out my waste can under that pitiful stream of water.

I studied the room for a minute. I was barefooted. I had to empty my bucket and shower in the same piece of floor in that dingy, dank cell. There had to be a way to do it without stepping in my own refuse. American know-how rose to the fore, and I stood on the bunks, one foot on each bunk, straddling the drain hole in the floor. Awkwardly, with my one good hand, I tipped the can and dumped its contents down the drain hole, then rinsed it and set it aside. When the drain hole was clear, I stepped down under the shower stream.

My arm in its crumbling cast and my dislocated shoulder made showering a difficult chore, but the torture room's stench of dried blood and sweat had followed me to my cell, and I was anxious to be rid of it. I returned to my cell wearing coarse, pajama-like shorts over skin that still burned from the lye soap I was given for washing. I would not be allowed out of my cell again until the next day's trek to the shower.

The first meal of the day arrived around 10:00 A.M. The guards opened the cell doors only a crack and shoved in a plate or dish of rice and pumpkin soup. I received the only other possession I would be allowed, besides my paint can and my drinking cup, and that was a tiny teapot filled with weak tea. There would be no refills until the next day. It became my daily challenge to make the brew last all day, through the night, and into the next morning.

Later in the morning, a guard opened my cell door and pushed me down onto one of the bunks. With dull and rusty clippers I wouldn't have used on a dog with mange, he hacked at my hair and clipped away at three weeks' worth of beard. It was my first experience of what became a monthly ordeal. Only years later were we given a razor and a bowl of water once a week and allowed to shave ourselves in our cells.

I learned that the Vietnamese here observed the same siesta period I had seen among peasants in the villages. From about noon to 2:00 P.M. the guards left for what we called "quiet hour." During those hours, Denton, Stockdale, and I could talk with each other almost freely. We looked forward to that time the way school kids anticipate recess. And I wondered, as I had before, why our military strategists didn't plan bombing missions during this time when we could have caught the enemy off guard. It seemed the intransigent theorists in our military system could not effect any intelligent or innovative tactic when the war was run from Washington, D.C., thousands of miles away.

The second meal of the day arrived around 5:00 P.M. The menu varied only if cabbage or boiled sewer greens, a slimy, seaweed-like plant that grew in river bottoms, were substituted for the pumpkin soup. The awful pigfat came only once a day in the early days of my imprisonment, and seldom was it without skin and hair. Never was it larger than a fingernail. Even during the worst days of my captivity, when I thought I couldn't endure another moment of hunger, I could not bring myself to eat the pigfat.

Camp routine included daily propaganda sessions, and they began for me immediately. Dressed in the pajama-like garb, I walked to the interrogation room the first morning after my shower, shave, and haircut. There sat Rabbit, and I looked straight at him as I encountered the first command I would openly resist.

"Bow," a guard ordered.

I refused. It would have meant acquiescence, agreement with their insistence that the Vietnamese were superior, and I couldn't bring myself to do it. It was a small act of defiance, and I didn't know what it would bring in the way of punishment, but I was determined to withhold any act that would suggest respect for these uncivilized captors. Oddly, at this point they didn't force me to obey.

The propaganda sessions were much as I had been taught to expect in survival school. I was lectured on the history of Vietnam, the evil oppression of the French, the glorious purpose of North Vietnam. I was surprised only by the fact that these people really believed that American prisoners would buy what they were selling. That we would readily believe their story and forget, even disdain, all we had known and experienced of freedom, democracy, and the capitalist system after a few hours of their propaganda lectures.

They asked me to write letters to the Congress and the president asking them to stop the war, and I refused. I was surprised when Rabbit sent me back to my cell without further punishment. Perhaps he thought I was so badly off already that torture would do little more than render me unconscious and useless to him.

On the third day, the guards offered me cigarettes. I didn't smoke so I refused their offer, and Denton and Stockdale roared.

"Take them for us," they begged, whispering and tapping down the empty corridor of Heartbreak. Six cigarettes per day, divided between the two of them, plus the few they were offered—a man could almost enjoy himself. But how would they get them from me? Then they told me of the secret hiding places in the washroom—the space above the window, the places under the bunks that still jutted out of the walls in the washroom, the cracks and nooks of the leg stocks on the bunks, and over the door there were holes in the concrete between the bricks. The hiding places were many.

I told the guards I had changed my mind about the cigarettes, and they gave me a whole pack of Vietnamese-manufactured Trong Sons.

Like the old World War II Camels, they were short rolls of tobacco without filters. Something a man would walk a mile for, or if not a mile, at least as far as the washroom. I hid six each day, and Stockdale and Denton took turns picking them up during their morning showers, then returned to their rooms to smoke and feel smug that we had put something over on the guards.

We bled each other for information in those early days and weeks together in Heartbreak. I wanted to know all they could tell me about the prison and the authority here. They wanted to know everything I could tell them about home.

We discussed the war and how it was being run. Each of us had believed it would be a quick war, but now we felt certain that, without a ground invasion in the North or some other big change in policy, such as nuclear attack, we would be here for a very long time. We wondered how we could survive the treatment the North Vietnamese called humane. We wondered if, by our responses to their harsh treatment, we might be able to effect some changes from within. We determined to continue to resist and, when possible, to encourage all other POWs to do the same.

It was difficult to get messages to Stockdale because he was so far down the hall. We learned we could tap very lightly and still be heard if we pressed an ear against the wall to listen. But punishment, usually leg stocks, sometimes days in handcuffs, or a beating, followed if the guards caught us. They often stood nearby, just out of sight, so they could burst in and pounce on us in the act of talking or tapping. Sometimes they pretended to leave and then sneaked back to try and catch us. Then they screeched and yelled and slammed their rifle butts on our shoulders. But they had no authority to order serious punishment. They had to tattle on us to the camp authority to get us locked into leg stocks or irons.

In many ways, they were like children. They followed commands and reported back to their superiors. They never acted on their own initiative. And they tattled not only on the prisoners, but on each other.

As with any totalitarian structure, the system of authority within the prison could survive only if it identified and eliminated all disobedience and objections. This created a unique system of spying among the camp guards themselves. Each was aware of the need for complete obedience, but he was equally aware of the rewards he might gain for reporting on any disobedience or dissent among his peers. They squealed on each other like kids in a kindergarten class hoping to gain favor with the teacher.

Air Force Major Jim Lamar joined us in Heartbreak during my first week there. He was shot down while flying an F-105. We were anxious to get him "on the wall" with the tap code so that we could find out what was happening outside, but it wasn't going to be easy. There was an empty cell between him and Stockdale, and that interrupted the flow of communication. Stockdale could clear for us, and we could whisper, but tapping was more difficult.

One day, I discovered that if I pressed the side of my face against the peephole and looked out through the tiny crack where the hinge latched, I could look down the hall and see my buddies. It wasn't easy, and the view was often sliced and obstructed, like the image of a slide placed wrongly in a projector. But there they were. I was not alone. I could see them when the guards walked them down the hall to the shower or to a quiz. Every day I looked forward to that glimpse of a friend. It worked until one day a guard caught me peeking out through the slit. He yanked the window cover open and slammed it shut again quickly against my ear.

"No look! No look!" he shouted from the hallway before he walked away. As soon as I was sure he was gone, I was back at the peephole again. But the ringing in my ear lasted for hours.

The guards didn't have to have a reason to harass us. They loved to pass through the hallways and slam their rifles against the doors or jerk open the peephole covers and then slam them shut. Their ruses to catch us communicating were as foolish as they were childish. They would stomp down the hall, slam shut the door to the cellblock, hoping to make us believe all the guards had exited, while leaving one behind to catch us in the act of talking to one another. It only worked once or twice. Stockdale's cell had a view of the hallway and the only door into the cellblock. He learned to listen and watch to see how many guards entered and then count to be sure the same number exited before giving the signal for all clear.

We learned from each other that entry into Hoa Lo via the torture room was standard procedure for all POWs. We had each spent about the same amount of time with Rat and his torture guard. We had all gone through his interrogation, torture and beatings, isolation, and deprivation. The pattern was the same: military interrogation until they were satisfied with something we told them, even if it was foolish. We had all felt the wind change when Rabbit entered the scene and began political interrogations. We came to call them quizzes.

One morning a guard entered my cell and ordered, "Put on," which meant I was supposed to put on the long-sleeved shirt and long pants for a meeting with Rabbit. In our tiny cells, Hanoi's summer heat baked us like pottery in a kiln, and we wore short pajama pants with a drawstring at the waist and no shirt at all in a futile effort at comfort. But a visit to Rabbit was considered a formal affair, and we were required to wear our long pants and put on our shirts and button them to the top.

My injured arms made me slow and clumsy. The guard grew impatient and hollered, "Quick-ee! Quick-ee!"

He watched with exasperation as I struggled. When I fumbled with the buttons, he made a disgusted sound, leaned his rifle against the doorframe, pushed my hands out of the way and finished the job for me.

I felt amost excited about leaving the dank, dismal concrete cell and walking outside across the courtyard under the blue sky, even if it was to a quiz with Rabbit. It offered a chance to breathe open air. And, in fact, I felt even a little stimulated at the thought of a battle of wits with Rabbit. I hoped he would inadvertently inform me of something significant about the war that I could take back to my buddies. All my senses were finely tuned to pick up something, anything new or encouraging.

"Bow," the guard ordered when he opened the door and ushered me in to face Rabbit.

I stood stiff and straight, still refusing to show any respect for the camp authority who refused to respect the Geneva Conventions. I had learned I could placate them with the slightest nod of the head. I told myself it was a signal to let the games begin.

Rabbit sat in a comfortable chair behind a large executive desk and motioned for me to sit on the tiny stool. It was built for men much smaller than I, and when I sat down, my knees folded up against my chest. Rabbit hoped to make me feel ridiculous and powerless, the better to intimidate and threaten me from his position of advantage, but I felt only relief. From Denton and Stockdale I had learned that if I was made to remain standing, I would be in for a tough, perhaps brutal interrogation session. But so far, the quizzes had not been too bad. I had the feeling Rabbit was toying with me, hoping to catch me off guard by his "leniency."

"Wouldn't you like medical treatment for your arm?" Rabbit asked me.

"Yes, I would," I answered cautiously. I knew there would be a price.

"Maybe we can get a surgeon to operate on you," he offered.

"No, I don't want to be operated on," I told him firmly. "I won't agree to an operation. I'd rather leave the arm as it is than submit to your surgeons."

Rabbit wanted to discuss the idea, but I was adamant.

"There must be other ways to take care of my injuries. I will not allow you to operate on me."

"You have no say in this matter," Rabbit said, and dismissed me.

A few days later Rabbit brought up the subject of surgery again.

"I'd rather just have you put it in a cast," I told him.

"We will do what we choose with you. You have no say!"

I had made him angry. Every muscle in his body was taut. He looked as though he might suddenly snap like a bow string tied too tight.

"We will determine what is to be done to you!" His voice rose to a shriek. "You have no say in this matter!"

It was a scary thought to take back to my cell with me. I had visions of Vietnamese in white coats sawing my arm off with a dull, rusty blade.

The arm was broken within and above the original cast, and what was left of the cast was loose and crumbling and useless. I knew one was a severe diagonal break—I could feel a space widening between my upper and lower arm where the broken ends of the bone had separated. I had to face the possibility that I would never regain full use of that arm. It had to be set and immobilized immediately.

*Please, God,* I prayed, *let them just put a cast on the arm.*

The Vietnamese had tried to persuade Stockdale to let them operate on him too, but he had refused. He recounted some of the horror stories he had heard about their primitive surgical techniques. He believed there was a good chance they would have amputated his leg if he had agreed to surgery. His leg was now fused at the knee, but at least he did still have the leg. He walked with a unique shuffle-drag gait that made him easy to identify in the hallway of the cellblock when we pressed our ears to the wall.

"Don't let them cut on you!" he whispered down the hall.

One night, after a quiz in which I had again refused surgery, a guard opened my cell door and commanded, "Put on."

*Oh, no,* I thought. *What now?* There were only two possibilities. When a prisoner was taken from his cell at night, it was to move him to another part of the prison or to take him to a torture session. Neither prospect appealed. Stockdale, Denton, and Lamar had quickly become important friends to me. I hated the thought of being separated from them. I also hated the thought of torture.

I stepped out of the cell dressed in my long pants and shirt and followed the guard out into the courtyard. He motioned for me to get into the back of a waiting jeep. He shoved a dark olive-drab army blanket at me and said, "Put it over your head."

"It's too hot," I answered. My clothes were already wet from the short walk in the humid heat of Vietnam's summer. I would swelter under a heavy blanket.

"Cover up," he ordered, and gestured to two other guards to throw the blanket over me and anchor it down.

The jeep engine sputtered as we drove out of the prison gate and into the streets of Hanoi. I managed to maneuver under the blanket so as to peek out and see that we were driving through the city. After about an hour we finally stopped at an old, deteriorating structure that looked like a Hollywood version of a French foreign legion headquarters.

The guard pulled me from the jeep, draped the blanket over my head, and walked me into the building. He sat me down in a hallway with the blanket still covering me. From beneath the blanket I could only see the floor. Scores of feet moved about, and I could hear the sounds of a hospital waiting room. Babies cried, children hollered and chased, and voices scolded in sing-song Vietnamese.

Under the blanket, sweat flowed down my body like little rivers. It was like sitting fully dressed in a sauna. After a wait that seemed interminable, a hand gripped my arm, walked me into a small room, and yanked off the blanket.

I looked around at what I guessed was an x-ray room, albeit a primitive one. The equipment resembled World War I vintage. A heavy, white-coated woman walked in and stood in front of me, studying me with a look of seething anger. She satisfied every stereotype I have ever known of a communist woman: overweight, frumpy, and unpleasant. Her white coat hung loosely over a drab dress that was too long and too big even for her large size. She adjusted her wire-rimmed spectacles and peered at me intently from round eyes that suggested some French blood had gotten mixed in with her Vietnamese heritage.

"Lie on the bed," she said. "We will x-ray your arm."

She gestured toward the dirty bed. As soon as I was lying down, she began her speech.

"Why do you bomb our beautiful country? You know you are a war criminal." It was like replaying a tape recording of all I had already heard. "You are interfering with our just revolution. You are killing innocent women and children." She leaned close to me, as if she could better convince me if she looked into my eyes. "Why do you fight a war on the other side of the world?"

I did not even try to answer. She shrugged with disgust and continued her tirade. "You are cowards who fight a small country. You would not think of interfering with Russia, yet you interfere with the wishes of the Vietnamese people. Why is that? It is because you are cowards!"

She was another version of the Rabbit. Another political officer of some sort, brought in to do the work of propagandizing. I was supposed to believe she was a doctor because of her white coat, but she never touched my arm. She spoke to a technician who took three x-rays, and then she sent me across the hall into another room with instructions to wait for the doctor.

For more than an hour I waited, observing the facilities my captors called a hospital. Filth lay over everything like a dismal coverlet. Dusty, stained sheets were draped over ancient pieces of equipment. Grime crawled up the walls from the floor. Gnats, mosquitos, and other insects flew in and out of large window openings that held no glass. I swatted at something that buzzed near my ear and thought, *How does anyone survive a medical crisis in this place?*

The woman returned with a "doctor"—he was wearing the requisite white coat—and upon entering the room she began her assault on the American military.

"The humane people of Vietnam have brought you to this hospital. You will be cared for." She paused, no doubt expecting to see some sign of humility and gratitude. Seeing none, she continued in a shrill voice, "You are a criminal! You must repent!"

She moved about the room like a practiced strategist, finding the best position for firing her next political salvo. All the while, the doctor fidgeted with equipment, studied my arm, and finally handed me the x-rays. Even to my untrained eye the severity of the damage was clear. The humerus, which should have appeared as one large bone, was in three pieces. A jagged chunk of bone looked as if it was floating in a space where broken pieces met in a V formation.

*What a mess,* I thought. *Now what?* And then, *Please, God, don't let them cut it off.*

"We will put it in a cast for you," he said.

I drew a deep breath. *Thank you, God.* He had heard and answered.

The old cast came off easily. When the last of the crumbled plaster was removed, the doctor laid my broken arm against my stomach. Then he began wrapping gauze around my upper body, binding my broken arm to my torso.

When I was wrapped like a mummy and my arm pressed and held flat against my stomach by all the gauze, he began layering the gauze with plaster. He ignored my left shoulder, which was still dislocated and sloping at a grotesque angle. But the rest of my upper body, from neck to waist, he completely enveloped in plaster. I wore my own personal sauna bath.

Perhaps sometime in the future I would be thankful for the body cast, as it probably aided the healing of my fractured vertebra. But that day, as I contemplated the horrible humid heat of my cell, I felt only dread. Swathed in plaster and already beginning to sweat. I had to choke down a rising sense of panic and claustrophobia.

*I'll be all right,* I told myself, drawing a long, unsteady breath. *In a few weeks it will come off, and I'll be all right.*

I had no idea the misery that awaited me. I had no way of knowing I would wear that heavy body cast through all of North Vietnam's sweltering, sauna-like heat. For the next six months I would be encased, like a turtle, in a plaster shell.

I stumbled from the hospital, weighted down by the heavy blanket draped over my head and the awful burden of the cast surrounding me. My chest felt as though a vise had enclosed it. Only the dampness of the new cast relieved the stifling heat of the summer night, but that small respite was not enough to dismiss the sensation that swamped me. I felt buried and lost in a primitive plaster furnace.

The woman followed me out to the jeep. She turned up the volume on her political lecture to be sure I could hear every word from under the blanket.

"You are a criminal, you understand. There is nothing your government can do for you now." She walked quickly to catch up as the guards prodded me forward. "You must repent. If you do not you will die here. Do you want to die here?"

From under the blanket I could see her feet hurrying and nearly tripping, trying to keep pace with me so that she could finish her sermon. The jeep's engine struggled to life and drowned out her cackling voice which cried after me, "Repent!"

Sometime around midnight I stumbled into my cell, exhausted and soaked with perspiration. Stockdale, Lamar, and Denton were waiting to find out what had happened to me. In whispers and muffled taps, I told them about the ordeal at the hospital. Somehow it seemed easier to bear because I was not alone.

A few nights later, Robbie Risner joined us in Heartbreak. Guards shoved him into the cell across the hall from me and slammed the door shut. We learned that he had been in "New Guy Village" and then moved to the Zoo, an old French film colony on the outskirts of Hanoi. He knew Larry Chesley and told me Larry had been interrogated and moved with the others to the Zoo.

Lieutenant-Colonel Robinson Risner, commander of the 67th Tactical Fighter Squadron, was the senior ranking officer among the POWs in Hanoi's prison system. He had been something of a problem to the Vietnamese. He had insisted on more rights under the Geneva Conventions. He had organized the POWs and gotten them to communicate, and he had been caught talking. He had been ousted from the Zoo and taken to New Guy Village to be punished by isolation. All this we learned in cautious whispers. He would spend most of his prison years isolated from the other POWs, and the mantle of leadership would then fall on Stockdale.

Stockdale and Denton both shared the rank of commander, and the same date of rank, but only one could be SRO. The decision was made based on class standing at Annapolis. Stockdale stepped into position. He too would be isolated from the others later, and Denton would take command. The organizational structure was in place.

Robbie was confused and uncertain about what was happening. He had been ordered to "put on," as if going to a quiz. But instead he'd been placed in a cell, and he had not been allowed to bring his bedroll, his can, or the few personal items he had been issued. It was all very curious. Our questions were answered about an hour later when the guards set up a large, old-fashioned radio in the hallway and tuned the station to Radio Hanoi.

The guards opened the little shuttered windows on our doors and motioned for us to come and stand with our faces at the windows. A voice crackled through the cellblock, and we made our first acquaintance with Hanoi Hannah, Vietnam's version of Tokyo Rose.

"This broadcast is especially for American boys," her strident voice blared at us. "Why should you keep fighting for a losing cause? This war is bad for the United States. It would be better for them if they had never involved themselves. It is an exercise in disaster."

Hannah lectured us for half an hour. Two guards stood in the middle of the hallway to prevent us from talking while our windows were opened. They peeked in every few minutes, checking to be sure we were standing by our doors, listening to every word. For us, the open window was an opportunity to see each other, to make eye contact. For the first time, I was able to put a face to the friendly voices that gave me courage. The only one I couldn't see was Denton, in the cell next door. But Lamar and I winked at each other in recognition. I nodded at Risner and got a small glimpse of Stockdale's eyes peering down the hallway toward me.

When the program ended, Risner's door was opened, and the guards walked him out of Heartbreak and back to isolation in New Guy Village.

The radio in the hallway was the precursor to the sound system that was eventually installed. Soon every cell had a loudspeaker hanging from the ceiling. Every prisoner listened to propaganda programs, and if he appeared to be inattentive, the guard banged his rifle on the door, or opened the door and banged his rifle on the prisoner.

In Heartbreak, we were trying desperately to remain upbeat about the war. In every quiz, every encounter with the enemy, we looked for a reason to hope. We took note of every incident that took place in the camp, regardless of how insignificant, looking for hints about the status of the conflict. Our guards told us nothing. Hanoi Hannah told us only lies.

Time began to stand still. I often stared at the scratches made in the wall to mark off the days spent in Heartbreak. I added mine to those of earlier prisoners.

"Don't do that," Denton said, when I told him what I was doing. "If the guards find it they'll beat on you for sure. Just mark the Sundays. They're easy to keep track of because the guards slack off then."

So on Sunday we scratched a mark into the wall—the end of one week in prison, the beginning of another. It seemed right somehow to pray together on that day. A bump on the floor was the signal, and in our respective cells we knelt beside our concrete bunks and prayed.

I could feel the faith that had waned during my teen and adult years begin to grow strong again. But with resurgence of faith came sadness. God was like a friend I had unkindly ignored, and I felt an intense need to ask Him for forgiveness. The reality of His presence in that cell was indescribable. I was calmed and uplifted.

During the quiet hour, when we could communicate without fear of being caught, the most pressing subject was: how can we get out of here? It was unreasonable to believe we could escape on our own. We would have to have help from someone on the inside. We would have to begin feeling our way along, finding out who might be interested in working with us.

Risner was alone over in New Guy Village, but every day guards walked him to Heartbreak for his morning shower. Stockdale's cell across the hall from the shower gave him a chance to talk with Risner if the guards stepped away for a few moments. He told Risner we were considering an escape plan, and we thought we had come up with a workable idea. We would begin with the interrogator. We would be subtle in the beginning, but we would try to interest him in escaping from Vietnam with us. We would arrange to get him to the United States, we would tell him, and we would take care of him. Risner agreed with the plan.

Stockdale and Denton had not been called to quiz much lately, and Lamar appeared to have finished his sessions for the time being. But Rabbit wasn't finished with me yet. Since I was the one spending the most time in interrogation, it was decided I would be the one to begin suggesting the idea of escape.

At the next quiz, as I sat on the stool facing Rabbit, I drew a deep breath and thought, *Okay, Sam, if you're ever going to be cool, now is the time . . .*

I was nervous, but I thought Rabbit was a better candidate for the inside job than the other camp officers with whom we had had dealings. We needed someone with authority to get us a vehicle and pass us through the prison gates and past the guards. Rabbit could do it. He was also somewhat literate and seemed genuinely interested in the United States. At times, he seemed to hint at dissatisfaction with the Hanoi regime. It could be a trick, of course, to catch us off guard and prompt a careless admission from us. But something about him triggered an oddly sympathetic chord in me. I believed he had decided Ho Chi Minh held no special regard for him and his talents. I saw him as a somewhat disillusioned puppet, perhaps willing to have his strings snipped. Perhaps he harbored a secret dream of freedom and the American way of life. Perhaps he would help us escape and save himself as well.

When I look back at it now, I'm aghast at my own naiveté. I can rationalize and say I acted out of desperation and irrational optimism, but the truth is, I was appallingly ignorant of my enemy's wiles. As the communist party official, Rabbit was the most powerful officer in the prison system. His authority went unchallenged, even by military officers who outranked him. But I had no idea, at that time, of the extent of his power.

"It sure would be nice to get back to the United States," I mentioned casually after Rabbit dismissed the guard who stood near the door. "Looks like the war is dragging a little bit. Wouldn't you like to visit the U.S.?"

"Yes, I would," he answered.

*This is great,* I thought. *Now, just leave it dangling like a little piece of bait on a hook.*

The next day I felt sort of excited when I was called in to quiz. I reminded myself this was a strategic military operation. I might have to stoke the conversation. I couldn't afford to antagonize.

"What are U.S. highways like?" Rabbit asked.

*Tell him something, Johnson,* I told myself. *Don't make him mad at you.*

"Well," I said, "We have cars everywhere."

"Everywhere?" he questioned. He didn't understand. In Vietnam there are bicycles everywhere but only a few cars.

"Yeah," I answered, acting casual and disinterested. "We ought to take you over there and show you."

Rabbit changed the subject and began talking about ridiculous, irrelevant things, and I thought, *He's practicing his English on me.*

"You know, if you could get to the States, you could really begin to learn English fluently," I said, as cool as could be.

"Yes, I would like that," Rabbit answered.

Over the next couple of weeks I dragged the bait and watched to see how close Rabbit would come. One day I asked him outright, "Why don't you help us get out of this prison? We'll take you back with us."

I waited, feeling as if I had just asked to take a ride on the Tiger from Niger. Rabbit just looked at me, didn't answer, and then changed the subject.

Two days later I asked him, "Do you want to go to the United States?"

He answered calmly, "Yes."

"Would you go with us now? Help us escape? If we could get out of Hanoi we could get out easily. We'll take you with us. We can be sure you are taken care of."

It was difficult to hide my excitement. I willed myself to sit still on that ridiculous little stool while I waited for his answer.

"No. Too many people; you would be recognized."

"You could get us out," I said.

We had a plan. If we could get out of the prison, we would head north and attempt to commandeer a boat and set out to sea. Stockdale and Denton, the navy men, knew the pickup points. It was an almost surefire plan.

Rabbit stroked the space above his thin lips where his sparse, coarse whiskers grew. He didn't answer. In a moment, he called to the guard waiting outside the door, and I was returned to my cell.

As soon as Stockdale gave the all clear, I reported that I thought things looked good. I thought Rabbit might help us. It was hard to contain the excitement I felt.

About three days passed. Rabbit sent for me again. He made his usual opening remarks. I listened from my perch on the stool and then brought up the subject of escape again.

"Will you help us get out of here?"

Rabbit stood up behind and planted his palms on the desk. He leaned toward me, and I felt myself begin to sweat.

"I am a communist," he said, his voice firm and his words deliberate. "I am the *communist party member* for the prison! You do not understand the importance of such a position. I could never leave this country."

He began walking around the room as he talked, pausing occasionally to search for the right English word. "I was thirteen years old when I was conscripted into the army. Men, women, and children all go into Vietnam's army, but only those of us who are quick and dedicated rise to the top." He smiled his smile of superiority. He was enjoying this recitation of his accomplishments.

"I was assigned to an artillery unit. I was with the glorious and victorious troops at the battle of Dienbienphu when the imperialistic forces of the French were routed. The party took notice of my devotion and my courage." He paused and stared hard at me, watching for my response. "I have struggled, but I have made a place in the communist party. I will never give it up! Never!"

And with a wide, flourishing gesture, he dismissed me and called for the guard to return me to my cell.

I knew it was over. Back in the cell I told the guys. Risner, Stockdale, Denton, Lamar, and I had been ready to go. We hadn't admitted to each other, even to ourselves, how hopeful we had allowed ourselves to become. Disappointment was bitter, but we would not give up. I wondered what would be the consequences of my actions in the interrogation room with Rabbit. In only a few hours I knew I had triggered a chain of events.

The next night guards arrived at each cell in Heartbreak and said, "Roll up." It was a new command to me, and I didn't understand. With gestures, they indicated that I should roll my prison clothes, mosquito net, toothbrush and drinking cup in my bamboo mat, pick up my teapot, and follow them out of the cell. In the future I would know that "roll up" meant I was moving out.

A guard tied a blindfold over my eyes, but I could push it up enough to see that the rest of the gang from Heartbreak stood in the yard with their bamboo rolls and teapots. The guards ordered, "No talk!" and quickly checked our blindfolds before loading us by pairs into waiting trucks. Stockdale and I made the journey together with a guard seated between us to be sure we did not talk. Sometime later we climbed out of the truck, still blindfolded, but we had been able to see well enough to know we were at the Zoo.

Risner had told us all about this place. The French had once enjoyed the luxury of a swimming pool here and had passed long summer nights watching movies in an adjacent theater. The swimming pool had long ago turned into a slimy green bog. Prisoners had named it "Lake Fester." Millions of mosquitos and other disease-carrying insects made their homes in the scum and debris that floated on the surface of the water, but that didn't deter the camp guards from raising fish in it for food. The auditorium had been converted into a cellblock, and beneath its stage the Vietnamese had built tiny, almost grave-sized cells to house prisoners deserving of special punishment.

Guards marched me toward a dilapidated building that stood just inside the camp entrance and put me in a small room turned into a cell. Each makeshift cell in that building opened out onto a veranda that ran the length of the building. Cracked and falling shutters hung over large windows that also looked out on the porch. They were supposed to keep us from being able to see out, but I could look through the cracks and into the yard where film cans, long since discarded, lay rusting on the ground. Old rolls of film, rotting and mildewed, lay about like sorry leftover streamers from a party ended in haste.

While POWs were led away to other facilities, Stockdale and I were isolated from the rest and placed in neighboring cells in this dingy building. The camp authority had pegged us quickly. We insisted on communicating regardless of their idiotic rules. And we had plotted an escape. We were troublemakers.

My cell was slightly larger than the one I left at Heartbreak, but no less dismal. I had two wooden bunks and a paint can. A single light bulb dangled from the ceiling and revealed a sticky layer of dirt and filth on the brick walls and concrete floor. (It was amazing to me that light bulbs never seemed to burn out. There was no relief from the dismal surroundings.) The stench of the stagnant pond lay over the entire camp.

Stockdale and I started tapping to each other immediately. When we had worn down our fingernails, we took up our toothbrushes. These left telltale markings in the concrete – markings the guards learned to recognize as evidence of our disobedience – so we began to tap using the soft pads of our fingertips. We learned that these soft taps could be heard down the length of a hallway if we used our tin drinking cups as amplifiers. We could place the mouth of the cup against the wall, lay an ear against the cup's bottom, and hear an otherwise almost silent transmission. We signaled danger by just a light bump of the shoulder against the common wall.

We were seldom caught. A room full of Asian prisoners separated us from the other American POWs in the building, and the guards seemed more interested in that end of the building than in ours. Often we were left completely alone for hours. Our only contact with other POWs was made when we were taken to the showers.

A cellblock we called the "Barn" lay just parallel to the showers. Its windows faced the open side of the makeshift shower stalls, and I could always feel my internal antennae rise when I walked past. My ears strained for taps, thuds, bumps – any sound that resembled the code. Sometimes it was possible, when the guards looked away (as they always did because they would not watch us bathe), to send a hand signal, or a message to the prisoners peering through cracked window shutters. Nearly every day I had contact with someone in the Barn. It was usually Howie Rutledge.

Navy Commander Howard Rutledge was the executive officer of Fighter Squadron 191 off the U.S.S. *Bon Homme Richard*. He was flying an F-8E when he was shot down in November, 1965. In the months he had been in Hanoi's prison system he too had earned a reputation as a troublemaker. We dubbed him "the Great Communicator." Nothing stopped Howie. Not even banishment to "Alcatraz." There, a few months later, he honed his skills. Not only was he a fearless communicator, but he also seemed to be able to discern and identify sounds that the rest of us never even heard. It was uncanny. He could hear footsteps on a dirt path or the concrete hallway of the cellblock and tell whether they belonged to a friend or foe. We all learned to identify the sounds of our compatriots – the way they walked was distinctive – but Howie was the master. He could almost read our minds by listening to our footsteps outside his cell door.

Navy Commanders Jim Mulligan and Harry Jenkins were in the

Barn that summer too. On my daily trips to the showers I discovered them to be fearless communicators, "hardcore" or "diehards," as the Vietnamese liked to call us.

Harry "Ichabod" Jenkins, with his hooked nose and skinny frame, stood tall enough to look over the top of the shower stalls and send messages and signals right over the guards' heads. He had endured horrible torture shortly after his shootdown in November, 1965. The Vietnamese had recognized his name from U.S. media reports, and he had become the first senior officer thrust into torture immediately. But he, like Rutledge and Mulligan, refused to adhere to the ridiculous rules of the prison authority. Not only did they refuse to obey, but they encouraged new shootdowns to learn the code and defy the camp authority. They, too, became known as troublemakers who would find their place among the "blackest of criminals" in Alcatraz.

Jim Lamar moved in with me early that summer. We had heard each other's voices in Heartbreak and had tapped out terse messages, but we really didn't know each other. Now that we were roommates, we discovered that we shared a common Texas heritage. I was impressed that I was living with a descendant of a man who had been one of the presidents of Texas before it joined the United States. We became instant friends.

My body cast and dislocated shoulder made me slow and awkward, and I needed help for even the simplest acts. Perhaps the Vietnamese put him in with me for that reason. He was always quick to do what he could for me, although between us we had only one good arm. He had suffered a broken arm too, and it had fused in an L position at the elbow. Still, he was able to help me put on a shirt when I was called in for quiz, and he poured water on me to help me bathe so that I didn't have to stand under the shower in my body cast. There was little I could do for him, and that bothered me, but at times I tried to hold his shirt sleeve while he slipped into it or help him tip his water bucket. He always said thanks, as if I had done him a great favor. It was little compared to all he did for me.

My joy at having a roommate was only shadowed by my sadness for Stockdale. He continued in solitary confinement. Though we tapped and whispered to him throughout the day, it was not the same. He asked the prison authority several times for a roommate, but every time the request was denied. I'm sure they delighted in refusing him the solace of human companionship. The more he asked, the firmer their resolve to say no.

Political interrogations continued at the Zoo. It was always the same. Like children who never tired of the same game, interrogators repeated the jargon and the threats.

"You must write to your president and tell him this war is unjust."

"I can't do that," I answered.

There was no punishment at that time. Though others were experiencing some torture, I was spared. The body cast may have deterred them from inflicting further abuse. But still, the quizzes continued.

"Song, you do not have good attitude," they scolded. "You must repent of your criminal acts against the Vietnamese people." ("Song" was the Vietnamese name the commander gave me. All prisoners were given names the Vietnamese could pronounce easily.)

"Song, you must choose. If you will cooperate, if you will repent, you will receive better treatment. Always there are some diehards. Not many, but some. It will not go well for them. It will not go well for you, Song."

Back in the cell, I listened to the loudspeakers that hung from the ceiling as they spouted the same rhetoric.

"You will be tried for your crimes. You will never go home. The just cause of the Vietnamese people will never be defeated. Even now the tribunal is being assembled. Your crimes will be punished."

I learned to tune it out, but some days listening to the childish and illogical doctrines of Ho Chi Minh's thinking, the half-truths and untruths spoken in pidgin English, grated on my nerves like fingernails across a chalkboard. On those days, I wished for two good arms to rip the speaker from its perch above the door.

It was an unsettling threat hanging over our heads. Would they really try us as war criminals? Would the rest of the world let them get away with it? I didn't believe it could happen. Lamar and Stockdale were not so convinced. We talked a lot about it, about our options.

"It's just for show, guys," I insisted. "More communist garbage. If they tried to try us as war criminals, the American people would react and they know it." I had to believe it. I refused to believe their threats any more than I would believe their promises of the glories of communism.

June 29, 1966, began like all other days in the Zoo. But within hours we knew it would be a day for history books. We first heard sounds of gunfire. Then sirens wailed and screamed as American F-105s roared into the sky overhead. Lamar and I peered out through the cracks in the shutters and watched the underbellies of U.S. fighter planes pass overhead, on the deck.

President Johnson had finally ordered the bombing of Hanoi. It was a strategic move. The petroleum, oil, and lubricants essential to Vietnam's military force were held in storage installations in Hanoi, and those installations were located all around the Zoo. For the protection of both the installations and Hanoi, twenty-five thousand troops surrounded the area.

We were sitting in the middle of a huge deployment of military force. Antiaircraft gun emplacements were situated in strategic positions around the oil storage facilities. Railroad yards just outside the walls of the Zoo lay adjacent to an operating airfield where Russian MiGs landed and took off daily. Being in the Zoo on that summer day in 1966 was like being the bull's-eye on a gunner's target.

For a bombing mission, it lasted a long time. For more than fifteen minutes battle sounds filled the air. We watched as huge oil storage tanks exploded and sent fire and smoke spiraling up into the air. The prison building shook as the bombs landed on their targets. I could see the airfield not far from the Zoo, and it appeared the Vietnamese were trying to clear it of their MiGs before the F-105s could destroy them all.

Our guards' faces were masks of terror.

"Under bed! Get under bed!"

Shouts in pidgin English bounced around the concrete walls of the cellblock as the guards ran from cell to cell, gesturing wildly with their rifles. Suddenly the enemy soldiers who would kill us on command were responsible for our safety. They were determined we should not be injured, and they screamed at us until we obeyed them and crawled into the narrow spaces under the bunks. I hated to give up my front row seat on this historic battle that would later be credited with the destruction of more than half of North Vietnam's petroleum resources. I wasn't at all afraid.

Bombs exploded so close that I could actually watch them fall from the planes' bellies, but somehow I felt that the American forces knew we were there—that each bomb was strategically placed so that we would not be harmed. It was, in fact, one of the only times that President Johnson, from his closed-circuit television twelve thousand miles away, ordered a strategic, surgical strike on the enemy. Perhaps the war would have made a significant turn if he had also ordered ground troops to follow up and seal off the enemy from all further supplies.

On July 6, exactly one week after the bombing of Hanoi, Lamar and Stockdale and I watched through the shutters as thirty-six POWs entered the yard and boarded trucks. They wore their "dress" clothes, sandals, and blindfolds. We tried to guess what was happening, but did not come even close to the right answer. Later in the afternoon, Hanoi Hannah told us the story of the Hanoi March. Her strident voice and pidgin English gave us the details Ho Chi Minh wanted us to have. Communications on the wall later in the prison gave us the bits and pieces that told the real story of U.S. pride and courage through the streets of Hanoi.

I listened to the tapping on the wall, sometimes erratic in its excitement, sometimes slowed and filled with pauses. Fifty-two prisoners, some from each Hanoi prison camp, arrived in the city by truck to be paraded through the streets for the amusement of Hanoi's citizens. Camera crews from several different countries recorded every step of the march of horror.

It seemed nearly every inhabitant of the city turned out to view the fifty-two prisoners, the token representatives of the "American aggressors," who were handcuffed in pairs and ordered to march down the street.

Air Force Captain Bob Purcell, a veteran of one year in Hoa Lo, looked at the crowds lining the roadway and quipped, "A parade! A parade! Oh boy, I love a parade!"

"Today you will see the fury and hatred of the Vietnamese people," Rabbit told the prisoners. "They will try to kill you. We cannot protect you. Show proper attitude for your crimes. If you repent, you will see our lenient and humane treatment. If not, the people will decide what to do with you.

"Show proper attitude," he commanded. "Show your shame for your criminal acts against the peaceful Vietnamese people."

"Bow!" the guards shouted at the soldiers, shoving them into motion with their rifles.

And then, with megaphone in hand, Rabbit directed his voice to the growing mob, turning a curious crowd into one suddenly filled with murderous intent.

"Repent!" cried the guards. "Bow! Show proper attitude!"

Never! was the answer the prisoners sent back with their squared shoulders and their heads held high. They walked through the street, looking straight ahead, unbowed and undaunted. The mob growing larger at every corner taunted them as they passed. Side streets fed more people into the crowd that pressed against them until thousands swarmed the parade route.

Men, women, and children pushed through a line of guards to get close enough to the marchers to spit on them and strike them. The prisoners bunched together, trying to lift the ones who had fallen, trying to shield themselves from the violent mob. Obscenities screamed in oddly accented English pierced the air. One by one, the Americans took blows that staggered them. The guards turned their rifle butts on the crowd. The thing had gotten out of control. They weren't supposed to let the people kill the prisoners, but they were powerless to stop them.

I envisioned the story as it unfolded in soft taps and clandestine whispers. I remembered my own march through a village churned into fury by communist propagandists many months before. The heated pressure of the crowd against my body, the sting of stones bouncing off my shoulders and back, the shrill sounds of shrieking voices—it all came back to me. But for the men who marched through the city streets of Hanoi, it must all be multiplied a thousandfold.

By now, the prisoners knew they were fighting for their lives. They drew on their last reserves of strength to fight their way through the crowd armed with clubs and stones and fueled by ignorance and hate. Pushing and shoving, lifting their fallen partners from the ground, they finally reached the doors of a large stadium where Rabbit stood waiting for them. When the crazed crowd was locked out behind them, they fell to the floor in exhaustion.

Bloody and bruised from their battle through the streets, the fifty-two men congratulated each other. Their clothes hung in torn shreds. Their faces looked like raw meat, but they were alive. They had pushed their way through the thousands and had held their heads high. Not one of them had bowed or shown shame for the actions of the American military.

Rabbit addressed the band of bloody men on the floor in front of him.

"Now. You will choose. Repent of your crimes against the Vietnamese people. Receive lenient and humane treatment. Today you must choose."

The Americans looked around at each other and shook their heads. Rabbit did not understand. The decision had already been made. They would never submit to the idiocy of the Hanoi regime. They would never denounce the actions of the American military in trying to protect South Vietnam from the insanity of this communist regime. They would never repent of their "crimes."

Injured, handcuffed, and blindfolded, the fifty-two POWs limped back to the waiting trucks and returned to their respective prison camps. They were strangely buoyed by the knowledge that they had survived the furious attack of several thousand enraged Vietnamese, but the euphoria was short-lived. Pain from fresh injuries mixed with the pain of realization that the bombing of Hanoi had not brought the war to an end. There was no invasion, no ground battle. The air strikes had angered Ho Chi Minh and, no doubt, slowed his effort somewhat. But routes through the mountains were still open. Hanoi's harbor was intact; and fuel, munitions, and materiel would continue to arrive. The war was far from over.

As the summer passed we refined our communication skills, creatively abbreviating messages. "GN" meant good night; "GBU" – God bless you. One night I tapped to Stockdale, "Don't let the bed bugs bite." The next night I shortened it to "DLTBBB." In time, it became a nightly exchange between many prisoners throughout the camps.

We became adept at transmitting and receiving not only letters and words in tap code, but also the feelings that accompanied our words.

Pragmatic, professional, career military officers—we were an unlikely sort to be able to pick up the subtle nuances of feeling, even in a normal conversation with those we knew well. Prison was heightening our emotional perception, and we found ourselves sensitive and receptive to the feelings of men we had just met, some we had seen only at a glance. By the length of the pauses in our tapping we indicated to each other that day's mood, whether it was one of uncertainty or optimism. Stockdale and I both learned to determine a man's authority and leadership by the manner in which he tapped.

Summer in the Zoo changed suddenly during a quiz one day. I was dressed in my long-sleeved shirt, thanks to Lamar's assistance, and sitting on the too-small, backless stool in front of the interrogator, ready to give the same answers and nonanswers to the same old questions he never tired of asking. He finished his propaganda speech, hurled a few "war criminal" comments at me, and then ordered, "You will write the history of the United States Air Force."

Jim received the same command during his next quiz. We were to work on it together in our cell, Rabbit ordered. At first, we were in a quandary. We turned to Stockdale for advice.

"If we could gain some advantage from it," I speculated, "maybe we ought to give them something."

Stockdale agreed. "Give them something, play along. See what comes of it."

We decided we would produce a "history" of the U.S. Air Force, but it would be unlike anything the U.S. military had ever envisioned. It was risky, but it was worth it. They were going to give us pencils and paper in our cell! *No one* had pencils and paper! We had been making ink out of ashes and water, sometimes mud and urine, and using the rough, coarse toilet paper to write the carefully guarded messages we hid in cracks in the bricks in the shower stalls for the other POWs to find. Now, at last, we had writing materials. We were elated.

Immediately our imaginations went to work. It became a game of misinformation, and we determined to make it last as long as possible. First, we found excuses to ask for more paper and extra pencils, and we squirreled them away in cracked bricks and covered the cracks with mud. The thorough once-a-week searches did not include a strip search at that time, so sometimes we hid scraps of paper under our clothing. We used the extra materials to make ourselves a chessboard and chessmen. We laid our history report on top of the chess board whenever the guards peeked in to see if we were busy at our assignment. And after weeks of writing and stalling and chess playing, we gave them a history of the U.S. Air Force.

It had originated during the Civil War, we wrote, with the Confederacy's use of hot air balloons. Being Texans, we credited the Confederacy with this ingenious idea. The Yankees discovered it and began making their own balloons. The first recorded "dogfights" took place in the air somewhere over the Mason-Dixon Line. Soldiers in gondolas suspended from balloons fired at each other. Union blue and Confederate gray balloons swung in the sky and swooshed toward the ground when bullets or cannon balls ripped through their silk. There was precious little to laugh about in the dark, dingy, seven-foot-square cell we shared, but for weeks we snickered and chortled, entertaining each other with insane battle scenes enacted from hot air balloons. And we played hours of chess.

After our weeks of playing and collaborating on the history report, a guard entered one day and demanded the work.

"Okay," I shrugged, "but it's not quite finished." I was hoping to get a few more days of entertainment out of the project.

"Is finished!" he barked, and held out his hand for the pile of papers.

Jim and I looked at each other. Now what? We waited. Nothing. No response. For several days we waited for something to happen, some punishment to be carried out. It was inconceivable that any thinking person would believe such a story, but whether our captors believed it or chose to ignore it, we never knew.

Shirley's birthday came and went in early September. I imagined her with the children, trying hard to make it a merry occasion, trying to keep smiling and carrying on in spite of her fear and loneliness. I wondered if she knew I was alive. I wondered if she had any idea of how much I loved her and missed her.

With the coming of autumn came a change in the U.S. strategy. Agent Orange was introduced from the American arsenal. The enemy lay so well buried under the jungle cover that bombing missions in the South were futile. It was impossible to find communist targets unless something could be done to open up South Vietnam's jungle and reveal enemy positions. Agent Orange spread across the forests. The density of the jungle foliage held it in the treetops, and it never penetrated the roots or the lower, sheltered plant life. Only the uppermost branches turned brown and died. The dense jungle continued to flourish.

Autumn in Vietnam was much like summer had been – hot and miserable. Some days I lay on my wooden bunk and imagined Colorado at this time of year, its mountains brilliant with the gold and red that signaled the arrival of autumn. I wished for cool mountains and brisk streams, but wishes were wasted in Hanoi's prison system.

Humidity and rains thickened the air. The skin inside the body cast chafed with rash. The plaster had absorbed my sweat like a sponge, and my own body odor rose up to assault my nostrils. Open sewers and the stagnant water of Lake Fester added to the awful smells that made breathing a chore. There was no relief.

For weeks I pestered the guard to talk to someone about removing my cast. I could feel that the bones in my arm had finally connected, but something was terribly wrong with my right hand. My fingers were paralyzed, and the longer I wore that cast the more atrophied my arm and hand would become. I paced the small space in my cell, wondering if I would have any use of that arm and hand.

"I've got to get this thing off," I said to Jim, scraping at the plaster cast that reeked of body odor and mildew.

"I know," Jim answered, grimacing, "but it might be giving you some protection. They don't beat on you in interrogation with that thing on."

"But I'm burning up in here, and I'm afraid if I don't get it off soon I won't have any use of my right hand or arm."

"You're going to have to ask the guards to do something about it."

For weeks the guard ignored my request to remove the cast. For six months I had carried that plaster turtle's shell, through the sauna-like summer and on into the fall. If someone didn't cut it off me soon I was going to begin chipping it off myself. It would have been a slow and tedious chore using a metal spoon, but I couldn't stand it any longer. I stepped up to the window and yelled, "Bao cao!" the Vietnamese phrase for "attention."

A guard ran to our cell to see what was wrong. Then he left quickly and returned with an officer who authorized the removal of the awful, smelly plaster cast. A man in a white coat showed up at my cell a couple of days later with a pair of scissors that looked like dirty hedge clippers. He motioned for me to leave my cell, and he walked me out into the yard. He turned me around a couple of times, then he jabbed the clippers into the plaster, taking with them whatever skin got in the way. He slowly clipped his way across my back and down my chest until the cast fell away like two large halves of a nutshell. The gauze underlayer, now mildewed and green, had begun to rot.

I stared at my body. I hardly recognized my own frame. The plaster body cast had hidden the effect of the near-starvation diet the Vietnamese served us. Now I could see it—I was more skeleton than flesh.

I looked at my skinny, misshapen arm and felt ill. A stray bone chip had settled above the elbow, and my dry, thin skin stretched over it like canvas over a tent pole. Both my shoulders were still out of their sockets. My right hand hung limp and flat, my fingers numb and paralyzed.

Fear and depression closed in on me. I could not let myself give in to them. They were as dangerous an enemy as the khaki-clad men who guarded my cell. Quickly I began to list the exercises I could do to rebuild the strength in my arms and hands.

I lay on the floor in my cell, placed my hands under me, and attempted a push-up. My shoulders failed and I collapsed on the concrete. I tried again and again until finally I held my weight up for a split second and then lowered myself without falling on my face. It was a moment of triumph. If I could do one push-up, I could do more. I would not give up.

My thirty-sixth birthday, October 11, 1966, I spent celebrating some small physical accomplishments. I could almost grip lightly with my right hand using my thumb and index finger, and I had worked up to two push-ups in a row. Every day I watched for some slight improvement, some increase in strength. I set small goals and felt encouraged with every little muscle improvement.

*I'm okay,* I told myself. *I'll get out of this and go on with my life. It will be over soon.*

Most of the time I believed it, in spite of the pain and constant hunger that gnawed inside me. But the direction of the questioning during a quiz one day shattered my fragile optimism. After the usual rhetoric, the threats and promises, the war criminal accusations, the interrogator ordered, "Tell us about the weapons the U.S. criminals are using."

"I don't know anything about weapons," I answered, but I began to feel uneasy. Why the sudden interest in my knowledge of weapons? Military interrogation had ended back in Hoa Lo after the first five days of questioning and beatings. Everything since then had been directed at brainwashing. Propaganda had been the name of the game for nearly six months now.

My insides turned into knots. Had the Vietnamese learned about my position as director of the Air Force Fighter Weapons School? I had manufactured all sorts of stories to make them believe I was ignorant of U.S. weaponry. If they had learned I was a weapons expert, what would they do to extract information from me? Would I be able to hold out under their torture?

I learned later that the United States had begun using anti-radar missiles to take out North Vietnam's radar systems and their SAMs. They wanted to know how it was being done.

"Be reasonable. Tell us what you know about the American bombers and their weapons. We can make things better for you. Or we can make them much worse." It was a time to be cool, to act ignorant. And to be convincing.

"I don't know about those things," I said again, feeling the prickle of sweat on my neck and hoping I looked dumb. I shook my head. "I just fly the planes. Other guys know about that kind of stuff."

It was the same story I had told back in Hoa Lo. And it worked again. I was getting pretty good at playing dumb. A few shrieks, a few threats, and the commander sent me back to my cell. I lay down on my bunk and thought back through the entire question and answer session. I worried that they might somehow discover how much I knew about the weapons that were being used against them; and that they might also discover my breaking point.

Thanksgiving approached. The Vietnamese were curious about this American holiday we celebrated so sumptuously back home. They had nothing like it in North Vietnam. During a quiz, they asked Jim Lamar and me to tell them about it. We had time to think about it in our cells and decide what we would say.

"It's the time for the Great Pumpkin," we said, our faces contorted to prevent a telltale smirk. "You see, every year at this time the Great Pumpkin rises out of the ground. People all over the country sit out in fields and wait. It's good luck if you see it, so people everywhere hope their field will be the one he rises from," we told them.

"I really wish I could be home for it," I added, sighing for effect. "It's a big deal back in the States." The Vietnamese listened with quizzical expressions on their faces. They asked no questions. They sent us back to our cell. Charlie Brown and Linus would have been proud.

December, 1966. It was cold. Our concrete cell held in the chill like a well-insulated icebox. I put on every piece of clothing I had: the long pants over the shorts, the long-sleeved shirt over the T-shirt. My feet ached with the cold. I wondered why some prisoners had socks, but I still had none. Only after months of walking around barefoot on the crud and filth of the camp had I been given a pair of "Ho Chi Minh" sandals, but these were no insulation against the cold that rose up from the concrete floor of our tiny cell. I wrapped myself in a thin, dirty army blanket they gave me, but nothing really kept out the cold. It penetrated all the way to my insides.

Christmas morning came. I remember it well. There were many reasons for sadness and loneliness, but I refused to let myself think about them. I determined not to give in to the awful feelings of depression that I knew could swamp me. There were reasons for giving thanks: I was alive. And I had a roommate. I would not be morose today. I would not give in to self-pity.

Early in the day a guard escorted Jim and me to a large whitewashed room. In the center a long, draped table held a dish of candy and a bowl of the small "monkey" bananas which grew everywhere in North Vietnam. A camp officer stood behind the table, looking benevolent. Christmas was another opportunity for propaganda, and we were offered another show of the "lenient and humanitarian treatment of the Vietnamese people."

I had seen this camp official before. "Chihuahua" was a good name for him. His large head sat on a skinny neck, and his eyes bulged beneath a broad, flat forehead. His khaki uniform fit loosely over his thin frame. He swept the room with a gesture meant to extend generosity and welcome.

"Merry Christmas to you. We honor your religious holiday." He smiled and nodded toward the dishes on the table. "Have some fruit and sweets. The Vietnamese people wish to show their leniency to you at this time when you celebrate your Christmas."

Lamar and I exchanged looks. Was it the stick-and-carrot routine again? We had learned that the Vietnamese never did anything "for free." Everything they did had a reason, a purpose. What was the price for the fruit and the sweets? A statement about the "just" cause of the Vietnamese people? We said nothing. We waited.

"Eat, please. It is for you." Chihuahua smiled and pointed at the dish of fruit.

We hadn't had fresh fruit in months, but what would it cost us?

"Take it, take it," he smiled, pushing the bowl toward us. "The people wish you to enjoy your holiday."

He asked nothing from us, and so we each took a banana. While we ate he regaled us with the glories of Ho Chi Minh's revolution. I tuned out his ramblings spoken in halting English, and I let my thoughts pass back to other Christmases, other expectations. This year I would have rejoiced just to see Shirley's handwriting, just to read her name on an envelope. Since our imprisonment we had not been allowed to write to our families or to receive mail from them. We were hoping at Christmas they would give us a letter from home or the opportunity to write one, but neither was offered. Instead, Chihuahua handed us each a bottle of Vietnamese beer.

"Take this. It is specially for you on your Christmas." His flat, round face beamed with good will. "The people of Vietnam wish it. It is their gift to you."

Jim and I looked at each other and decided to try a swig. The stuff was awful. Another mouthful would have gagged me. I set the bottle down on the table and waited for the guard to return us to our cell. We spent the remainder of the day as we did every other day that winter — moving about and trying to keep warm. We were both quiet with our private Christmas thoughts.

I visualized Shirley and the children spending Christmas without me. I felt their loneliness, and I wondered how much they knew about my situation. I wanted to reassure them, to let them know I believed I was going to be okay, that I would get out of here somehow. I knew Shirley was doing all the right things in my absence — she always did. She was being strong, I knew. But she was hurting too. I ached to put my arms around her, around them all, and to feel their warmth in my arms. I had to continually remind myself of my resolve not to feel sorry for myself.

The war would be over soon. I had to believe that. Few wars in history had ever lasted this long. It had to be over soon. I comforted myself with these thoughts. And I prayed. For Jim Stockdale, still in solitary confinement, and for all the POWs, and for Shirley and my children in far off Texas.

I had been doing a lot of praying lately. In the first few days after my capture, I had felt hindered by guilt for being the kind of man who calls on God only when he is in trouble. I regretted the years of indifference, when my family and career were moving along without crisis, and I had believed in my own sufficiency. The long, quiet hours of isolation and pain at Hoa Lo had made me intensely aware of my need for God.

Early Bible teachings returned to my memory, and I began to understand the deep significance of forgiveness. Using the Sunday School terminology I'd learned as a boy, I'd talked to God and rediscovered His mercy and peace. Bible stories and verses I had learned as a child had flooded back to me, and prayer had become as natural to me as breathing. God was very real to me during that first holiday in prison. I felt confident that He was with me, and that the God I had known as a boy had never let me out of His sight. His presence seemed to fill the tiny, dark cell, opening a window of hope for me.

In the days following Christmas my feelings of hope swelled. I learned from Stockdale that he had discovered a way to communicate with the U.S. military. Through surreptitious taps he tried to explain how it was to be accomplished: invisible carbon sent in a letter from his wife. It was hard to explain the process fully on the wall, but just knowing we could send and receive news from home was a boon to my spirits. It would be several weeks before I understood just exactly how it was to be done.

The new year began with a decision by the camp authority to move Lamar and me away from Stockdale. We speculated that the Vietnamese felt they could control and prevent our relaying communications from Stockdale to the prisoners in the other cellblocks. Carrying our bedrolls and teapots we marched out of the cellblock. The guards' rifles prodded and directed us toward a tiny, windowless room in the Barn. The cell was little more than a dark hovel, but it was down the hall from the master communicator, Howie Rutledge, and the other diehards, Jenkins and Mulligan. I figured we couldn't beat the company.

Prison life resumed its monotony. Lamar and I were allowed to exercise together, and every day guards walked us to a small enclosed area outside, about fifteen feet by twenty-five, where a circular path had been worn by rubber-tire thongs. It was adjacent to what we knew to be the torture room, and our telegraph system had sent word that a POW had been ensconced inside for several days. We decided to try to get some encouragement to him.

I stood where I could see any approaching guards, walked around a little, and cleared for Jim to go over to the building and tap a message of "hang on." For a couple of days we kept this routine going, but we weren't certain the guy in the torture room was hearing us. Jim would have to bang on the wall to be sure he could be heard. It was dangerous—guards were usually nearby—but we decided to try. We had to let the guy in there know he was not alone, that someone knew and cared.

"I'll clear," I offered.

Jim approached the wall closest to the torture building. A peephole in the enclosure wall would tell me if any guards were close enough to hear Jim's banging. I found one and stepped up close and put my eye against it to look outside. A black, narrowed eye stared back at me through the hole.

I gasped and jumped back quickly. "Jim, get away from that wall!" I hollered before Jim could pound out a message. The guard in the outer yard screeched something shrill and furious and ran in through the gate, gesturing and poking the air with his rifle to punctuate his command, "No communicate! Keep silent! You keep silent!"

He yelled as if he were crazed. He eyed us and circled us and, like a ramrod on a cattle drive, he herded us back to our tiny cell in the Barn.

We had broken the single most carefully enforced rule. We had tried to communicate with another prisoner. We would have to pay. Our exercise privileges ceased. Our only exercise became the walk to the showers every morning and the pacing we did in our cells when the walls tried to close in on us.

# SEVEN

# Iron Shackles

January, 1967. Ten months of prison life lay behind me. I was coping with the filth that clung to every wall, every space, every part of my body. I was beginning to see some small improvement in my arms and hand. I found I could wake up to rats running across my chest and not scream. Most days I felt somewhat upbeat about the war. Even the ridiculous prison rules, instead of frustrating me, challenged me. They summoned from me my most creative resistance. But I could not get used to being hungry.

I thought about food all the time. As the meal portions dwindled, so did my optimism. Pitiful drippings of rice mixed with mashed corn twice a day were not enough to sustain a man's body or his spirit.

Lying on the floor in my cell, I could peek out into the hallway through the the crack under my door or through the drain hole. I could see my buddies walking like zombies, the guards' rifles jabbed into their bony backs. Their gaunt, ashen faces and their emaciated forms mirrored my own skinny frame. I wondered how long we could last on this diet. I knew we had reached the bottom of the food barrel one day when the evening meal consisted of a fish head.

I picked at the gills with my metal spoon. "What do you think, Lamar? Suppose fish eyes are good for you?"

"You're not going to eat those!" Lamar was appalled.

"We eat fish eggs, why not fish eyes? Besides, I'm too hungry to care."

I held the fish head still with my limp, partially paralyzed hand, and used the other hand to dig at the eye with my metal spoon. After some clumsy poking, I finally put a fish eye in my mouth and felt it pop between my teeth like a garden pea fresh from the pod. Lamar gagged and shook his head.

"I can't believe a guy who won't eat pigfat will eat a fish eye."

"Two fish eyes," I corrected him and popped the other one in my mouth. "Probably pure protein."

And pure desperation. I had never been that hungry. During the next quiz I complained about the food. Chihuahua, the interrogation officer, listened from his chair and then, before the last word was out of my mouth, he leaped to his feet and strode across the room until he was standing over the small stool I sat on. Glaring down at me, his bulging eyes flashing with fury, and his dark, angry face just inches from mine, he shrieked at me like a banshee.

"Your American bombers have destroyed our rice paddies and our levees! Our crops are damaged! Our stores are depleted! If you are hungry complain to your American criminals! They are the ones to blame!"

*What a coup!* I thought. *We destroy their food supply and their transport systems. We starve them into submission while they steadily exhaust their military strength and Ho Chi Minh has to end his assault on South Vietnam.*

"Do you think we will take the food from our own people's mouths to feed criminals? You are hungry? Good. You can write your congress and tell them enough of this bombing. You can tell them you want them to stop this illegal and immoral war!"

It would have been a brilliant move, strategically, to destroy the North's food sources while cutting off all supply routes to the North, but there is no evidence that the U.S. military deliberately set out to do that. If it *had* been a tactic for winning the war, however, it would not have made our hunger any easier to bear. We were watching ourselves slowly die of starvation, growing weaker every day.

Our hunger became a tool in our captors' hands. They worked on us with variations of the old theme.

"This war is going to be long. It may never be over," the interrogator said from his chair in the quiz room. "You might as well accept this life. Quit fighting us. Repent and accept leniency. You must have a good attitude."

"Have a good attitude." It was a favorite phrase and one we understood well. It meant simply, do what we want you to do and you will have an easier time here. That included better food. A very few capitulated.

A handful of prisoners stopped communicating and agreed to write letters home in exchange for the promise of better food and treatment. They accepted the bribes of the enemy and feasted on eggs and drank lousy Vietnamese beer as a reward for their collaboration. The prison authority put them together in a large cell, gave them playing cards and some other games to amuse themsleves, and allowed them more lenient exercise privileges. It seemed so little to receive in exchange for their honor. We called them turncoats.

Most of the POWs knew the threats and promises of rewards and leniency were a deliberate ploy to drive a wedge among us, to break up our unity with jealousy and distrust. Perhaps it would have worked if we hadn't been constantly on the wall, telling each other of each new development in the guards' behavior, each new slant in the interrogator's rhetoric, each new tactic employed to try to work us against each other.

A few diehards were given a tiny piece of meat and an extra portion of rice to make it appear as if they had cooperated with the enemy, to try to make the rest of us believe they had changed sides, and thus influence more of us to join them. But these men simply refused to eat the extra portions. They made it clear that they had not done anything to receive lenient treatment and would not eat the extra food unless *all* the prisoners received an extra portion. We continued to be hungry and grow weaker.

Winter's damp cold seeped through the walls and turned our brick and concrete cell into a meat freezer. Many days Lamar and I huddled close to each other on one of the bunks, trying to share the little body heat we were able to retain. We layered ourselves in our pajamas and wrapped ourselves in the thin blankets, but North Vietnam's cold nevertheless penetrated and chilled us to the bone.

We were still being denied our exercise privileges. We had no relief from the monotony. No relief from the sense of bondage. Only in my thoughts could I escape the noncolors of gray and mildew and faded khaki. Only when I thought of home and Shirley did I remember color and beauty. All else was ugliness and barrenness.

Some days I thought I could feel the life draining out of my body, and I feared I really would die of starvation. I feared using up the few essential calories my body needed just to stay alive, yet I could not stop myself from working my arms and hand in the cramped space of our cell. Other days, that little energy needed to tap my fingers on the wall was more than I could muster. I learned, during those horrible days, that sometimes the spirit can override the body, and from somewhere deep inside, from a hidden spring, comes fresh strength for the moment.

Our captors were freezing us and starving us, hoping we would slow or stop all our communication efforts. But instead, we increased them. And the guards increased their vigilance to try to catch us. Like hall monitors in a junior high school, they cruised the corridors, listening for soft taps, watching for violations of their rules.

The resulting punishment, whether a beating, or a day or week in leg stocks, had nothing to do with the war. We were committing no sin, no breach of military conduct. Again, it was simply the fact that we had resisted the communist methods of brainwashing: isolation, deprivation, and torture. We had to be punished for not cooperating with objectives of the communist regime.

After dark, on January 26, a guard entered our cell and ordered, "Roll up." Lamar and I gathered our bedrolls and other meager items and, when the guard stepped into the hallway, we quickly dug into the cracks in the bricks for our chess set and the extra paper and pencils we had managed to hide. We didn't know where we were going or why, but we weren't going without our stash.

Blindfolded and with our hands cuffed in front, Lamar and I walked into the yard and waited, listening to the sounds of other POWs milling around us. In a few moments I was separated from Jim and shoved into the back of a truck.

"No talk! No talk!" muttered a guard who climbed in to sit across from me and the prisoner next to me. I moved my cuffed hands cautiously until my fingertips could just brush against my companion's thigh. With almost invisible motion I tapped, "Johnson."

In another few seconds I felt the same small taps against my leg. "Jenkins."

I felt a silly grin spread over my face, and I ducked my head down to hide it. *Ichabod. How'd they ever get a blindfold to stay over that nose?* I could feel Harry grinning beside me.

"No talk!" the guard screamed. "No talk!"

The grins faded when the guard, like a schoolyard bully, picked up a stick from somewhere and began pounding on our heads and shoulders.

The truck stopped half an hour later and, with a guard for each prisoner, we were led into a building. I heard doors creak and sandals slap against the soles of bare feet. We walked a few yards, turned sharply, went a few more yards, then turned again, as if making our way through a labyrinth. It was, in fact, a painstakingly built maze. We were back at Hoa Lo, and the entire camp had been remodeled to prevent communication among the prisoners.

It was like a confusing rabbit warren. None of the tiny cells in the newly built structure shared a common wall. All were separated by these narrow, oddly perpendicular hallways. But, as I saw when my blindfold was removed, each tiny cell had a drain hole that opened into the hallways. We were once again in business. Within minutes we had identified every man in the building.

Lamar and I were together, just as before, in a cellblock dubbed "the Stardust." It was in one of the four buildings in the newly built complex we called "Las Vegas." The others were the "Mint, "Desert Inn," "Thunderbird," and "Riviera." Our cell, about three and a half feet wide by eight feet long, was the last one on the end of the building, nearest the Desert Inn, but separated from it by another room. Two bunks jutted out from a side wall, one above the other, cutting the standing space in the cell to no more than about eighteen inches. We had to turn sideways to move past each other if we both stood at the same time. There was about a foot of space at the end of the bunks for our waste cans.

A large, high window in the back wall of our cell looked out at the moat-like passageway between the building and the outer wall of the prison. It was lined with half-inch steel bars, but it was uncovered. Sunlight poured in, and for the first time we could look out, but we could see little more than the tops of trees that stood higher than the wall. The real action happened out front, in the center courtyard, but we had no view that way. Our only access to the front was the tiny window in the door that opened into a hallway. We used it to clear for guards when we wanted to communicate with prisoners in other rooms. The hallway was watched and paraded constantly by ever-vigilant guards. But undeterred as always, we began immediately to try to find out where our friends were and how we could get information to them.

The showers were in the center of the courtyard, little stalls separated by concrete walls, and each had a little wooden door and a washroom-type sink. The brick floors were uneven and crumbling, offering good places for hiding messages. The rusting faucets in each stall trickled with only a thin stream of water. Once a week we were allowed to go in and shave and shower and wash our clothes. And once a week we had opportunity to make contact with other POWs.

Lamar and I were taken to the showers together. One of us could clear while the other sent a message. The guards caught on right away that we were tapping on the shower walls. They started leaving an empty stall between us so that we couldn't hear each other. They stationed a guard outside each door while we showered, and they watched for our heads to appear over the doors, hoping to catch us trying to send messages.

I was often struck with the ridiculousness of it all. The camp authority had carefully redesigned the entire Hoa Lo facility to better isolate its prisoners from each other, yet they had built the shower stalls with common walls, planned the buildings so that each cell had a hole that opened into a common hallway, even if it was just a drain hole, and they had laid out the buildings in such a way that prisoners had to be walked in front of the cells to get to such places as latrines, showers, quiz rooms, and exercise areas.

There was no way they could keep us from seeing each other, though they tried various means to prevent it. At times they used the shower stalls as holding places. To avoid the risk of one prisoner seeing another, a guard often placed one man in the showers and then watched to be sure he didn't turn around and look at a passing prisoner. It was all so foolish and so futile. And so childish.

Within a few days after our arrival at Las Vegas, Lamar and I figured out that the large room next to ours was a holding tank for new prisoners. We knew there was a guy in there, but he would not respond to our efforts to communicate. If he was like most of the new shootdowns, he did not know the tap code. We would have to teach him. We tapped a few times, waited for him to tap back, but nothing happened. The initial contact was always the same: tap — tap-tap-tap — tap, to the rhythm of "shave and a haircut," and then we waited for a response of tap-tap. But he made no response.

During the guards' siesta I stood at the back window and yelled toward him, thinking he would get up and go to his window and talk to me, and I could tell him about the tap code. I had to get him into the system so we could get some encouragement to him. He had probably been beaten, maybe tortured with the ropes. We had to let him know someone cared. We had to break into his isolation.

"He's scared, Sam," Lamar said, as we waited for him to respond.

"Yeah, I know. But we've got to get to him," I answered, and I tried talking through the window again while the guards were resting.

"There's no telling what they said they'd do to him if he gets caught communicating. He probably thinks they'll shoot him or something."

"All the more reason to keep trying," I answered.

I remembered my first few hours in Heartbreak Hotel, when Stockdale and Denton had called out to me and refused to let me give in to the desolation I felt. I had to do the same thing for this man. I owed it to all the men who had tapped on walls and hollered down hallways, at risk of punishment, just to tell me I would be okay, to teach me how to communicate, to assure me that I could make it.

And so we kicked off a tedious, time-consuming project. "Shave-and-a-hair-cut," wait, then "two-bits." Wait, then slowly tap twenty-six times on the wall, a tap for each letter of the alphabet. Every day, three times each day, we tapped out the same ditty, then twenty-six slow, deliberate taps. Every day, for a week, we persisted. The second week, after the same routine, we tapped eight times for the eighth letter in the alphabet, H. Then a pause, and nine taps for the ninth letter, I.

Still no response. For three more weeks we persisted in the same routine. We had nothing else to do with our time, so we continued to tap, always the same. At the end of the third week we heard a light tap from the next room. Lamar and I quickly put our ears to the wall.

Tap-tap-tap-tap-tap-tap-tap-tap, for the letter H. Then another nine taps for the letter I. He had finally figured it out. But the procedure was only an introduction. It took another thirty days to teach him the abbreviated code for each letter. We took him through each letter, according to its position in the alphabet, and meticulously taught him the other system, using the twenty-five-letter alphabet and the grid. We called it the Smitty Harris Code. Smitty, a fellow POW, had heard in survival school how some enterprising POWs in Korea had created a code that could be tapped on pipes or walls. He was quick to put the code to work in Hanoi.

We had used up all of February, March, and most of April teaching our neighbor how to communicate within the Stardust. As May passed, we taught him how to carry messages to the showers, how to get information to the other cellblocks. We told him how to write notes on the toilet paper, how to hide them in the cracks in the showers. By this time we had collected the names of about two hundred POWs. Everyday, each man reviewed the names he had memorized. If even one man was able to get out, he could take all the names back to the U.S. government.

I never learned why our neighbor in the holding room was so slow to respond to us when we tried to initiate contact with him. He was moved out of the holding room shortly after he finished his orientation course with us, and he never told us his story. Whether the camp authority had so frightened him, or whether he was ill and unable to get on the wall, I never understood. I had already learned, however, that every man has a different philosophy toward the military code: some would honor it and abide by it at all costs. Others would not.

I had also learned that every man has a different threshold of pain. And I soon heard on the wall that the North Vietnamese had brought a cadre of Cuban torture experts to Hanoi to help them explore that threshold. Prisoners brought to Hoa Lo from the Zoo told stories of savage beatings and torture at the hands of a Cuban they dubbed "Fidel."

In a morbid sort of way, it fascinated me that the North Vietnamese had discovered a kindred spirit with the communists of Cuba and invited the Cubans into their shop of horrors to help direct the punishment and torture of POWs. Though they continued to reject all offers of assistance in this area from the Chinese and Soviets, they asked the Cubans for advice. The Cubans could understand the tiny Southeast Asian country's need for some show of independence from its huge and somewhat domineering communist neighbors. They, too, had wanted to be recognized as independent. They had fought the imperialist capitalists to the north and could identify with North Vietnam's struggle for independence, unity, and sovereignty. They came to the aid of their philosophical brothers, and they enjoyed the part they were asked to play. Their philosophy was simple: beat a prisoner and he'll do anything.

Under Fidel's direction, a group of POWs was separated from the rest of the Zoo's inhabitants and used as a sort of test group. Their floggings, torture, and mental abuse was some of the worst experienced in Hanoi's prison system. In the end, one man in the "control group" lost his mind under the constant barrage of brutality. The others nearly lost theirs. Their own beatings were severe, but they were also forced to observe the savagery inflicted against one of their own. He was beaten and tortured beyond recognition and coherency, then thrown in with his friends to be tended and cared for, then yanked out of their hands again for more savage beatings and torture. In horror, they watched him suffer and lose his grasp on reality, never to regain it.

The Cuban claimed that he could make them all surrender and co-operate with the North Vietnamese regime. In the end, they "surrendered" only the most useless misinformation their well-trained military minds could invent. The Cuban's test failed miserably, but that summer at the Zoo would never be forgotten.

Meanwhile, the daily routine at Hoa Lo seldom varied. The monotony was killing—except for one particular morning when a guard decided to roust us before dawn for our daily trip to the latrines. Around 4:30, he opened our cell door and commanded us to get our cans. He prodded us with his rifle and pushed us out into the courtyard, past the showers and toward the Mint, a cellblock of only three tiny cells next to the latrines. I was still half asleep when I reached the small step up into the latrine area. My Ho Chi Minh sandal caught on the step, and as I fell forward my can flew out of my hand. I watched, stupefied, as the can sailed through the air, end over end. The guard threw himself back and shrieked. It all happened in a split second, and yet it played out in front of me like a home movie shown in slow motion. Just before I landed face down on the concrete floor, I looked up to see the entire contents of my honey bucket drench the guard from the top of his khaki-capped head to the bottoms of his disheveled pants.

"Stop! Stop!" the guard bellowed.

Others rushed in and began yelling, spewing the few English curse words they knew. In seconds the latrine area was a swarm of furious North Vietnamese. Laughter was begging to explode inside me. I dropped my head and felt my shoulders shake with the effort to control a loud guffaw. A guard spitting fury yanked me to my feet and shoved a mop into my hands.

"Clean up!" he ordered.

While his rifle poked into my ribs, I swished circular motions in the mess and kept my face turned away so he wouldn't see me grinning.

A guard shoved a mop into Lamar's hands too, and he began mopping furiously. I sneaked a look at him, hoping the guard wouldn't see me grinning. Poor Jim! He dared a quick look in my direction and shook his head at me, like my dad used to do when I misbehaved in church, and then he quickly looked away. His face was white. He thought I had laughed outright at the sight of the guard, and he thought we were in for another miserable spell of punishment.

"I didn't laugh," I whispered to him, with my head down and my eyes intent on the floor. "I must have hollered as I was falling, but I didn't laugh, honest!"

"No talk! No talk!" The rifle butt dug a little deeper. "Shut mouth!"

I swished my mop up against Lamar's and stepped close to his shoulder. "I didn't laugh," I muttered again under my breath. Lamar shook his head and continued mopping.

The guard dripping with refuse stomped away to change his uniform. We finished mopping and washed out our cans. The only consequence of the incident was more cursing and the impatient prodding of our guard on the return trip to our cells. The whole scene was seemingly forgotten, except by Lamar and me. We waited for punishment, but none came. I wondered if the guard was too humiliated to acknowledge what had happened, too humiliated to address it in front of an officer, even if it would give him a reason to see me punished.

When it was evident that we weren't going to suffer for it, Lamar finally began to enjoy the whole thing. We described the scene to each other over and over again, and with each retelling of it, the picture of the dripping guard got even funnier. For weeks afterward I lay on my bunk and chuckled, thankful for something to laugh about in this awful, stinking place.

The radio speakers that hung from the ceiling in each cell played hour after hour. We had begun to be able to tune out the voices and the words, but during the summer of 1967, some propaganda broadcasts began to trouble us. The voices of American POWs speaking the rhetoric and jargon of our communist enemies played in our cells. At first, the tapes were played only for other prisoners, then they were put on Radio Hanoi for all the city to hear. U.S. intelligence could tune in as well, and hear the voices of Americans lauding the communist regime.

We felt fairly confident that the tapes were being made in other camps — we knew of no prisoners at Hoa Lo who were submitting to pressure to cooperate. Jim Stockdale, SRO because of Risner's isolation from the rest of the POWs, felt the time had come for a specific statement of policy for all POWs to follow. It would have to address all the issues that faced us as prisoners of a communist regime, yet it would have to be easy to remember under duress and torture. It was just that: BACK U.S.

> B — Bowing. Don't do it in public, unless the prison authorities force it. Be sure that any observers recognize we will not submit to any government that refuses to respect the Geneva Conventions.
>
> A — Air. Do not make any statements on the air. This means no propaganda tapes of any kind.
>
> C — Crimes. Don't even say the word! Make no admissions. We are not criminals, we are soldiers.

K – Kiss. Don't kiss up to the communists. Don't show gratitude for anything they do. Even at release, do not "kiss them good-bye."

U.S. – Unity over self. Our greatest strength lies in our unity. We must be together, united in our efforts to resist. Basic trust in each other must be maintained at all times.

The policy was implemented quickly among the POWs. It was understood that the degree of torture meted out, as well as each man's capacity to endure pain, would determine how closely he could adhere to every point of the policy. Only a small handful would ignore it completely, placing self above the good of the whole.

Shortly after the policy was implemented, I was called in to quiz. A camp commander I hadn't seen before presided at the large desk in the stark interrogation room. There was something about this man, a different air of authority than I had seen in other, younger officers. He was about sixty, with graying hair and an inscrutable expression suggesting that, until now, I had been dealing with mere kids. I felt a shiver of fear. Things had been heating up at the Zoo, and I wondered if Hoa Lo was about to be the scene of increased torture. Was this an indication that harsher treatment was in store for us?

He wore a dress parade hat, or "garrison cap," throughout the quiz. His stiff posture matched the creases in his khaki uniform. His eyes, barely discernible slits in his frowning face, sent out thin shafts of ice that chilled me. He motioned for me to sit on the small stool that forced my long legs to fold until my knees nearly touched my nostrils. He tapped his fingers for a moment, then began his questioning through an interpreter. His Vietnamese words flowed quietly. He looked at me and waited while the interpreter spoke in English.

"You are to write your congressman."

He listened, his head slightly cocked to the side, while I gave him the standard answer. The interpreter repeated it for him. He retorted, waited, then spoke again. The interpreter repeated the command. The commander sat stiffly in his chair behind the desk and watched as I shook my head.

A heated blast of words erupted, and then the interpreter said, "You know this war is wrong. Even some of your own senators have agreed. You should too. You will not receive leniency until you write a letter to your senators!"

"I can't do that." I willed my voice to be calm. Inside I was shaking.

The conversation continued, first in Vietnamese, then English, then my uncooperative answers. Suddenly the commander shoved his chair back and stood to his feet. His broad chest heaved with fury. In almost perfect English, he said, "You are obstinate! You are still a diehard! We are going to kill you! Return to your cell!"

Back in my cell a few minutes later, I drew a long breath and tried to steady myself. Then I sent a message on the wall.

"The commander speaks English. He doesn't want you to know it, so be careful."

It was one of the many bits and pieces of camp information we circulated among us. Anything that would help us in an interrogation, anything that would better equip us to survive and resist effectively we passed around.

The threat to kill me was just that: a threat. I knew from spending time with Stockdale, Denton, and Lamar, that in most instances, if we stood up to them, they would back down. We had learned that those who gave in were pushed for more. Denton had said, "Just say no. Say no to everything. They will have to back up and regroup." It worked. I had seen it happen many times. They would curse me, threaten me, and finally dismiss me.

It was all part of a learning process for Ho's regime. Except for the Cuban experiment in brutality at the Zoo, the North Vietnamese remained adamantly independent of outside assistance and advice when it came to interrogation. Their style of trial and error gave us at Hoa Lo some small advantage, a sort of respite as they returned to the drawing board to rethink their procedure for the next encounter.

The punishment that came a few days later, however, had nothing to do with my refusal to write a propaganda letter to the States. We were tapping on the wall, communicating with a man in the room next door when a guard caught us. He yanked Lamar by the shirt and marched him off to stand before an officer to have his punishment pronounced. A short while later he returned Lamar to our cell, pushed him down onto the lower bunk, and locked his legs in the stocks.

It was unusual and unjust—to punish only one of us and not the other, but we had long ago learned that they had a purpose for everything they did. In this it was evident: by punishing only Lamar, they hoped to make him angry and resentful toward me. Their intent was always to disrupt any kind of unity among the POWs. It didn't work on us. We knew the ruse. They also hoped to scare me into obeying the rules. That, too, was useless. Lamar and I knew their game and we refused to play. As soon as the guard exited we were back on the wall.

It was a little more difficult to communicate without one of us to clear for the other, but we went on as before. I tried to clear for myself; and Lamar, from his bed, tried to watch for shadows under the door. The risk factor increased, but we wouldn't be quieted.

We played chess and kept up communications, never missing a beat, for three more days. Then it happened. It was noontime, the guards' siesta, when we expected to be able to communicate without much chance of being caught. I was on the bunk with my ear pressed against my cup and the cup against the wall when I looked up and saw a khaki uniform in the back window. It was too late. His bloodcurdling shriek echoed through the cellblock. He jumped off his perch on the back wall where he had been stationed to spy on us and ran into the building and down the hallway to our cell.

I figured the guards knew the only way they would catch me was to set a trap. We had been careful to watch for shadows under the door. I had listened at the rat hole for the sounds of footsteps, but I had never even checked out the window that opened to the back wall and the moat. It never occurred to me that they would position a guard there to watch us. And it did no good when I tried to pretend I'd just been drinking out of the empty cup I held in my hands.

"No! No! You communicate! You are caught!" the guard shouted as he poked his rifle butt into my back. In moments I was standing in front of an enraged officer and listening to my punishment decree: leg stocks.

We spent a week with our legs anchored fast under the steel bars and our ankles tightly held in the wooden forms. We were not allowed out of them for any reason, not even to use our cans. I felt bad for poor Lamar below me, when he handed me my can and then pressed himself flat against the back wall, out of range, while I rolled over to use it. There was nothing else we could do.

The guards brought our meals in to us and grinned when they set them down just inches beyond our reach. Then they stood and watched while we stretched, scraping our ankles against the steel bar and wood of the stocks, trying to get a tip of a finger on the tray so we could pull it toward us.

Lamar dug our chessboard out of its hiding place and put the pieces in place so we could play to pass the long hours of each day. We called out each move to each other, and, like children, we took turns being the one to hold the board and make the moves for each other. Only once did the guards come in and catch us playing. Then they shouted as if we had done something that would threaten the entire North Vietnamese war effort, and they tore up our chessboard and confiscated our materials. Moments after the door closed behind them, we made more, using the coarse toilet paper we had squirreled away in hiding places and making more ink out of water or tea mixed with mud.

It was a long and uncomfortable week, made even longer by the fact that Lamar won every chess game we played. I was a lousy chess player, and an even worse loser. It made for a potentially volatile combination. When I lost the twenty-fifth consecutive game, I was furious. I wadded up the toilet paper chessboard and threw it off the bunk. It floated through the air and settled gently on the floor. That made me even angrier. I wanted to break something, to bang and shout and slam something, *anything* against a wall. I wanted noise and impact and response. But all that came of my exploding emotions was a silent, sailing piece of toilet paper that landed quietly on the dirty concrete floor. A wise and somewhat subdued Lamar, instead of railing at me for being such a jerk, lay back against his bunk and stayed out of sight while I simmered silently for a while.

The night we came out of the leg stocks, guards told us to roll up. Lamar and I looked at each other. What was happening now? We had only a second to say good-bye. They took Lamar out of the cell first, and then they came back for me and walked me to a "holding cell" in the showers. Moments later a guard blindfolded me and walked me around, probably to confuse me, and then thrust me into another cell. When the blindfold came off, I was standing in a cell in the Thunderbird, face to face with Jim Stockdale.

Jim grinned, and his eyes filled with tears as he looked at my oddly sloping shoulders and limp hand. I was skinny and stooped and as gaunt as a specter, and before I could put down my can and bedroll, he enclosed me in a smothering bearhug.

It was like a homecoming. Since my first night in Heartbreak Hotel, many months before, Jim Stockdale had been with me, tapping out encouragement, suggestions, and orders, as well as entertaining me with his intellect and his humor. My eyes stung with tears too, when I stepped back and studied him. To me, he was a perfect pattern for the navy's stereotype: a salty seagoing sailor. He'd been hefty and sturdy-looking when he arrived nearly fifteen months earlier, but now his skin hung on his broad, squarish shape, and his hair had grown nearly white. His craggy face was creased like that of a man twice his age, mirroring my own haggard visage.

Our cell, twice the size of the one I had shared with Lamar, was on the end next to the Mint. Built for four men, it offered more space for exercise, but the filth and the rats and the darkened, covered windows made it a good deal more dismal than the cell I had just left. The walls were covered in dirt that clung like glue to the brick walls now sticky with summer's humidity. The hot, damp air and the darkness would have depressed me if I hadn't been instantly buoyed by my feelings of friendship for Stockdale. We were glad to be able to talk to each other without the threat of punishment hanging over us. We had names of POWs to exchange and add to the growing list of prisoners held in the North Vietnamese prison system.

The prison authority's practice of mixing and moving prisoners was again working against them. They thought they were creating chaos in our communication system, but in fact they were improving it. The constant rotation of POWs from prison to prison, and within the cellblocks in each prison, made plausible, and perhaps possible, the idea of contact with every single U.S. prisoner of war in North Vietnam's penitentiary system. Contact and unity. It was a heady thought, and one that made us aggressive and bold.

One POW had passed on word of some U.S. Army fellows who had been taken captive in South Vietnam and then transported north to Hanoi. He had shared a cell with them and alerted us to the fact that they were in the North's prison system. We added their names to the growing list of prisoners for whom Hanoi would have to account when this whole thing was finally over.

And Jim had a way of getting the names of the POWs out of North Vietnam and into the hands of the U.S. government. Now I would learn exactly how it was to be done.

The camp authority had given Stockdale a letter from his wife, Sybil, at Christmas, while we had been at the Zoo. She had written and said she was enclosing a picture of Jim's mother, but the woman in the picture was a complete stranger. Stockdale was puzzled at first, but then decided that there must be a reason. He didn't really believe he had endured so much that he was losing his mind. That woman was *not* his mother. So somewhere in that picture was a message for him. He had studied it for hours. Maybe the message was somewhere in the layers of the photo paper. He decided to play "secret agent."

He had placed the photo in a shallow mixture of tea and urine to make the layers separate. He waited and, as the pieces of paper came apart, he found a message and instructions from the Navy. Sybil's letter had been written on paper that was invisible carbon. When the North Vietnamese gave him a form to write home on, he was to lay Sybil's letter on top of it, a copy sheet on top of the carbon, and write his message in lines perpendicular to the penciled words the North Vietnamese could see. He was to begin his letter home with "Darling" if the letter carried a carboned message. It was an unfamiliar and stilted endearment, one he and Sybil had never used. But by using it, Jim would be telling Sybil that the letter must get to the navy for deciphering.

It could work! We could get the names of the POWs back to the states. If the North Vietnamese did actually mail his letters. If he did not get caught. It was risky business, playing spy. If the communists caught on, he could be charged with espionage and placed in front of a firing squad. He decided it was worth the risk. Anything to try to beat the enemy. Our spirits were high with this new challenge.

We had a feeling of success, of victory. There were ways to win, even in this place that smelled of human waste and fever and filth. One POW, a stubborn air force recalcitrant, Captain Ron Storz, had beaten the enemy soundly. In this bevy of POWs, where the navy seemed to have the other military branches outnumbered, I was especially proud of Storz. He had earned a reputation as a difficult prisoner while in the large holding room between the Desert Inn and Stardust. He kept up a constant communication with the four cells with which he had common walls. He got caught but kept on tapping. This called for leg stocks, but there were none in that cell, so the camp officer ordered him tied up with ropes.

Storz just wouldn't give up. And he wouldn't accept this blatant disregard of the Geneva Conventions. He refused to eat. After about three days, the camp authority buckled under and took the ropes off of him. Their obsession with world opinion would not allow them to let a prisoner die of starvation, so they relented. It was the first hunger strike at Hoa Lo. It was our first experience with that kind of resistance, and our first introduction to another diehard. We added his name to the list of POWs, and he joined us in Alcatraz a few weeks later.

The Vegas complex teemed with new shootdowns. Heartbreak Hotel couldn't hold them all. The last six rooms of the Thunderbird became a holding area for the overflow. Stockdale and I could hear them coming in. We made it our ceaseless task to communicate with these new guys and let them know the policy, BACK U.S. The new arrivals brought us news from home too. One of the new shootdowns sent word down the hallway that he had seen Stockdale's wife, Sybil, and that all was well at home with Jim's four sons.

We tapped on the walls, hollered down the hallways when the guards were at siesta, and used every trek to the showers or the latrines to collect and pass on news. It was inevitable that we would be caught. Our punishment: no baths for a week. Our response: big deal.

One day we detected movement in the cellblock and discovered that the guards were moving prisoners around in order to leave empty rooms between all occupied cells so that they could break up our "party line." Within a day or two there were only a few of us left in the T-bird. The guards, now paranoid that we were talking to the other cellblocks too, hurried us through the halls and past the latrines, to be sure we didn't bump against a wall or doorway. Even an inadvertent rub against a wall earned me a sharp jab from a guard's rifle and a scolding in pidgin English.

It was absurd, but the tactics proved effective. We were finally cut off from the rest of the camp. We couldn't get through to the Mint, and we couldn't get down to the buildings the other direction. Our only chance to stay in contact was while we were in the showers. Jim and

I took turns clearing for one another, while one of us whispered through a tiny space to the shower on the other side. The short guards couldn't see our heads above the stalls.

We had to be more creative, but we were still consumed with trying to gather data and pass it on to other POWs. Any alteration in camp routine, any change in a quiz, anything, regardless of its seeming insignificance, had to be circulated among the POWs. Knowledge was both a shield and a sword for those of us fighting the enemy without benefit of conventional weapons.

By summer's end, I could see more signs of improvement in my arms and hand. I was determined to regain the use of my limbs, and every day I used the air force five basic exercise program (5BX). It was a predecessor of the doctrine of aerobics, and in the tight, cramped space of a prison cell, where only one could work out at a time, they were just right. I stretched to loosen up, then ran in place to kick my blood pressure and heart rate up, all the while reviewing the list of POWs I had memorized. But my progress was halted when boils erupted all over my body.

Malnutrition, filth, and the prison's grossly inadequate conditions finally took their toll. No part of my body was spared the huge, hot boils. Every movement was painful. I couldn't sleep or eat. The rough, coarse fabric of my prison clothes scratched and irritated the already oozing sores. The prison authority offered no salve or antibiotics. I fantasized about a basin of hot, soapy water and a clean cloth, but I had to make do with the shower's thin brown stream of water. I imagined the infection coursing through me, and I wondered if I might die.

Stockdale, too, was covered in boils. His back looked as though it was encrusted with bird droppings. There was nothing we could do for ourselves, nothing we could do for each other. For weeks we did little more than lie on our bunks in quiet misery.

While I was in the Thunderbird, the camp authority began using Vietnamese women to work in the prison. They were little more than beasts of burden around the camp. They cooked and delivered our meals, carrying them down the hallways on poles and buckets that hung from their shoulders. We had seen women in the other prison camps, but they had been peasant farm women. These girls were military. They wore the same unkempt khaki uniforms as their male counterparts. The same creased and stained caps sat above dirty strands of long black hair. They carried rifles, and we could occasionally watch through the cracks in our boarded windows and see them sprawled on the ground for rifle practice.

Of the many young women who walked down the hallways of our cellblocks, only one attempted to communicate with the prisoners. Like the others, she spoke no English. She tried to use sign language, but no one understood. I don't think anyone ever figured out what she was doing, or what she intended to do. Only one other woman attracted our attention, and we called her Miss Piggy. She tied her long hair back in a straggly ponytail that reached her waist. Her baggy uniform, filthy and foul-smelling, hung on her thick, shapeless body. When her grimy hands shoved my food at me in the cell each day, I nearly choked with revulsion.

*Oh, Shirley, do you know how much I miss you?* I thought every day. *Do you know how much I love you?*

By late August, I sensed that a change was in the wind. "Cat," the commander over all the prison camps, called me in to quiz.

Large for a Vietnamese, Cat was broad and bulky, unlike so many of the guards and officers who were slight and wiry. He moved with a sort of cat-like stealth, and he posed his questions with a slyness that was a little disconcerting. His pointed questions about Stockdale made me especially nervous.

Until that day, I had never been questioned about the activities of my fellow prisoners, but Cat wanted quick answers to his questions about Stockdale, his policies, and his commands to the U.S. POWs. I discovered that he had asked the same questions of other prisoners, and then tortured them with leg irons or ropes in an attempt to get them to talk about Stockdale's orders. I had a feeling these were merely omens of what lay ahead. I also had the feeling that my days with Stockdale were numbered. We would be moved again soon, I was sure.

My instincts were right. Things were heating up at Hoa Lo. The prison authority had decided to toughen up on us. They had begun to see how tightly organized our resistance really was, and how far-reaching. They had learned, somehow, about the POW policy, BACK U.S. And they were determined to break the chain of command among the prisoners. Because Stockdale was the SRO, they were determined to break him.

"We will make him into a domestic animal," Cat hissed, as he quizzed me.

He leaned close to my face, and I could smell his acrid breath. Then he spun away and strode back to his chair behind the huge desk. He was furious. We had been able to counter his every move. He was also frightened. I could see his neck straining against his shirt collar. His orders were to isolate all prisoners, deny them communication, and weaken them until they repented of their "war crimes" and acknowledged the justness of the Vietnamese cause. He was failing pitifully in this endeavor.

I stared back at Cat, silently vowing not to say a word that could be used against Jim. Cat snarled and stood to pace the room. Then he sent me back to my cell.

A few nights later, we heard the sound of feet in the corridor, and the window on our cell door snapped open. Rabbit peered in while a guard fumbled with the lock on the door. As Rabbit stepped into the cell, Stockdale rose and stepped forward, his large body colliding with Rabbit's smaller one. Rabbit staggered back a few steps, and the guard nearby caught him before he could fall to the floor.

"You attack me!" Rabbit blustered furiously. "You will be punished!"

I stared appalled at Jim. Like the sturdy sea captain that he was, he stood silent and still, daring Rabbit to make a move toward him. Rabbit backed away from the menacing look on his face and continued to scream, "You will be punished!"

Rabbit straightened his shirt and pulled on his sleeves. "Roll up!" he said, glaring at a still silent, unmoving Jim. "I say roll up!" he screeched.

With deliberate motions, Jim rolled up his belongings, shook my hand, and walked out of the cell with a rifle point in his back. Moments later he stood before Cat.

"You are instigating a revolt," Cat stated. "You and Song are threatening to overthrow the Vietnamese government. You are going to be punished."

It was an astounding accusation. That two men, one lame and the other a cripple, housed in a tiny concrete cell inside an impenetrable prison, could be considered a legitimate threat to the entire North Vietnamese political regime was almost beyond belief. But the camp authority believed it. And they acted on that belief. Stockdale and I were moved into separate cells in the Mint.

Cell is perhaps too kind a word for the tiny, brick room I entered. It was more like a small, dark cage. What had been built as one cell had been cut into thirds, so that each cell in the Mint was little more than three feet wide and eight feet long. The two large windows in my end cell were arch-shaped and striped with bars. From outside they were tightly boarded so that only pencil-thin shafts of light sliced the dimness.

A guard shoved me down on the single bunk in the end cell and then walked out and locked the door behind him. I heard another door slam shut, the sounds of shuffled feet, some stomping and shoving, then all sound ceased. I pressed my ear to the wall to listen for tapping, for some assurance that I was not alone.

I knew I had now reached the worst that Hoa Lo had to offer. The Mint's horror was renowned. Only those prisoners deserving of the worst punishment spent time there. And because I was accused of collaborating with Stockdale to threaten the security of the North Vietnamese government, it was only fitting that I should be locked up in the Mint.

Events in the Mint, as we soon found out, were being carefully orchestrated by Rabbit, our old nemesis who found himself under the claw of the Cat. The orders were to catch us communicating red-handed. Where better to accomplish that than in the Mint? With its three tiny cells, our communications would be easily heard and our disobedience finally and completely squashed.

The empty room between Stockdale and me was filled, then emptied, then quickly filled again with POWs planted there to catch us tapping. They were expected to squeal on us, or be tortured until they did. But the prisoners placed in that cell between us never lasted long enough to "get the goods on us." They deliberately caused their own trouble, antagonizing the guards and the camp authority until they were moved out, one after the other. It was a circus-like routine. If the center performance didn't quite live up to its billing, it was removed and replaced with another hopeful. But none was willing to perform. Finally, Howie Rutledge was moved into the center room. It was like another homecoming.

"There's no way to clear in here," Howie said. He was in the Mint for a return engagement, and he knew its every problem and possibility. "You gotta watch out 'cause they like to catch you from behind, and there's no way you can cover yourself."

"I've been caught from behind, Howie," I answered quietly, remembering the days I spent in the leg stocks in the Stardust.

We talked softly each day during the guards' siesta period, but we couldn't tap often. I felt the sense of isolation more than ever before. It had been so long. So long without sunshine, so long without open sky.

Six years later, Shirley told me of the many nights she had sat outside on the porch and looked up at the stars in the Texas sky. She knew, somehow, that I was alive, but held captive where I could not see the stars. So each night she gazed at them for me. She told herself there was little else she could do for me; at least, this was *something*. Years later, when I learned of her nightly vigil, I cried.

Rutledge, Stockdale, and I were completely cut off from all the other prisoners. Even trips to the latrines were no help–our cells were right next to them, and we didn't pass any other cellblocks. We had no news, no fresh information. We felt desolate and discouraged.

In early September, the camp commander began his assault on Stockdale again. His spirits plummeted when he was again moved, this time to a tiny hovel called "Calcutta" where he was even more isolated than before. The guards moved Rutledge down to the Mint's end cell and late one night they moved Jerry Denton into the vacant cage in the middle. I heard the sounds that meant a prisoner was being moved, but a short while later I heard the sounds of a prisoner in distress.

"Bao cao! Bao cao!"

An American was in trouble. The only way to get the attention of a guard was to shout that Vietnamese phrase. And it had to be pretty bad to risk hollering down the hallways of a cellblock. For several minutes the shouting continued until finally I went to my door and shouted back.

"Jerry, is that you?"

"Yeah, it's me."

"What's wrong?"

"They are denying me my food and harassing me. I want an officer to come!"

A guard pushed open the door to the small cellblock and shouted, "No talk! Keep quiet!"

Jerry answered with another shout. "Bao cao!"

"Keep quiet! You be punished! Put bat in mouth!"

It was just the challenge we needed. Howie and I joined our voices with Jerry, and we all three shouted loudly, "Bao cao! Bao cao!"

The guard stomped up and down the hallway for a moment, screeched again, screamed into my cell with a threat of the "bat in mouth!" and then marched out.

The threat of the "bat in mouth" was an empty one. They did not follow through with it. I knew about the Vietnamese habit of wrapping a stick in cloth and holding it in place with cloths tied behind the head, but Jerry had experienced it personally. It was an effective tool for silencing a noisy prisoner or for quieting the screams of a man in torture. We would not have welcomed it, but it wasn't enough of a deterrent to stop us from calling for help.

Jerry never saw an officer. And he was moved out again shortly. Howie and I were now the sole inhabitants of the Mint.

The dismal reality of solitary confinement settled on me heavily. The ever-vigilant guards made communication almost impossible except during the short siesta hour. In the tiny cramped footage of the cell I could no longer exercise. I spent most of the time lying on the concrete bunk, trying to think of ways to stay mentally stimulated.

The antics of two tenacious spiders provided great entertainment during the daylight hours. I discovered them early one morning when thin shafts of sunlight lit up their web in the corner of the windowsill. The intricate threads glinted like a tiny neon sign just about to short out.

Every morning I pulled down the spiders' lacework and then lay on my bunk and watched while they rebuilt it. Like determined squatters, they returned to the same corner of the window every time and tirelessly spun another web. When the work was done they patiently sat and waited for a fly or some other unsuspecting insect to get tangled in the almost invisible sticky threads.

"Howie, I got a construction job going on in here. It's pretty interesting," I whispered to Rutledge. "Watch the spiders in your cell. It passes the time."

"Yeah, and you can eat 'em too," he answered. "It's pure protein. Not bad. Try some."

It was not appealing, but I was starving. Our meals were growing skimpier everyday. The Vietnamese were scrounging for staples such as rice and corn to feed themselves. Whatever pitiful amounts were left over they fed to us, and the portions grew smaller with every serving. Often my stomach's gnawing woke me during the night. Though I lacked Howie's appetite for spiders, I did try some of the water bugs that found their way into my cell.

Listlessness and depression hung on me. I had no energy. I lay still much of the time to try and conserve the few calories I consumed. I was afraid of losing any more weight. I estimated that I had already dropped from 190 pounds to about 130 pounds. I was more a skeleton than a man.

For the first time since my capture I had to fight to retain my sanity. Beatings, propaganda tapes, and threats had not come close to breaking me, but hunger combined with the Mint's awful isolation was taking a terrible toll. I struggled to think cohesive thoughts. Memories became all-absorbing. In that dark cave of a cell, surrounded by the stench of death, the present was unbearable and the future almost unthinkable. Only the past had meaning. I brooded on memories. I recalled events from my past that I did not know I remembered. I dug back into my childhood for memories long ago dismissed as trivial. They suddenly had great significance.

I was amazed at what the mind could retain and reclaim after years of storage. I remembered Bible stories from Sunday school. Songs and verses I hadn't heard since grade school came back to me with perfect clarity. I was able to picture, in living color, toys I had played with at three and four years old. Family outings, family members I hadn't seen in more than three decades came rushing back to my memory. I replayed them in my consciousness, fine-tuning every detail of every recollection.

Sometimes I wondered if I was really the child I saw in those mental images, or if my mind had created a scene for me to savor in this desolate place. It didn't really matter, of course, but still I wondered. And I grasped at anything that might provide diversion or stimulation.

"Howie," I whispered one day. "How many bugs do you think we kill every day in these stinkin' cells?"

"Oh, I don't know. But we oughta find out. Let's start keeping count. See who can kill the most," he answered.

And so for a while, starting at the first light, we kept a running tally of the number of mosquitos and insects we killed each day. Each evening we counted up and declared a winner. One night I won with an incredible score of 211.

We were a captive audience for Vietnam's small and abundant lizards known as geckos. They crept up the cell walls and lay in wait for flies to settle within range of their long, skinny tongues. Then, in one silent, almost speed-of-light flick, the geckos claimed their dinner.

I watched this routine and figured out that the reason the gecko could catch the fly is that the fly cannot see things that are straight ahead of it. If a gecko could kill a fly with its tongue, then I could certainly do it with my finger. I entertained myself a few minutes every day by trying to move in on unsuspecting flies. I learned that I could get my fingers as close as a quarter-inch from a fly's head, and then knock it silly. It would roll over, kick its tiny legs, then flip back over and wobble for a minute before it finally flew off.

Sometimes, while the fly was still stunned, I would pull off a wing and place the fly back on the wall just beyond the reach of the gecko's tongue. Then I'd watch the fly try and escape across the wall with the gecko in hot pursuit.

I noticed that if a fly was able to shoot straight up and away when the gecko went on the attack, the gecko could not catch it. This fascinated me! It was exactly the means fighter planes used for evading attack. It was a perfect miniature of our maneuvers: up and over and out of distance. If only my plane had been able to accomplish that maneuver.

If only . . . I summoned all my emotional strength to fight against the futility of such thoughts. I could not waste my limited energies grieving over what might have been. I forced my thoughts away from anything that might produce more frustration.

I turned my attention toward God. When the guards increased their patrols and their vigilance and my talks with Howie had to be stopped, I could still talk freely to God. I knew with certainty that He was present in that dark, cramped closet of a cell. He listened when I prayed—this I *knew* without doubt. He answered me. When Bible stories and verses of comfort came into my thoughts, I knew He placed them there. I was comforted and encouraged. And I began to know my Creator in a way I had never known Him before. I know now, in retrospect, that God's intimate interaction with me in the Mint strengthened me and built my faith, so that I would be able to trust Him in the darkness of the terrible days that still lay ahead for me.

Occasionally, I was called in to quiz. I discovered a sort of ambivalent excitement stirring inside me whenever a guard came to escort me out of the dark, awful monotony of my cell. It was an excitement tinged with danger. I felt stimulated at the thought of human contact, even if it was with the enemy. I was alive to the challenge — to guard my every word, control my every expression, weigh my every response. Always, there was the possibility I would bring anger and more punishment down on myself, but I welcomed a chance to walk outside into the sunshine, even if it was only across a courtyard to an interrogation room.

I was surprised to see Chihuahua seated in the interrogator's chair during a quiz session one day.

"You in very great trouble, Song," he told me. "We are very angry with you. Your collaboration with Stockdale is going to make things very bad for you."

I listened quietly and wondered what charge they were going to concoct. *Don't answer yet,* I told myself. *Careful, careful . . .*

"Your attitude is very bad. You cannot afford to continue in this manner. You are already in very great trouble," he repeated.

*Trouble?* It was crazy. *I'm sweating and starving to death in a tiny box of a cell, completely cut off from everyone, and I'm in great trouble?*

I forced myself to look unconcerned, but I was puzzled. Lately, my isolation had been almost total. The guards seemed everywhere at all times. They had even begun taking their siestas in shifts so that they could keep us from communicating. For weeks I had hardly been able to tap a "GBU" to Howie.

"You are to be punished," Chihuahua continued. "You must be put in leg stocks. Probably you will be locked in them for the rest of your imprisonment."

I walked back to the cell angry, but I would not allow the guards to see it. I played a game with myself. Its rules required that I never show the enemy any sign that they had succeeded in troubling me. That would have pleased them, and I didn't want to do anything that would give them pleasure. It was my little extra means of resistance: frustrate them by acting as if all their efforts at punishment were nothing to me. I acted well. I made Chihuahua furious. He despised my nonchalance.

A guard locked my legs in the wood and steel clamps that fastened me to the bunk in my cell. I could lie flat on my back or I could sit up. Nothing more. Even the luxury of getting up to use my waste bucket was denied me. Chihuahua ordered the guards not to unlock the leg stocks for any reason.

"You get good attitude, Song," the guards liked to tell me when they came in to dump my waste can each day. "Then you won't have to live like this."

"Yeah, right," I answered.

My ankles were swollen and scraped from the tight fit of the stocks. My buttocks were sore. My skinny body had no fat for cushion anywhere on it, and some days I thought I could not sit still another second. I tried to exercise my arms and shoulders, but any motion scraped my already raw ankles against the stocks. Some days I ignored the pain and forced myself to do sit-ups anyway. Within a couple of weeks the inflammation in my ankles became infected, pus-oozing cuts.

Two months passed. Some days I lay in silence, oblivious to everything, almost as though I was wood and stone, a part of the bunk I lay on. I felt nothing, saw nothing. On other days, I fought furiously against claustrophobia. It clawed in my throat like a fierce caged animal. I thought, what a cruel joke: to pin down a man whose life has been spent in the sky, defying gravity and crashing through invisible barriers to soar above oceans and continents.

On the evening of the seventy-fourth day in stocks, I stared at the boarded up window in my cell. It had been so long since I had seen the sky and the sun. My eyes blurred with tears, and at that moment, I felt suddenly finished. It was over. I couldn't fight any more. I remember thinking, as I fell asleep, exhausted and defeated, *It would be okay if I never woke up again.*

Late that night, a typhoon tore through the city of Hanoi, ripping roofs off of buildings and lashing the prison courtyard with wind and slicing rain. I awoke to the sounds of breaking glass and slamming window shutters. The floor of my cell filled with water, and I huddled against the wall, as far away from the incoming rain as the leg stocks would allow me.

The violence of the storm stirred something inside me, and I began to pray like I had never prayed before. Long after the storm subsided, I lay on my bunk, drenched from the rain, and strangely at peace in the darkness.

I awoke the next morning to see my cell flooded with the first bright streaks of dawn. The storm had ripped the boards off my window, and for the first time in more than two months, sparkling rays of light danced a celebration in my tiny room. I had an overwhelming sense of the presence of God in that moment. He was with me, and He would be faithful. His fresh supply of mercy was pouring into my cell with all the reality of the sun's shining rays. I understood the Bible verse I had learned as a child: His mercies are new every morning. I was convinced that He would be sufficient for me. He would see me through.

The despair of the night before was gone. The leg stocks would come off soon, I was sure of it. And I knew I was going to be all right.

In only a few hours, a guard entered my cell and removed my legs from the stocks. For a moment I just sat there. My legs throbbed. There were deep imprints of the wooden stocks in my flesh. I reached down to massage my swollen ankles, and the guard hit me with his rifle.

"Get up! Dress up!"

I swung my feet toward the floor and, at my first attempt to stand, my legs collapsed. If I was going in to quiz, I would have to be dragged or carried. After seventy-five days in stocks my legs would not support me. Two guards picked me up and half-dragged me to a quiz room located in the cellblock called the Riviera.

Chihuahua sat at the large desk and motioned for me to sit down. I crumpled down onto the small stool.

"Stockdale has confessed," Chihuahua stated. He held his head high as if he were announcing an important state message. He waited for my response.

"What are you talking about?" I answered, surprised, but not impressed—I knew Jim too well. Yet I felt uneasy. If they had gotten some kind of propaganda garbage from him, it was only after severe torture. He would not be an easy man to bend. *Please, God, let him be all right.* I willed myself to stay cool and unperturbed. I prayed I would answer wisely. I didn't want to make things worse for Jim, nor did I want to go back into the stocks again.

"He has confessed to everything you and he have been doing in this camp to instigate revolt and disobedience."

"If he has confessed to anything it is because you forced him, you made him," I drawled, knowing I was angering Chihuahua, but I didn't care. "He didn't do anything voluntarily."

"That is not so. Here, see for yourself. Here is his confession and his signature."

Chihuahua lifted a sheet of paper and then laid it down on the desk.

"If it's his, I'll recognize it. Let me read it."

"Oh no, that is not possible," Chihuahua answered.

"Then obviously it isn't his," I argued.

Chihuahua looked intently at me, shrugged, and then he leaned across the desk and handed me the "confession." His fingers never let go of one end of the paper.

The confession stated that we had plotted to overthrow the Vietnamese government. It "admitted" that we were in constant communication with other American prisoners. The signature at the bottom was sloppy and almost unintelligible, but I could see that it was Stockdale's writing. I knew he had been tortured. He had given the enemy something the United States would recognize as ridiculous information, but only after he had suffered horribly. I tried not to let myself show the emotions I was feeling.

*Oh, God, help him.*

"That may be his signature," I said, "but I can tell from the way it's written that it was forced from him." I looked into Chihuahua's smug expression, hoping my concerns were well veiled. He mustn't think he had me cornered.

"You must write *your* confession now," Chihuahua stated, as if he had not heard me.

"You don't need anything from me if you've got Stockdale's. I'm not going to write anything. If you want anything from me, you'll have to force me."

Chihuahua's eyes flashed and his neck swelled against his tight khaki collar.

"You are very obstinate." Then silence, while he gathered himself up straight and marched around the desk to lean over and stare down into my face.

"This camp has decided you are to be killed! Go back to your cell!" And he waved his arm in a gesture of dismissal.

The two guards hauled me to my feet and started me toward the door. Chihuahua's voice spoke from behind me, and the guards paused just before opening the door.

"Before you die, the camp authorizes you to shower and shave."

Was I hearing right? Was the condemned man being given a "hearty meal"? Even in their threat of death there was a sort of perverse comedy. I almost laughed out loud. Like the villain in an old melodrama, I was being granted one last cigarette, one last meal.

The guards on either side dragged me back to my cell. With razor in hand, I stumbled to the showers. The thin stream of tepid water flowed down my body, and I closed my eyes and felt something almost like ecstacy. After seventy-five days of living in my own filth I felt rank. I focused only on the feel of the water on my body. I saved thoughts of Chihuahua's death threat for later.

Back in my cell I wondered, had someone in authority actually ordered my execution? I didn't *really* believe they would kill me, but it was an uncomfortable thought to try to lie down with.

*Killing POWs would damage the carefully constructed facade of leniency and humanity they wore before the nations of the world,* I assured myself.

*Maybe they don't care anymore,* I argued back.

*But that's ridiculous. . . . world opinion is important to them. That is the only reason for all the propaganda pressure. They don't dare damage their image as an honorable nation. They can't start killing off their prisoners.*

The arguments went back and forth. I prayed and determined I would trust God; and then, just when peace would settle over me, the insidious fears and questions would begin again. Finally, after many hours of uncertainty, I understood they were not going to kill me. They had decided, instead, to bury me alive.

# EIGHT

# The Eagle and the Arrow

"It's a lousy war, Sam."

"You're right, Mom," I answered. "It *is* a lousy war, but it's the only war we've got."

It was one of the last conversations I had with my mother-in-law before I left for Vietnam in April, 1966. She stood in the doorway of the bedroom with her hands on her hips and frowned at me while I packed my suitcase. We had reached an impasse.

She hated my going to Vietnam, and she couldn't understand why I had asked to be assigned to a fighter squadron. I watched her shake her head and then walk out of the room, leaving me to load the last few items into my bag. In a few hours I would begin the journey to the air base in Ubon, Thailand.

My parents, too, struggled with my decision to return to the war. It seemed only my fellow pilots understood. And my wife.

Shirley hated my going, but she understood why I felt I had to go. She took a deep breath and calmly handed me my shaving kit. Our fingers met, and I grabbed her hand and squeezed it tightly.

In peacetime, fighter pilots are nothing more than sparring partners for one another. Everything we do is just practice. Like shadow boxers, we jab and punch at the air, simulating our moves and countermoves until, on cue, we enter the ring. For us, that ring can be as high as forty thousand feet above the ground. As for any fighter, contact with the enemy is the ultimate test of our skill and our courage.

I could already feel that rush of adrenaline that surges through a pilot's system as the afterburner ignites and the plane roars to life. I could feel the force of acceleration thrust my shoulders against the seat. I imagined the heady mixture of altitude and speed, as intoxicating as wine. I could close my eyes and feel the plane climb until finally, breaking through the blanket of clouds, it soared into the clear, thin air of the blue sky. I could feel the heat of the cockpit as the sun poured in through the canopy, baking me until my eyes stung from the streams of sweat. My heart pounded as it always did when I prepared to engage the enemy, when I had to fight first with myself, to subdue my aggressiveness and force it to submit to the calculated, technical details of dog-fighting; I knew the strange, almost mysterious sensation that sets in when the body and mind are overtaken by sheer survival instincts.

Mixed in somewhere with the addictive sensations of flying fighters there was another element: a deep patriotism which I knew most of my fellow pilots shared. Some of it was a natural product of having grown up during World War II in a nation that had fought hard for its freedom. And some of it was the result of our training which sought to instill in us a sort of "Hurrah for God and country" mentality. But I was honest enough to admit that, for most pilots, the passion of patriotism pales a little next to the fervor of our competitive, ego-driven natures.

I saw that nature in myself; I sensed it in the pilots I trained, and I learned early in my career not to tamper with it. It is that nature which drives us to live in the superlatives of speed and altitude, to strap on an airplane and pit ourselves against gravity and enemy gunfire.

In many respsects, our lives are fraught with contradictions. As pilots, we defy, and at the same time utilize, the physical laws of nature to nose our planes up to altitudes of thirty thousand feet and above. As warriors, the spiritual laws we embrace when we laud God and country appear violated when we carry out our missions as ordered. Yet, most of us, at some point, make peace with these seeming contradictions, both in the air and in the soul.

Perhaps it was easier for me than for some. I guess I always believed there were things in life worth fighting and dying for; and for me, the American system of government was one of them. That it was a simplistic view which did not answer all the complexities of the Vietnam War, I know. But the military officer lives and moves in a simplistic, narrowly defined system, where rank defines duty, and commands often superseded individual conscience.

The early years of my captivity gave me many long hours to search out the truth of my political and spiritual convictions. I had to find purpose and meaning in what I had done, what I was doing, or lose my sanity. In the dark, putrid, squalor of my concrete cell, I reexamined the path that had led me to this place in my life. I walked back and forth through the maze of experiences that had finally culminated in my capture and confinement in Hanoi.

I felt certain that I had not violated any Biblical principles by becoming a fighter pilot. I had a personal sense of the wrongness and evil of communism and its coercive methods of government. I felt I was part of an effort to keep that evil out of a land that, without aid, would be forced to live under a cruel and harsh totalitarian regime. If Ho Chi Minh took South Vietnam, he would purge the country of all who held differing political viewpoints. He would murder, "reeducate," or remove all those who were not in agreement with his policies and politics.

Ho Chi Minh's brand of communism was already carrying out similar purges in North Vietnam to rid his regime of all obstacles and opposition. Intelligence reports indicated that many of his own troops had begun to doubt Uncle Ho's veracity as a leader. Refugees continued to pour out of the North into the South to escape the murder and destruction they saw in their own villages under the heavy hand of Ho Chi Minh. No, I felt no need to apologize for my part in fighting Ho Chi Minh. I had no sorrow over any damage I might have done to the likes of him and his insidious ideology.

And I was not disturbed by the fact that we were embroiled in battle so very far away from America. Historically, the American military has had as its objective to fight the enemy as far away from American soil as possible. With the exception of the attack on Pearl Harbor, bombs have never exploded near an American city. Our farmlands have never been cratered, our children never threatened by enemy fire. Since our independence was fully and finally secured in the War of 1812, our seat of government has never again been under siege by a hostile, foreign power. The role of the military, through the years, has been to guarantee that such terror and catastrophe never reach our homeland.

Our strategy: engage enemies elsewhere. Fight them and defeat them in their own countries. Since our beginnings as a nation, our goal has been to battle the enemy on its ground, not our own. Even the war with Mexico over Texas was fought on Mexican soil. Fifty thousand volunteers arrived from all over the United States to fight for Texas. They pushed the Mexican forces all the way back to Mexico City and held the capital until treaty negotiations returned it to Mexico. In 1898 we held off the Spanish and confined the Spanish-American War to the Caribbean and the Philippines. We intercepted the Germans in Europe; we countered the Japanese invasion in the Pacific; and although we did battle on U.S. protectorates and the Alaskan territory, we were able to hold the enemy away from our borders.

World War I and the rise of communism in 1917 saw the United States thrust into a major role as a defender of freedom. Our long-held beliefs in democracy and free enterprise, as well as the fact of our political and military dominance, placed us in a prominent position as a bold opponent of communism around the world. It was from that position that we stepped into the fray in Vietnam.

Containment had a historical precedent. That we were thousands of miles away from American shores was not a problem to most career military officers who were involved in the war. We believed we were living up to our SEATO obligations. We believed we were engaged in an honorable endeavor, in the beginning. But as the war progressed, I began to doubt the honor of our endeavor.

Had it been honorable to participate in a deadly coup to remove an undesirable leader in South Vietnam? Did the people in the South want or even understand the workings of democracy? Had we, with a sort of political superiority complex, arbitrarily determined that our brand of government was best for the South Vietnamese? These questions plagued me as the war dragged on and victory eluded us, and I could find no clear answers. But it was the total ineptness of the war strategy that made me nearly crazy with frustration.

I could table the subtle questions and the political nuances to be examined some other time, some other place. I knew there would be many different philosophical stances. But I could not stop wrestling with the oddball way Lyndon Johnson was fighting this war. Once committed to the battle, why would he not allow us to fight it to a victorious end?

Interrogations with Rabbit constantly pointed out that the United States was not really intent on winning this war.

"We know you have supply ships off shore near Saigon," he said once. "We know there are tactical nuclear weapons on board, just in case your government decides to use them. But we also know they will never have the resolve to do it. That is why we call the United States a paper tiger. We know your strategic statements will never be carried out."

I knew, even as we spoke, that we should have stopped Ho Chi Minh in his tracks already. A few well-placed weapons would have closed all the passes and the DMZ to any traffic, stopping all resupply, and it could have been done with few or no losses to the U.S. military and to North Vietnamese civilians. Ultimately, the Johnson White House decided against such action because of fear of China's possible retaliation. The only feasible plan to end the war victoriously was crushed.

Fear of the Chinese had also stopped us from decisively closing out the Korean conflict. General MacArthur had known the Chinese were massing above the border. He also knew they could be stopped with nuclear weapons—one bomb, strategically placed, would end the war. When he made that recommendation to President Truman, Truman fired him. The Chinese overran our position, captured many Americans (many of whom are still not accounted for), and massacred thousands more. The great irony is that, in that instance, as in Vietnam, China had no nuclear weapons with which to retaliate if we had in fact determined to stop them. Massive retaliation would have ended the war at that time, but instead, MacArthur's successor ordered the U.S. forces to pull back, drew a line, and the fighting and killing continued for two more years.

China's interest in both Korea and Vietnam was that they be buffer states, but they did not have the weaponry to ensure their wishes. The United States, by backing away from victory, made China's wishes easily obtainable.

"You know that the United States is about to commit more atrocities," Rabbit told me another time.

"What? You mean we have finally decided to win this war?" I answered. *Is it possible? Has Johnson ordered the bombing of strategic targets at last?*

"No, you will never win this war. Our resolve is to fight forever if we have to, even from the jungles and in tunnels in the hills. You can never win."

Again, I thought of General MacArthur. His statement that there is no way to ever neutralize a jungle environment rang in my ears. I wondered. I worried.

"Your country is planning an amphibious invasion near Vinh," Rabbit informed me once. "They will destroy our cities and murder our women and children. We will withdraw to the hills and never allow them to advance. We will kill them all and all their replacements. Your country will give up. Already your people are rising up against this unjust war."

He was right. We could hear it in the reports from the United States, in the news from new shootdowns. The evidence was growing. People at home were rising up against this war. Many American voices railed and ranted against any actions that would appear to be an escalation. The nuclear option, the attack from the sea, was shelved. The reason given was the shallow coastal waters, but again, Korea and MacArthur came to my mind. His successful landing at Inchon, Korea, had been made under the same dire warnings of shallow waters.

The Vietnamese propaganda war was succeeding in Hanoi as well as in the outer world. We could see its impact on some of our fellow POWs. Our ranks grew wobbly as we learned that some officers in middle levels, such as captains and majors, had begun to doubt the value of resistance and became collaborators with the North Vietnamese. Why not go ahead and do what the enemy wanted? We would only be adding our voices to thousands of other American voices that decried this war. Why hold out? Why not cooperate and live out the remainder of this ridiculous war in some sort of comfort? What was the point of resistance any longer? Theirs were the voices we heard, clear and loud, reading propaganda statements over the air—statements which were freely given without torture. To this handful of POWs, resistance now seemed a futile pursuit, empty of meaning when measured against the actions and policies coming out of both the Pentagon and the oval office.

Lyndon Johnson and his staff directly questioned the on-the-spot decisions in the war zone, calling their shots from in front of television sets on Capitol Hill. What might have been sound military decisions coming out of the Pentagon were suddenly subject to comparison with the advice of the State Department. A change had come over the American military system. The Joint Chiefs of Staff had begun to function much like pseudo-foreign affairs experts. Military expertise gave way to political expedience. And the indecisive, inept war strategy fed the antiwar sentiment among Americans.

U.S. forces continued to make thrusts into enemy territory in the South and then withdraw, letting it fall back into Vietcong hands while the ground was still wet with American blood. The Soviets used Vietnamese air space as a testing ground for their aircraft and air defenses, while the United States issued some new gadget to the troops for tests of our own. The Secretary of Defense believed we could win this war with superior technology.

In the North, our leaders continually sent our air arm out over territory we never intended to occupy, mistakenly believing that ground forces occupation was not essential to successful war strategy. The bombings left hundreds of elephants dead on the jungle floor, but Ho Chi Minh's forces continued to thrive. Strategic enemy targets survived and operated with few interruptions, while U.S. pilots wasted themselves, their fire power, and their airplanes against junk targets, like vacant truck parks and empty supply roads.

At this point, America was involved in a full-scale war, though LBJ refused to admit it. He refused to involve the nation in an endeavor that could only succeed with the full support of the American people. He mistakenly thought he could divide the country's resources between a full-scale war halfway around the world and the domestic programs he had earmarked for his Great Society.

History shows us a president who coveted the creation of a political legacy for himself. He vowed to "end that bitch of a war," freeing himself to "court the woman I really love"—his Great Society.[1] His jealousy for her robbed him of enthusiasm for winning the war in Southeast Asia. His ambivalence for fighting forcefully and decisively fueled the already well-oiled machinery of the peace movement.

Just as sparks from a forest fire can ignite a distant meadow, the war in Vietnam sparked scores of domestic conflagrations. At first there were only a few small hot spots, but by 1967, portions of every American community felt the heat. Politics at the highest level were stuck at a stalemate over the matter of the war in Vietnam.

In September, 1967, while I was locked in leg stocks in Hoa Lo's Mint, President Johnson revealed his famous "San Antonio Formula": "There is a positive movement toward constitutional government [in South Vietnam]," he stated. An elected government and an elected senate and legislature would be installed in South Vietnam, he prophesied. The war's toll had been high, he told his audience. American casualties thus far: 13,500; wounded: 85,000. However, there were signs of progress, he reported. "The tide continues to run with us. But the struggle remains hard."[2]

Vague wording. No absolutes to report. "Progress" compared to what? Were we killing fewer people than we had before? Had we finally and permanently closed off any supply routes? Had we destroyed any strategic targets that would limit the effectiveness of the enemy? It was true that for a time the communists had appeared to back off, but then they came back more strongly than before. Their philosophy was two steps backward and then one giant step forward.

Letters that flew between Washington, D.C. and Ho Chi Minh in Hanoi revealed the great philosophical chasm that lay between the opposing forces. Ho Chi Minh called the American action a "war of aggression against the Vietnamese people . . . a challenge to the countries of the socialist camp . . . a threat to the national independence movement, and a serious danger to peace in Asia and the world."[3]

LBJ offered a "cessation of bombing against your country and the stopping of further augmentation of U.S. forces in South Vietnam as soon as I am assured that infiltration into South Vietnam by land and by sea has stopped."[4]

Ho Chi Minh's acceptance of such an offer would have meant a concession speech, a humiliating declaration of his defeat. This war was about geography: reclaiming the land of South Vietnam that was lost to Ho Chi Minh after the routing of the French in 1954. It was about infiltration: turn the thinking of the South Vietnamese to accept the politics of Hanoi's regime. It was about unity: erase the line drawn at the seventeenth parallel, and present to the world a united, independent country, sovereign and free of western interference, and governed by Marxist-Leninist doctrines.

It was a standoff. Neither side could graciously concede on any point and still remain true to its ideological stance. It became a question of who could fight the longer. Would the United States, with its superior arsenal and military expertise, pound away until the communist enemies of democracy finally gave up their fight for South Vietnam? Or would the North Vietnamese, tenacious and determined, continue to harass and, as a cartoonist once depicted it, drive out the "imperialist beast," like mosquitos could drive away an elephant? Only time would reveal the answer.

U.S. domestic difficulties made world headlines. The regime in Hanoi was in a state of absolute glee over the dissension in America. Nothing could have pleased the North Vietnamese more—unless, of course, they had received a notice of the surrender and withdrawal of all American troops from South Vietnam and a cessation of all further aggression against North Vietnam.

Theirs was a war being fought on two fronts: the first, the geographic battle zones in North and South Vietnam; the second, the invisible stadium of world opinion. As more and more Americans renounced U.S. intervention in Vietnam, the cause of Ho Chi Minh gained acceptance among the other countries of the world. He valued his propaganda winnings even more highly than his military victories.

In an ironic and perverse sort of way, every account of American antiwar activity supplied the enemy with yet another weapon for use against the POWs. While we were fighting their abuses and their total disregard for the Geneva Conventions, they were reloading to attack us with the verbiage of our own countrymen.

Aesop's "The Eagle and the Arrow," told the story of the eagle who, upon seeing "the fashion of the shaft" that struck him, exclaimed: "With our own feathers, not by others' hands are we now smitten." The American POW in North Vietnam could have said much the same thing. The communist propaganda machine was succeeding. I listened in horror as Hanoi broadcast news of the violent clashes between blacks and whites back home. The peaceful reforms initiated by Martin Luther King were being rejected in favor of more militant means of protest. It sounded as if our country was aflame with anarchy, hatred, and violence.

Stokely Carmichael stunned the troops in Vietnam when he made his statement on Radio Hanoi in 1967. To the black American fighting the ground battle, he said leave this war to the "white man . . . it's his war. Let him fight it." Hanoi Hannah played the message over and over, urging the black American troops to desert their companies and align themselves with the North Vietnamese.

With every horror story our fears multiplied. Was the dissension enough to propel the administration into a unilateral withdrawal? What would happen to us if the United States just quit and walked away? The North Vietnamese knew this possibility was our worst nightmare. They played on it with daily messages intended to weaken our resolve to resist.

"Your country is tired of this war," Hanoi Hannah said. "Your own people have come to believe in the cause of Vietnam. You think about it, GI Joe. Get out of Vietnam. You do not belong here. Refuse to fight. Insist on withdrawing now, before more of you have to die uselessly."

Hanoi, a quick and ready advocate of the antiwar movement in the United States, sent annual appeals to the U.S. peace movement and praised its recognition of the rights of North Vietnam to claim the South. While the FBI, CIA, and congressional investigations could prove no direct link between the antiwar organizations and the communist regime in North Vietnam, there was a spirit of cooperation and support between them that was nearly the undoing of many POWs in Vietnam.

I was shaken by the messages delivered by the antiwar activists. Many came in person. Celebrities such as actress Jane Fonda, jouranlists Harrison Salisbury and David Dellinger, activist Tom Hayden of the Students for a Democratic Society, and Herbert Aptheker of the American Communist Party were the most troubling. And the most destructive.

They returned with reports that identified the Hanoi regime as "competent, even representative of Vietnam," and proclaimed that the POWs were being treated well. They returned to the States committed to convincing people that our presence in Vietnam was immoral and illegal. Their pronouncements gave fuel to the North's assertion that we in captivity were, indeed, war criminals. That we were, in fact, guilty of war crimes, and therefore deserving of all the punishment and torture that the prison authority was capable of inflicting upon us. Deserving even of death.

Those representatives of the peace movement who were allowed to meet with POWs in Hanoi saw fiction, not truth. They returned home with reports of prisoners dressed in clean clothes, sitting at tables heavy with fresh fruit. They saw carefully selected prisoners; only those whose injuries were not crippling. The facade suggested good medical care, proper nutrition, and humane living conditions. Behind that facade were prisoners who had been tortured and beaten into submission—prisoners whose bodies were doctored to appear whole so that the visitors' cameras would record a false image, an image of humane and lenient treatment given by the North Vietnamese. They spoke with men who, only days before, had been tortured to ensure their cooperation in front of those cameras and in the presence of the peace representatives. In some cases, a POW knew one of his friends hung from the meat hook in the torture room and would receive further abuse if he did not cooperate in the propaganda ruse. There were a few POWs, however, who spoke gladly with the peace envoys. They were willing conspirators, ready to give a good report of the communists who held them captive, and rewarded with better treatment in exchange.

The peace activists believed what their eyes told them. Although history lay on the page in front of them and contradicted Hanoi's claims, they refused to see it. China, purging herself of dissenters, had only recently rounded up her intellectuals, artists, musicians, and scientists and locked them away where their influence could not be felt by the working class. Those individuals whose broader knowledge of the world and its workings would clash with the totalitarian tenets of Mao Zedong were imprisoned, murdered, or simply drowned in the blood of revolution. All independent thinking was, at that moment, being squelched in China and in North Vietnam. All their citizens were being brought down to the same low level of slavery to one totalitarian premise.

I found it almost impossible to believe that American peace envoys and antiwar activists could be so naive. To us in prison it was obvious what was happening. But again, it was with our military training that we interpreted all these things. We had studied the text of a speech by Dmitry Manuilskiy at the Lenin School for Political Warfare. Most of us in the POW camps in Hanoi could quote the paragraph written in 1931 and still used in Moscow's military schools today. We remembered, and we cringed:

> War to the hilt between communism and capitalism is inevitable. Today, of course, we are not strong enough to attack. Our time will come in 20 to 30 years. We shall begin by launching the most spectacular peace movement of record. The capitalist countries, stupid and decadent, will rejoice to cooperate in their own destruction. They will leap at another chance to be friends. As soon as their guard is down, we shall smash them with our clenched fists.

We could see it clearly. The antiwar protesters were propaganda tools in the hands of North Vietnamese communists. I am not so cynical as to be unable to understand that, among the dissenters back in the United States, there were genuine pacifists, those who for reasons of religion were against war and all violence. Through the centuries, there have always been authentic believers who have chosen some other form of service to their country in lieu of military and combat service. But among the demonstrators and peace activists, these were few in number. The vast majority of activists had no pure sentiments about violence and war. They would (and did) gladly engage in violence to make their views known.

Some of the most vocal encouraged the violent overthrow of the U.S. government if that would ensure the end of the war. One war to end another, they seemed to be saying. I found it hard to listen to "peace" rhetoric against such a background of violent intent. It appeared that their philosophy was not so much *for* peace as it was *against* the U.S. political system.

The sit-ins, riots, and civil disobedience in America fueled the mental war the communists were waging against us, their captives. With every new report of American disenchantment over the war, the torture in Hanoi's prison camps intensified. We were like marionettes, dangling from the hands of indecisive, ambivalent politicians and peace activists, to tell the story our captors wanted told.

Strangling in communism's vicious bindings, we were gasping for our breath. We were seeing, firsthand, its insidious lies in action. To most of us, the thought of relenting and giving approval to such an ideology was preposterous. With a perverse sort of logic, the increased torture only fueled our determination to resist our captor's pressure. It strengthened our resolve to refuse to admit to any crimes. We would do nothing to help elevate the cause of this regime. We would not willingly cooperate in any way with Ho's campaign to gain honor and recognition.

If LBJ's philosophy toward the war was crippling, militarily, his philosophy toward the POW issue was devastating. His advisors, naive concerning the communist mentality, believed we would be better served by quiet, private diplomatic dealings. All information that came in concerning us was classified. Our plight was not a matter of national interest, it appeared. The attention that could have (and, we later learned, definitely *would* have) had an impact on our treatment was quelled.

LBJ brought no pressure on Hanoi for our release, nor for an exchange of prisoners, nor even for an accounting of our numbers and our treatment. He accepted the reports of those decidedly left-wing thinkers who had visited North Vietnam and brought back stories of humane treatment. Hanoi was accountable to no one for its abuses. It appeared to the regime that no one cared about us. We were the war's expendable commodities. We were of no concern to anyone except the families and friends who mourned us.

## Notes

1. William Appleman Williams, Thomas McCormick, Lloyd Gardner and Walter LaFeber, editors, *America In Vietnam* (Garden City: Anchor Press/Doubleday, 1985), p. 221.
2. Ibid., p. 265.
3. Ibid., p. 262.
4. Ibid., p. 260.

# NINE

# The Alcatraz Story

I heard the guard's footsteps in the hallway. He stopped at Howie's cell, and I laid my ear against the wall to listen for sounds that would tell me what was happening. It was pitch dark and past our bedtime; much too late to be taking Howie to the showers. Maybe to quiz? The door slammed shut again, and I heard Howie moving about in his cell. I heard the clank of a waste can against the wall, the scraping of a metal cup across the bunk, then soft shuffling sounds, like the ones a prisoner makes when he's gathering his few things to roll up in his mat.

*Oh, God, no,* I thought. *They're moving him out. I can't stay in this place without Howie . . .*

For the first time I thought about being absolutely alone. I could feel the threat of panic rising inside me. With Howie gone, I would be completely cut off from contact with all but the guards and the camp authority. There would be no one to hear me if I cried, "Bao cao," no one to tap encouragement to me. No one to know or care if they decided to carry out their sentence of death against me.

But maybe the worst was over for Howie. *If you're leaving, I'm glad for you, buddy.*

Just then I heard a faint tap. I held my breath and listened.

"I don't know what's happening," Howie told me on the wall. "I'm rolling up to move out, but I don't know where. It doesn't make sense. You got any ideas?"

"I don't know," I answered. It was puzzling. We had had no contact with other prisoners since we had been isolated in the Mint. We were completely cut off. We had no clues about life beyond our tiny dark world.

I heard footsteps outside the door, and Howie quickly tapped, "Good-bye."

"Good-bye," I tapped back. At that moment I felt more afraid and forlorn than I had ever felt. I squeezed my eyes tightly against burning tears and slumped back on my bunk. In the next moment, the guard opened my cell and commanded, "Roll up."

*I'm going too!*

I started to shake. My hands couldn't move quickly enough. I was leaving this awful, stinking hole of a cell. Half an hour later, the guard returned to blindfold me and cuff my hands in front of me. He shoved my bedroll into my arms and prodded me ahead of him toward the court-yard. Muffled whispers and the sounds of bodies shuffling about told me that I was one of a small group of POWs rousted for some late-night encounter. With an executioner, perhaps? Were these under the threat of death, as I was?

No one knew what was happening. Blindfolded and stumbling, we milled about in the little yard and determined that there were only a few of us being moved out. After colliding hard against a sturdy, square-shaped body and hearing a whispered curse, I was able to identify Stock-dale. He, too, was confused about this late-night rendezvous. The most reasonable explanation was that we were being moved to someplace like the Zoo again to make room for new shootdowns.

In recent weeks, the United States had increased bombing missions over Hanoi. The sounds of planes "going downtown" reverberated over our heads constantly. Lately, we had lain on our bunks and listened to exploding bombs, trying to guess their targets. The number of new shoot-downs, once only a trickle, had become a steady flow, and the prison now bulged with prisoners of war. At this rate, soon every cell in every prison facility in North Vietnam would be filled.

I heard the clanking of metal tailgates dropping and felt myself shoved and pushed out of the way. In a few moments, truck engines coughed and chugged out of the yard, leaving several of us standing, waiting to take a ride on the shuttle to the unknown.

In a little while, the trucks returned, and a guard poked his rifle bar-rel into my back, prodding me forward. I felt myself falling. The bed-roll in my arms cushioned my landing on the truck bed. I lifted my foot, not quite high enough, and the guard prodded once more until my feet met something solid. I finally climbed in and crowded close against someone who whispered, "Harry Jenkins."

"Sam Johnson," I answered, almost smiling. I was among friends. I leaned back against the taut canvas of a canopy.

"Shut mouth!" a guard scolded, as he crawled into the back of the tiny truck that was cramped with just the three of us in it. In a mo-ment we were bouncing over Hanoi's rutted streets.

We stopped less than twenty minutes later, and after we climbed out of the truck, it left again immediately to shuttle the next pair of prison-ers. For only a moment I stood and listened, trying to orient myself to new surroundings. The familiar night sounds of the city echoed around me.

*So, we are still in Hanoi. The driver purposely twisted the route, circling and backtracking to confuse us, but we're not far from where we started.*

And yet, there was nothing familiar about this place. We thought we knew of all the facilities in the Hanoi prison system—even the remote ones, such as Briar Patch—because of the prison authority's practice of moving prisoners from place to place. We had been able to collect data on every place of incarceration, but we knew nothing about a place such as this. Wherever we were, it was not on the regular POW itinerary.

I took a few uncertain steps down what I guessed was an alley. I could look straight down and under my blindfold to see the ground, and if I turned my head just a little, I could see enough to make out large, three- or four-story brick buildings on either side. We stumbled across an open space, probably encircled by the large buildings, I figured, and then I felt myself shoved through a narrow gateway. My legs were still wobbly from the seventy-five days in stocks, and I stepped forward tentatively. When my foot met nothing but air, I lurched for something to grab onto and bumped into a guard.

"Move!" he growled, as he pushed me away.

*Stairs! Slow and easy now.*

Cautiously, I set each foot down, blindly gauging the distance for each step. The guard prodded me forward, jabbering Vietnamese words, and I placed one foot in front of another, counting four or five steps down. When the ground was again level, I took about three strides before I was shoved into a cell. The guard yanked off my blindfold and exited, slamming the door shut behind him. I stood in total darkness. With my first tentative step forward, I banged my shins against a solid slab of concrete and again fell forward, landing facedown on my bedroll.

I stood and inched my way about in the darkness. It seemed there were about two feet of standing space in front of the door. Then, jutting out into the room was a large concrete slab, probably for sleeping on, but it filled the remaining square footage of the cell. I stepped up on the concrete platform and found that I could stand up to my full height. Perhaps the high ceiling would provide some ventilation. But as my eyes adjusted to the darkness, I saw that, above the door, the cell's only window was covered with a perforated metal grill. There would be no breeze in this tightly sealed box of a cell.

I sat down on the concrete slab and rubbed my bruised shins. The stale air was hot and stifling. The sharp, stinging prison smells were faint, as if time had blunted them. I listened for the sounds of prisoners, the sounds of pain; but there were none. I had the strange feeling of being in a prison where only ghosts remained.

Outside my door I heard the clanking sounds of metal banging against metal. The cell door opened and a guard stepped in. Above the door, a single light bulb came on and revealed an ominous-looking steel ap-

paratus dangling from the guard's hands. He removed my handcuffs, and then he reached for my ankles.

*Leg irons!*

My chest muscles tightened. My heart began to pound. I closed my eyes tightly while the guard grasped my legs and fumbled with the steel horseshoe-like clamps. Finally, with a curse, he stomped out of the cell.

*He can't get them on! My ankles are so swollen from the stocks, the irons won't fit!*

I lay back on the bunk and drew a deep breath. In the light, I could see that this cell, with its sloping tin ceiling, was slightly larger than the one I had just left in the Mint. The dirty concrete walls glared like blank billboards. The metal grill over the window seemed to tease with the promise of light and air, but I knew only pinpoints of sunlight would be able to enter. And unless a violent wind ripped through Hanoi and tore off the grill, there would be no air circulation in this hole.

The door opened again. The guard entered with his hands full of irons and steel rods. He pulled my ankles forward and began again fumbling with different sizes, trying to affix a pair to my grossly misshapen ankles. Finally, he shoved a U-shaped piece on each ankle and connected them with an eighteen-inch steel rod. It was still a tight fit. The puffy, discolored flesh squeezed into the irons, but I felt grateful that at least I could stand and move about. I thought I was much better off than I had been in the stocks.

The sounds of guards outside the door finally faded. It was safe to begin communicating.

"Irons! They've got us in leg irons!"

One by one, every man vented his anger and frustration against the wall, tapping out messages of indignation.

I whispered to Jenkins, who I learned was next door, "Pass the word: It could be worse. I've just spent over two months in stocks. At least in irons we can stand and walk around."

In a few days I would actually be grateful for having worn the leg stocks. The swelling in my ankles would go down, the irons would become loose, and I would be amazed to hear myself thank God for the leg stocks. Because of them, I would be a little more comfortable in the irons.

I also knew that my months in the Mint had probably helped to prepare me for this place. In that dark, tiny hovel, I had felt what David the Psalmist wrote about: "There is no one who regards me; There is no escape for me; No one cares for my soul." I had already experienced hell, and I figured almost anything would be an improvement. Even during the uncertain moments of our arrival at this strange, unknown prison facility, I had had the feeling that I was being reunited with friends.

I was again a part of a whole, a member of the team. And an impressive team it was, indeed.

For hours, that first night, we tapped to one another, identifying ourselves, and trying to find some common denominator that would explain why we were all here together in what we determined was an L-shaped block of cells somewhere in downtown Hanoi.

It was a confusing mix of men — some navy, some air force, some high-ranking officers, some junior grade. There was Jim Stockdale, the SRO, and Jerry Denton, his sidekick and next in rank; myself, the highest ranking air force officer of the bunch, and good buddy of Stockdale and Denton — I knew our names had been blacklisted together as hardcore resisters, enemies of the Ho Chi Minh regime. We had dared to plan an escape, and we had consistently opposed the prison authority and encouraged other POWs to do the same.

There was Jenkins, who was famous for his daring flights off the U.S.S. *Oriskany,* and who became famous among us for his zany sense of humor. Rutledge, who had killed a man during his capture, was a spirit who could not be dominated by the Vietnamese. Mulligan, another navy commander, had earned a reputation as a strong resister and powerful communicator. All these fit into the category of diehards, as the camp authority liked to say.

Ron Storz, who had made himself a nuisance and an embarrassment to the North Vietnamese by his hunger strikes, was just two cells down from me. The tall, skinny New Yorker just wouldn't relent. Neither would he survive the conditions in this hell.

Lieutenant Commander Shumaker was next door to me. His diligent efforts at resistance made him a standout among the hundreds of POWs. The second shootdown of the Vietnam War, he was always on the lookout for some innovative new way to communicate.

There were three more men, all younger than the rest of us, and of lesser rank. Lieutenant Commander Nels Tanner, a pilot off the carrier U.S.S. *Coral Sea,* earned his place among us with his penchant for creative storytelling. After several torture sessions with the ropes, sessions that left his arms purple and swollen and useless for several months, he and his fellow airman, Lieutenant Ross Terry, decided it was time to placate with misinformation in order to save their limbs, and quite possibly their lives. Pushed for propaganda statements, they created a farcical story about two pilots from their carrier who had been court-martialed because they disagreed with the United States involvement in Vietnam and had refused to fly combat missions. Their names: Ben Casey and Clark Kent.

To round out the story, they added the account of a man whose wife violently opposed the war and divorced him because he was bombing

North Vietnam. They let Hollywood's Tom Ewell play that part. They read their script for a team of Japanese journalists and cameramen gathered in a large room at Hoa Lo.

The Vietnamese were delighted to have the support of such credible individuals as naval aviators. Rabbit beamed with pride while the Japanese listened, wide-eyed, to the propaganda statements featuring a comic book hero, a television character, and a movie star. When the Japanese press reported the story, *Time* magazine picked it up, and six weeks later, the Vietnamese knew they had been duped. Tanner was blamed for the ruse, and a few months later he found himself locked up with the "blackest of criminals."

Lieutenant (j.g.) George Coker was the youngest of our gang and the only one who was not a pilot. He was a cocky sort, a bombardier-navigator, and Stockdale dubbed him "Cagney," after the James Cagney of the big screen. He was short and square and sometimes bigger than life. He and George McKnight, a fearless air force captain with a huge booming voice and swashbuckling style, had planned and executed a daring prison escape to earn "criminal" stature. Two weeks later they were loaded into trucks and driven out to this mystery prison.

After hours of tapping the pattern emerged. We were all troublemakers. Every man in our group was what the Vietnamese would label a hardcore, a diehard. We had offered constant irritation to the prison authority, had been anxious to foil the enemy at every opportunity, and had incited others to resistance as well.

When exhaustion finally brought our conversations to a close that first night, I lay down to sleep on the concrete slab and felt something I hadn't felt for a long time. It was a strange sort of elation, an excitement almost, that I had been categorized with such valiant men as these. It was like being selected to serve with an elite company of warriors, and I felt honored and challenged. Of course, there were others among the hundreds of POWs who also deserved to be here, but the Vietnamese had chosen only eleven. And I was among them. It was an honor, a medal I would wear in my heart.

My first glimpse of the place by daylight explained the grave-like feeling that had come over me during the first moments after our arrival. In the center of Hanoi, amid the three- and four-story buildings that comprised the North Vietnamese Ministry of Defense, a 2,500-square-foot area had been dug out in the center courtyard. In that sunken hole, a cluster of tiny prison cells had been built and surrounded by a half-earth, half-brick wall. Barbed wire and glass embedded in concrete lay across the top of the east wall. The other three walls were less forbidding, but guarded at all times by sentries.

The prison, built by the French, had not been used since the 1950s when it had housed high-profile political prisoners who had most ardently opposed French rule. It was a secret, high-security system for the country's arch criminals. It was inescapable. And incongruous.

The large buildings that surrounded our dugout prison facility were the equivalent of the U.S. Pentagon—the administrative center of the military arm of the government. And beneath its windows, in a corner of our dugout yard, was a small, rickety pen filled with pigs. Nearby, a three-foot retaining wall encircled an earth-covered, dugout bomb shelter.

Every morning about nine, my cell door was opened and a guard removed my leg irons. About an hour later he returned to give me my food, which he handed me from the doorway. Around 4:00 P.M., guards returned with our last meal, and an hour later the dishes were picked up and the leg irons put on for the night. Once a day I walked a short distance to empty my can in a bomb shelter that had been turned into a makeshift toilet. Once a week I walked to the opposite corner of the yard to stand at a sink and sponge off my body's stench and filth and then douse myself with a bucketful of tepid, dirty water.

The sense of isolation was overwhelming. For the first time since the early weeks in Heartbreak Hotel, there were no radio speakers in our cells. There were no propaganda programs, no interrogations, no quizzes, and hence, no torture; but there was also no opportunity for gleaning information about the war. We had no incoming prisoners and no way to contact anyone outside the walls of the Ministry of Defense. We had only one source of information: the American fighters who flew their daily missions over Hanoi to bomb the Daumer Bridge and the power plant near Dirty Bird. Their roaring engines and exploding firepower reassured us, for a time, that the United States hadn't pulled out and left us. Within the walls of Alcatraz we existed in a virtual vacuum.

Our days and nights were a confusing blur of cold, gray hours. A bare light bulb above the cell door burned all night, casting a garish light all around. By day the light was turned off and the cell was dim, lit only by the pinpricks of light from the grill over the window and the shaft of light that spilled in through the space under the door.

The sounds of the city could be heard in the early mornings. I could lie on my bunk and identify gasping motor engines, high-pitched voices, and the bells and squeaking wheels of the city's trolley cars. At night I lay and listened to the roar of fighters overhead, going downtown. Air raid sirens whined, and I could hear the whoosh of missiles flying through the air toward the ground. The Ministry of Defense was well protected —antiaircraft gunfire erupted all around us.

The Daumer Bridge and the power plant nearby were favorite targets. I wondered about their significance to the total war effort. Had LBJ finally ordered strategic strikes against the enemy? If so, maybe my instincts about the war were right. The heavy bombing would drive Ho Chi Minh to the bargaining table to begin to talk peace. Surely the war was nearly over. I continually tried to convince my fellow inmates of this, but I was often the only one with such certainty. Mistaken certainty, as it turned out, but it kept me going and sometimes steadied my buddies as well.

In the first few days at Alcatraz we were all consumed with the need to get acquainted with each other, to communicate. We spent every possible moment tapping or whispering to one another in a frenzied effort to prove to ourselves that the enemy could not completely cut us off from human contact.

"Hey, Jenkins," I whispered to my neighbor, when the guards were out of earshot. "Find out how Coker and McKnight escaped, will ya? I'm dying to know."

"Me too," Harry whispered back.

The idea that two prisoners could actually get outside the walls of one of Hanoi's prisons intrigued me. Since we had arrived at Alcatraz and met up with these two, I had been waiting for a chance to hear all about it. How did they do it? How far did they get? I had to know.

A primitive sort of party line carried the story.

"We were in the 'Dirty Bird'," Coker tapped up the length of the cellblock.

We all knew about the Dirty Bird. It was a hastily built camp erected near a belching, smoking power plant. Its residents were the overflow from the other, bulging camps, and its cadre of guards were poorly trained, probably all new recruits. The time was ideal for an escape attempt.

"The locks on the doors were easy to open, so we decided to go for it," Coker told Tanner, and Tanner passed it on. "We used the old stuff-your-clothes-under-the-blanket trick after the guards made their final check for the night. Then we opened the doors and slipped out and put the locks back on the doors from the outside."

I couldn't believe it. They just walked out of their cells! Over the wall and across rooftops, they had stealthily made their way through the shadows and the back alleys that would lead them to the Daumer Bridge and the Red River. In the dark and nearly empty streets, they crept the short distance and then followed a ditch down to the edge of the river. Using a drawstring from their pajama-like pants, they tied their wrists together so that they wouldn't get separated in the river's current, and waded down into the muddy water.

"We figured the current could carry us out toward the ocean. We estimated by daylight we'd be far from the city, and well on our way to the beach and maybe a navy rescue," Coker continued, "but we didn't figure on the river twisting and turning so much. After all night in the water we'd gone nearly fifteen miles, but we were still on the edge of the city. We decided to get out of the river and hide in a mudbank during daylight while the river was crowded with boat traffic. We'd get back in the river after dark. It probably would have worked, but McKnight got fidgety in the mud and had to stand up. Some peasants spotted us and there was no place to hide and no place to run." In less than two hours, Coker and McKnight were back in prison.

"We thought they were going to kill us, but they just threw us into solitary and said we'd die if we tried it again." There was no opportunity for a second try. Two weeks later, on October 25, 1967, they were moved to Alcatraz with nine other diehards. There would be no more escapes.

For nine of us in a line of cells, communication was fairly simple, but for Mulligan and Stockdale it was more complicated. The guards put them in the three-cell block that lay perpendicular to our nine-cell unit and separated them by leaving an empty cell between them.

After two weeks of frustrated, limited communication, Stockdale was down on the floor in his cell looking out under his door when he saw Tanner under *his* door. Over the next few days they adapted the tap code to a flash code. Moving a hand across the crack under the door to interrupt the light, they could signal and send messages.

Stockdale issued orders to all of us to discipline ourselves to some kind of physical exercise every day. I had already started a walking regimen in my cell in the small space between the slab and the door. Some days I estaimated I walked at least five miles. My shoulders were still weak, but I could do three consecutive push-ups, and that made me feel good. Except for an occasional flare-up, the awful boils I had suffered in earlier months had finally subsided. My worst complaints were hunger and the miserable, damp cold of the North Vietnamese winter.

We were cold and hungry all the time. We gulped down a cupful of dry, sticky rice and corn mixture in the morning and still felt ravenous when it was gone. Sometimes sewer greens replaced the rice, but it was always less than a cup. The guards picked out and ate any tiny pieces of meat and pigfat they saw in our servings, leaving us nothing of substance. Our emaciated bodies had no strength or stamina to withstand the cold weather. The sloping tin roof overhead gave no insulation against temperatures that often hovered near freezing. Wind and rain swirled in under the door, and many days I sat on the concrete slab and shivered, too cold to walk or talk. The little energy we had we used only for tapping, to keep ourselves alert and busy with something useful.

I was desperate for the sight of a friend, but the guards were meticulous about not allowing us to see each other. They were obsessive about trying to make each man believe he was here alone, though they must have known we weren't fooled. I knew Tanner, Stockdale, and some of the others had managed to get down on the floor in the small space in front of the cell door and peer under it. But I was too tall to fold myself up like that, and I feared my injured shoulders would make me slow at getting up if a guard happened by. I had to figure out some way to get a window on this world to which I was condemned. I had to see beyond these walls. The tiny cracks in the wooden door of my cell beckoned me like sirens, but they were too small to offer more than a skinny shaft of light.

*So do something! Make yourself a peephole, Johnson!*

I looked around for something to dig with, something that could gouge out some of the wood splinters and enlarge the tiny cracks so I could see out of them. I had only the spoon I ate with, and I was allowed to have it only during mealtimes. It came and left with the guards who brought my dishes. I always ate quickly – like a ravenous animal – and then sat and listened to the still-hungry rumblings of my stomach when the tiny portion of rice had been devoured. Now, armed with purpose and a spoon, I began working at the cracks in my door, instead of sitting and feeling sorry for myself. I picked away at the old, rotting wood. I knew if I got caught I would be beaten, or worse, so I worked carefully, quietly. At the sound of footsteps I stopped and placed the spoon in the dish. After a few days, I had removed enough tiny splinters from the door to be able to watch my friends come and go from the latrine and the showers. It was one small pleasure, and I guarded it carefully.

The sense of isolation and deprivation at Alcatraz was, for most of us, the supreme test of our sanity and strength. In the beginning, there were no interrogations, only an occasional "attutide check." No overt torture, although the solitary confinement and the prison conditions were, themselves, torture. There were no conversations with Rabbit or Cat, or anyone else who might be able to inform us inadvertently of what was going on in the war; of what was going on in the world. We had to do something to revive our spirits and keep ourselves from giving in to despair.

"We'll teach each other what we know," Stockdale ordered. "Whatever your expertise, share it with the rest of us."

The command came across the yard to Tanner, and he sent it up and down the walls. Each man would share his special talent or interest with the rest of us. We would stimulate our minds and help each other pass the horribly long hours that never seemed to separate distinctly into night and day. The curriculum began immediately.

The navy guys taught the air force guys, Storz and me, the unique aspects of flying off a carrier at sea. I taught about precision flying, the way it's done in the Thunderbirds. I had flown solo for the Thunderbirds, and had written a manual to train other pilots: how to fly inverted, and how to fly loops and rolls in formation. Though most of the "Alkies" were pilots, they were fascinated by the idea of such ultimate precision, and it made for good conversation on the wall.

I'd always wanted to learn French, and Shumaker, next door to me, was proficient. I determined to learn ten words per week, and if the pessimists were right about the war, I figured I'd be conversant by the time of our release. He was a math whiz as well, and he took us through a review course of algebra and calculus.

Jenkins knew auto mechanics. We methodically took apart an automobile engine and put it back together again, without ever lifting a wrench. He was an avid sailor too, and he taught us about different types of sailboats, nautical terminology, and equipment.

In those early weeks at Alcatraz, we were forced to put our lives into some sort of focus. We were caged, like animals, but we could think and analyze; we were alive and able to help one another; we were physically weak and hungry, but not defeated. We developed especially close ties with the men who were next door to us. We told each other things we probably had never spoken of before—things about our childhoods, our family lives, our wives. There was little we didn't learn about each others' wives. In later years, we all sensed that our wives were uncomfortable with the fact that others had such intimate knowledge of them. But we had held back nothing, so great was our need to communicate and be close to another human being.

Christmas approached, and Rat, the camp commander, wanting to demonstrate the benevolence of the Vietnamese people, honored our holiday by allowing Shumaker to make chessboards for each of us on small scraps of coarse paper, but he would not allow us to move in with each other to play. He knew we would play with one another, directing our moves with taps on the wall, but communication was still "forbidden."

Christmas carols blared into our cells from a radio speaker hung on the wall of a building within the compound. We tried to memorize the words of every one. "O Holy Night" was the favorite of the radio's programmer, and it played continually. When the phrase "fall on your knees" rang out, I tried to block out the perverse picture that came to my mind: beaten and bloody prisoners falling on their knees, trussed up with wet hemp rope, with bamboo poles shoved between their legs.

On Christmas night, Rabbit entered Mulligan's cell and announced, "You are going to a Catholic mass." The rest of us were given a chocolate bar. Mulligan was, at first, reluctant to go if we were not all going to be allowed to go. But if he could see another POW from another camp and get the word out about where we were, it might not be a bad idea. He went without resistance.

The service was held at the "Plantation," and twelve other POWs were present. Mulligan recognized one of them, Jerry Coffee, and managed to inform him of the tiny gang of prisoners hidden away in a place called Alcatraz. It was another year later before any of the other camps learned of our whereabouts.

That Christmas night, 1967, soft taps and muffled whispers flowed through the walls and across the yard as we sent out greetings to each other.

"Merry Christmas."

"GBU."

We were all quiet and subdued, consumed with longings for family and friends. I had prayed for a letter from Shirley, but there was none. I looked at the naked, dirty light bulb burning above the door, and then at the grim, bare walls of the cell. What a contrast to other Christmases lit up by twinkling, colorful lights on the family Christmas tree. I tried to remember the scent of pine boughs and the sound of my children's laughter. I huddled deeper into my thin blanket, but I could feel no warmth. Suddenly, my thoughts were interrupted by the soft, bass sounds of Christmas carols coming from the far end of the building. Jerry Denton. He was singing. I bowed my head, overcome at the sweetness of the sound.

The new year began for us without fanfare. We continued to do the things that, for us, were essential to life. Communication was our main endeavor. We had long ago adapted our tap code so that we listened for a message in every sound. A cough or spit or the swish of water in a bucket could send a word or abbreviated message. In every way possible, we sent information to each other. We played listing games with one another. I issued a challenge to someone to name the books of the Bible, and I was startled that I could remember all sixty-six of them. I could close my eyes and see myself as a small boy sitting in "church school," a sort of junior church that the children were sent to during the adult worship service on Sunday mornings. I recalled learning the divisions of the books of the Bible: the Pentateuch, history, poetry, and the major and minor prophets. I could sing the little jingle we had learned to help us memorize the books in order.

We created a precursor to the game of Trivial Pursuit, asking each other to name the fifty states of the union and their respective capitals. We challenged each other to name animal species, books and authors, and of course, the seven dwarfs—anything that would make us think and draw our focus away from our misery was fair game.

One day a strange message came up the line.

"Did Rabbit offer to bring a woman to your cell?"

I tapped back, "No."

"Well, he made the offer to Denton and a couple of others. They all turned him down. Pass it on."

The word went up and down the wall. Rabbit had made one of his frequent visits to Alcatraz and brought with him an offer he felt sure no man could refuse. None of us would even have considered accepting the offer of "company" in his cell.

Spring finally came to Alcatraz. We exchanged bitter cold wind and rain for multitudes of stinging insects and stifling heat. With the change of season came other changes. After months of silence and isolation, guards appeared one day and hung radio speakers in each cell. The voice of Hanoi Hannah, raspy and sarcastic, bounced off the dingy walls and told us news that had rocked the world three months earlier: the TET offensive.

"Now we are going to allow you to hear about the war because of the Vietnamese people's policy of good treatment," the voice on the radio blared. "Your president has announced a bombing halt. He has admitted defeat. The American imperialists are defeated. You will see the success of North Vietnam. You will see the demise of the American aggressors."

On January 30, 1968 — the Vietnamese new year, known at TET — the communists had launched a massive, coordinated assault on nearly every populated province and military installation in South Vietnam, and we had sat through it in silent ignorance. Six months of detailed planning had culminated when communist forces had entered every major city in the South, shattering the fragile security of the civilians and altering the course of the war. The battles of TET left the South Vietnamese civilian population reeling under casualties that numbered as high as thirty-eight thousand. Their confidence in the U.S. forces' ability to protect and secure their freedom was badly injured as well.

The communist forces also suffered excessive casualties, but their leaders had convinced them that their deaths would be honorable, a worthy sacrifice for the unity of Vietnam. This was to be the ultimate battle, the "greatest battle in the history of our country" — it would "split the sky and shake the earth." The Year of the Monkey had begun with ferocity.

U.S. military intelligence had seen clues of a huge enemy buildup throughout the summer and autumn of 1967, but had not fully grasped the scope or magnitude of the coming events. In North Vietnam, Ho Chi Minh had ordered the celebration of TET to be observed a day early, on January 29. He would not desecrate the national holiday, so he arbitrarily changed it. On the following day, the actual holiday, the battles began. Once before, in 1789, a Vietnamese hero had driven Chinese enemies out of a garrison in Hanoi. The surprise attack had occurred during TET. Ho Chi Minh hoped to see history repeat itself.

Hanoi Hannah informed us that the TET offensive had brought the United States to its knees. To the troops in the fields and jungles, she said, "Why do you want to fight against the just cause of Vietnam? You can see you are losing. You put yourselves in the position of criminal aggressors."

"Lay down your arms! Refuse to fight! Demand to be taken home, now! Today! Do you want to die in a foreign land, twelve thousand miles from your home?"

And to the POWs, she said, "The American criminals have bombed Vietnam's dykes and dams and flooded the country. They are killing innocent women and children. Our food supplies are destroyed, our crops wiped out. You will pay for the crimes of your countrymen."

It was propaganda, and we knew it. But it made for uneasy thoughts, especially since we had noted that the bombing missions over Hanoi had ceased. Hannah wanted us to believe that we had been left to die by a country that had lost interest in a war it could not win. That we were buried forever in this grave-like prison in North Vietnam. I could not believe that was true.

My own interpretation was more optimistic: that the TET offensive had been less than successful for the communists, and that they had finally agreed to peace talks. That would explain the sudden silence in the skies over Hanoi. No more low-flying fighter planes. No more sounds of gunfire and exploding bombs. Surely North Vietnam had finally been convinced to sit down at the bargaining table and talk peace.

Years later I learned that LBJ had called a partial bombing halt in the North, an unprecedented unilateral move, politically expedient in the United States, hoping to draw the North Vietnamese into diplomatic negotiations. Instead, however, Hanoi used the quiet of the bombing halt to continue troop buildups and to feed supplies and materiel from Soviet and Chinese sources into the South to strengthen their next big offensive.

At Alcatraz, interrogations began again. One by one, we were escorted from our cells into an interrogation room, our first time out of the dug-out compound since our arrival at Alcatraz, to view Ho Chi Minh's victory. The walls were plastered with posters and photographs blown up to show the "victorious forces of Ho Chi Minh." Black and white combat photos of officers shaking hands with South Vietnamese, pictures of soldiers standing over masses of bodies, assumed to be enemy forces, covered every square inch of wall space.

The photo gallery was manned by a young sergeant who was charged with the task of informing us of the North's perspective of the war. His English was poor, and I figured him to be sort of an apprentice at this task. He met me at the door of the room, dismissed the attending guard, and began his speech without demanding the requisite bow from me.

"So, you heard the radio," he said. He gestured to the black and white combat photos that plastered the walls. Then he began to walk me up and down the room, pointing out various scenes, and narrating each battle. At first, I felt cautious, uncertain of what was expected of me, but as he spoke carefully and somewhat haltingly, I began to understand.

*They're going through the motions,* I thought. *Following orders—put the propaganda program into effect in all the camps. But we're dead men, as far as they're concerned. They don't have to convince us, just keep us isolated from the other POWs.*

"What do you think?" the young man asked me. His hand swept the room, indicating he wanted my opinion on this vast array of evidence of the North's inevitable victory.

"I don't know," I answered, shaking my head, and shrugging.

"Look around you," he said. "You can see we are winning the war. How can you think the war will not be over soon? The United States will retreat and go home, and we will be the winners."

The pictures were haunting. Torn and bleeding bodies lay in sharp focus against a background of city buildings. Twisted vehicles and crumbled, demolished structures gave evidence of intensive battles fought, not in the jungles, but in cities and heavily populated areas. Something inside me would not let me believe what I was seeing. I couldn't come up with a reasonable explanation for where the photos had come from, but I refused to believe that these represented the total annihilation of the South Vietnamese and American troops. I held to my earlier belief: it was a last ditch effort. The North was flailing at whatever lay within reach, making one last stand before they had to give up in defeat.

Each of the prisoners at Alcatraz walked through the photo gallery. Our conversations on the wall were no longer trivia games. We discussed in detail what it all meant. We were sure it was propaganda, but it was a strange sort of soft-sell program. My outlook, as usual, was rosy.

"Look at the signs," I said. "It's just like it was in Korea. This is their last gasp. They want us to think they've wiped out all the American troops and sent us bleeding and dying out of the country. Obviously, they want us to think they are winning. I think they are making their last blast." I was convinced we were going home soon.

While their propaganda program was failing miserably to convince the majority of POWs in Hanoi, it was working splendidly in the United States. Peace activists were marching against the war, insisting that LBJ pull our forces out of Vietnam and leave it to whatever fate destiny had in store for it. LBJ could muster little or no support from Congress for further offensive action in Vietnam. His advisors insisted on continual troop withdrawals. Ironically, he secretly initiated an intensive troop buildup throughout that summer, and the number of U.S. troops swelled from 486,000 to 535,000. North Vietnam matched the buildup, almost man for man.

The following weeks were filled with trips to the room of photos. Pictures of peace marches and student rallies in the United States were added to the walls to hang alongside the morbid battle scenes of the TET offensive. The propaganda officers stepped up their efforts to convince us that our country had lost interest in this war. We didn't have a true picture of what had happened on January 30, 1968, and the communists wanted it to stay that way.

The North Vietnamese side of the story said that the TET offensive was only the initial assault. Battles of like intensity were, at that very moment, in full force, and would continue throughout the remaining months, until the American troops were routed. It was years before we learned that TET had been a bloody and extensive assault, but its duration had been mere days. Militarily, the TET offensive had been a victory for the American and the South Vietnamese forces, but it was a short-lived victory which was almost immediately identified as defeat after a heavy propaganda barrage from the North.

A wave of battles, a sort of second TET, occurred in early May, sending up fresh photos of the destruction of Saigon. Though it was not as all-encompassing as the first TET, it was a devastating blow to the already shaken confidence of the South Vietnamese people. Their capital city lay in ruins. U.S. forces had brought in helicopter gunships in the effort to wipe out the Vietcong who barricaded themselves in city buildings, and the destruction of Saigon was massive. The heated battles spilled into the quiet neighborhoods, destroying shops and businesses and leveling more than eight thousand homes. Forty-eight hundred civilians were injured, and 160,000 new refugees fled the city.

The people of South Vietnam could not endure many more such assaults. Their allegiance to President Thieu's leadership was shaky, as was their acceptance of the U.S. presence and continued fire power in their country. Though the communists were driven out of Saigon without a military victory, they had scored a psychological win: the people of South Vietnam were weary. They no longer believed they could survive the continual assaults by the North. They believed their defeat and domination by the North and Ho Chi Minh's communists was inevitable.

"Our just cause is winning!" Rabbit was proud. It was another of his visits to Alcatraz, and he was pompous as he took charge of the interrogation. His chest swelled as he drew in a large breath and declared, "Now you can see!"

I looked up at him from my seat on the low stool in the center of the interrogation room.

"What do you mean?" I asked.

"You have seen proof! Our photos, our radio! The United States has given up and will lose the war in Vietnam!"

"I cannot believe your photos or your radio."

"The bombing has stopped. Your country has deserted you. You will never go home. You have been left here to die."

"I can't believe that." I shook my head, and refused to let Rabbit think I was bothered by his comments. "Time will tell."

He nodded, as if wisely guarding a secret. "You will see. We are right."

Back in my cell, I got on the wall quickly. I learned that Rabbit had tried to feed all of us the same stuff. We all agreed it was propaganda.

"The U.S. will never give up on us," Stockdale flashed to Tanner, and it passed up and down the walls.

And Denton tapped, "Never happen. They won't leave us here."

Through the summer months, the physical conditions at Alcatraz grew unbearable. The tin roofs overhead served as solar conductors and radiated heat that broiled us in our cells. There was no respite. The grills over the windows kept out even the smallest motion of fresh air, and the concrete cells became ovens. Suffocation seemed a very real possibility. When I allowed myself to think about it, fear made me gasp at already shortened breath. I remember standing with my mouth against the cracks in the door, trying to suck in air.

Hunger and heat produced a frightening lethargy in me. I had no energy for tapping or even whispering. Sweat poured off me at the smallest amount of exertion. The walk to the latrines was a chore that left me soaking wet and nauseous. I noticed that even the rats that usually ran up and down the power lines above the walkway seemed slowed by the heat. Their bold races became sluggish and faltering.

One morning, after another sleepless night in the suffocating cell, men arrived at each cell to remove the grills on the windows. They laid large tropical leaves across the tin roofs and planted fast-growing vines alongside the buildings to help insulate them from the high temperatures. The relief was moderate but immediate. At least we could breathe.

I learned from Denton that Rat was responsible for our slightly improved conditions. In his wily manner, Denton had congratulated Rat on his clever plot to kill us by letting us suffocate in our cells. Rat's surprise answer supported what we had already figured out. "We were not told to kill you," he said, "only isolate you." Soon after that conversation, the cell improvements were made.

It was a difficult summer for Americans back home too, we learned. The radio speakers in our prison cells blared the news of Martin Luther

King's assassination, and then Bobby Kennedy's; and we bowed our heads with sadness. The hot, impassioned slogans of antiwar activists in the States were juicy propaganda pickings for our enemies. They made much over the confusion and student unrest. The demonstrations and militaristic uprisings across the country confirmed their view that the United States was a decadent, imperialistic nation at war with herself.

The Democratic Convention in Chicago produced dozens of pictures of violence and political chaos. The National Mobilization Committee to End the War in Vietnam ("Mobe"), headed by David Dellinger, planned and carried out an assault on Chicago that brought more than ten thousand demonstrators into the city. Assisted by SDS leaders Tom Hayden and Rennie Davis, Dellinger had hoped to draw a million demonstrators together to indicate to those in power the force and magnitude of antiwar feelings, and to influence the convention to adopt the peace platform. He fell far short of his goal.

Peaceful demonstrations were the strategy, but violent confrontations erupted between mobs holding ground in Chicago's Lincoln Park and the police and guardsmen sent in to drive them out. Police billy clubs and clouds of tear gas drove the demonstrators through Old Town and into Grant Park, where they made their final stand outside the Conrad Hilton Hotel, the headquarters of the Democratic Convention.

I stood and studied the photos on the walls in the gallery. Rat, standing nearby, seemed pleased. He gestured proudly at pictures of guardsmen wielding clubs and spraying tear gas against a defiant and determined mob. Locked in battle, students hurled rocks, bottles, and sticks at police instructed to meet the provocation with force.

I could not drag my eyes away from the awful scenes. I felt my chest tighten. What was really happening back home? I recalled the blurred and faded Civil War photos in history books—images of Americans fighting Americans. Could it be happening again? I returned to my cell feeling appalled and forlorn.

Uncertainty settled on all of us in Alcatraz. Rat was replaced by an officer we dubbed "Softsoap Fairy." His thin, effeminate manner was almost laughable in contrast to the military pomp he tried to project. He was intelligent and appeared to have been well educated, and life at Alcatraz went on much as it had under Rat. Only when "Mickey Mouse" took command were we thrust back into torture that rivaled the early days in Hoa Lo.

Fall, 1968, arrived. Back home, our friends and neighbors were standing in line to buy tickets to see Dustin Hoffman in *The Graduate*. Students and other peace activists continued their sit-ins and seized administration buildings on campuses from Los Angeles to Atlanta. News of violent clashes between police and demonstrators were commonplace in headlines and newscasts. The presidential candidates, Hubert Humphrey and Richard Nixon, made their campaign speeches and swept the cities with their promises and their plans for a prosperous and peaceful nation.

Alabama's Governor George Wallace took advantage of the confusion and disunity in the Democratic party and, as an independent, challenged Humphrey for the vote. At first it appeared his aggressive platform might pose a real threat, but comments by his running mate, General Curtis LeMay, quickly buried all his chances of leading the country. LeMay's suggestion that now might be the time to unleash nuclear weapons dealt a killing blow to any chance Wallace might have had for the presidency.

Massive retaliation was not a popular strategy in the American political climate, and Wallace's campaign for the presidency ended almost on the spot. The Vietnamese radio announcers sighed with relief. When Wallace was later shot in an assassination attempt, they declared, "Governor Wallace stands against the will of the American people. He should not even be on the ballot. And now the people have spoken."

The camp radio played constantly with news of U.S. politics. We were intrigued with the reports, and, of course, always skeptical of their truth. The newscasters gushed over Hubert Humphrey. He was the choice of the North Vietnamese.

Ambassador Averell Harriman and Deputy Defense Secretary Cyrus Vance began secret talks with the North, to try to put together a workable plan for peace. It was the first time the negotiations had been constructed on a four-party format. The North, the South, the United States, and the communists in the South were all involved. For a time, it seemed there might be a chance for peace. Suddenly, the talks sank into a quagmire over issues that were impossible to resolve. Concessions would not be made on any side.

About a week before the election, President Johnson ordered all bombing in North Vietnam to cease, and our fears were compounded. They were giving up and giving us away. We couldn't help but be uneasy. It was, in fact, one last effort by the Democrats to create the impression that they were closing down the war. It was, again, a political decision that stood in absolute opposition to any strategic military decision that might have aided the U.S. fighting forces in Vietnam or hindered the aggression of Ho Chi Minh and his communist forces in the South.

It was a futile gesture, even in the political arena. The Democrats were defeated. Richard Nixon was the victor.

Ho Chi Minh and his comrades were uneasy. Humphrey's attitude toward the war would have made him their choice. His position on the war was more tenable to the North; his actions would have been predictable. But Nixon was a question mark. His election campaign had not fully addressed the issue of Vietnam; he had focused on the serious domestic issues instead. When probed for his intentions regarding the war, he had stated only that he "had a plan."

The regime in Hanoi responded to America's new politics with changes of its own. The soft-sell propaganda program of photo gazing and lectures made a 180-degree turn. Our hiatus from interrogation and brutality was over. The thinking of the North Vietnamese seemed to be that it was possible to speed up the withdrawal of American troops by drawing propaganda statements from prisoners. Mickey Mouse was the perfect choice to implement Ho's new policies. A steel-minded communist, he replaced Softsoap as the camp commander and carried out the harsher system with enthusiasm.

Tension among the Alkies soared to a dangerous level. Our emotions were strung out on a tightrope which, at the slightest aggravation, could have tossed us into despair. The games we had made up to keep us stimulated and united became small battlefields. Some guys grew frustrated with each other and refused to tap or communicate for hours, even days at a time. We were all edgy with fear of the unknown.

Our communications, which the guards had all but ignored for over a year, were now cause for a beating. The guards were suddenly everywhere, and always alert to the first soft tap or the first soft whisper of a message.

McKnight was the first to go through the purge. His session in the interrogation room lasted for days, and I watched from the crack in my door when he was dragged back to his cell, bloody and half-conscious. After a long and painful siege, he had finally given in to the demand to write a letter of apology to Ho Chi Minh for bombing his beautiful country. I knew the torture must have been horrendous for a resister of McKnight's caliber to finally succumb.

The prison authority wanted a similar letter from all the Alkies. Denton was taken in next. He was accused of communicating, and he had to be punished. For two days and two nights he stood in leg irons, forced to hold his hands above his head, and on the third day, his answer was still a strong no. Mickey Mouse would have to press harder.

Denton knew all about the ropes—he had suffered them in Hoa Lo. But the torture experts had invented a new, more sadistic apparatus, and Denton soon knew that the ropes had been kindergarten fun compared to this. Trussed up in poles and ropes that cut off all circulation to his limbs, and beaten and booted until he was bloody and crazy with pain, Denton passed in and out of consciousness for the next day. Finally he agreed to write an apology.

Jerry returned to his cell too sick to stand or eat. His second round a few weeks later produced an incoherent jumble of words the prison authority hoped would sound like a persuasive radio speech. The words were badly mispronounced and his voice hardly recognizable. Instead of a useful propaganda message, it was a frightening warning to all prisoners: They will not give up until you give them something. There will be no mercy.

While Denton was still bleeding, Mulligan was hauled in to the torture room. A few days later, his letter to Ho Chi Minh joined Denton's.

We learned that propaganda efforts were in full force in the other camps around Hanoi too. Many POWs were relenting without having to be pressured or tortured. They were beginning to believe the propaganda garbage the communists were feeding them. They offered little or no resistance to the demands of the prison authority. More and more prisoners acquiesced, agreeing without argument to read propaganda statements over the radio for all to hear. The voice of an American puppet warrior on the air carried much more weight than that of a Vietnamese.

About that time, Harry Jenkins got sick. We heard him writhing in his cell, screaming from the pain of intestinal worms. A guard yanked his cell door open, and we heard the sickening thud of a rifle barrel against flesh and skull.

*They're beating him! He's sick and asking for a doctor and they're beating him!*

I put my mouth close to the crack in the door and shouted, "Bao cao! Bao cao!" Almost in unison, everyone began yelling and banging on the doors in protest.

"Shut mouth! Shut mouth!" The guards ran up and down the walkway, banging on our doors and shouting.

The ruckus subsided. Jenkins lay and moaned throughout the night, and in the morning, Stockdale ordered us all to participate in a two-day hunger strike in protest. That day we sent our two meager meals back uneaten. The next morning, guards entered Stockdale's cell and ordered, "Roll up." I watched as he limped out of his cell, his cuffed hands clutching his bundle of belongings. I knew he could feel our eyes on him, I hoped he could feel our prayers too.

We had no idea where he was being taken or what would be done to him. I was sick with worry for him. He was the SRO, and the prison authority would hold him responsible for instigating the most heinous crime in communism: organized resistance to established state regulations. His punishment would not be light, but only months later would we learn the nightmare dimensions of his torture. He was returned to Hoa Lo and immediately thrown into the maelstrom of a violent propaganda program.

At Alcatraz, the mantle of leadership fell on Jerry Denton. What was he going to do about the hunger strike? Stockdale's order extended to one more day. Denton's decision was, "Carry on."

Immediately he was met with opposition.

"What's the point?"

"We're all dying of starvation . . . Harry got his doctor . . . Let's eat!"

Denton faced a dilemma. He had settled on a course: to finish what Stockdale had started, to show the camp officers we would not quietly accept their abuses, especially the abuse of a sick prisoner. But it was true: Harry *had* gotten his doctor. In fact, we had all had a medical exam of sorts, complete with a few pills and some innocuous-looking salve. We had each been assured individually by Mickey Mouse that Jenkins was *not* beaten. We had been told what they wanted us to believe, and now we had medicine. So, what was the point of not eating?

The ten united souls became angry, irritated individuals, and Jerry's first command was in jeopardy.

"It's only for the rest of today," I tapped to Shumaker. "We can make it. Do it for Stockdale. Do it to show we don't believe their lies. We *heard* them beat Harry!"

I was in full support of Jerry's position. He wanted to finish what had been started. As angry messages moved up and down the walls, he began to question his decision. I knew most of us could have held out another day, in spite of our emaciated state, but Storz was already half-dead from malnutrition. We were all worried about his condition. Some days he had to be ordered to eat. An extended hunger strike would kill him, and we all knew it.

Jerry tapped out a new order, "Everybody eat."

With the coming of the new year and a new presidency, peace negotiations took a new turn. Rabbit told us that Hanoi was considering releasing some American prisoners. In fact, Hanoi had agreed to send home about one hundred POWs, but they would be carefully handpicked POWs; they would be sympathetic to the cause of North Vietnam. They would be prisoners who had been brainwashed successfully by propaganda. Their return to the United States would guarantee that the message of Ho Chi Minh would be told, just as he wanted it told.

What followed was a furious season of pain and misery for us. I wondered if they were sizing us up, measuring to see if any of us would break, evaluating us to see if we could be released to speak for Ho Chi Minh. Denton was thrown back into the torture room for sessions which lasted for weeks at a time. We learned from him what we should expect: beatings, followed by days of isolation, and then more beatings.

"They want us to write letters asking Ho Chi Minh for amnesty," he said. "If they're working on some kind of release, they can't just turn us loose without losing face. They have to have some kind of justification, some kind of admission of guilt. Then Uncle Ho can forgive us. Don't make it easy for them. Hold out as long as you can."

Rutledge went into the torture room next for a week or more of isolation followed by severe beatings. Then Jenkins was taken in for the same. Guards returned Rutledge while Jenkins was still out, and I learned in labored whispers from Rutledge what to expect when my turn came a few days later.

When the guard opened my cell door and motioned me to follow him to the interrogation rooms, I tried to forget the screams of agony that had risen from that place in recent weeks. Each cry that pierced the quiet prison yard had been a painful stab in my own heart. I had spent hours each day praying for the men in those rooms. I could feel their prayers for me now.

"The United States is going to leave you here, you know." It was Softsoap. He was back. He sat facing me, his thin, effeminate hands folded on the desk in front of him.

"The Vietnamese people love you, Song. You do not understand that. They want to let you go home. But we cannot unless you write a letter of apology for your crimes."

"I can't do that," I answered.

"You will think about it," he commanded, and he left the room.

For days they kept me in the interrogation room, cut off from all possible communication with my friends. There would be no encouragement, no tapped assurances, no friendly sounds to boost my spirits. I was completely alone. A guard brought me my waste can and my teapot and delivered my rice in the mornings. I slept on the concrete floor and huddled against the wall for some small warmth. During the day, I sat and practiced my French and prayed to keep my thoughts off the inevitable moment when I knew they would tire of my obstinacy. Each day Softsoap came in and gave me his speeches.

"The Vietnamese people cannot let you go unless you write a letter to Ho Chi Minh asking for release," he repeated. "You must decide. If you will agree to write and ask for amnesty the Vietnamese people will consider letting you go home."

Day after day I continued to say no. As a unit, we had long ago decided we would not admit to crimes; we would not request amnesty; and no man would accept an early release unless the same promise was made to all the POWs. I resolved again to stand firm. That resolve had cost Denton, Rutledge, and Jenkins a rough round of torture, and in the end they had finally written a pitiful facsimile of an apology. I would resist at least as hard as they had. I would hold out as long as I could.

"I'll wait until the United States government releases us at the end of the war," I told Softsoap again after about the fifth day in the interrogation room. He stared hard at me and then dropped his eyes to look down at his slender hands. I sensed his patience with me was thinning, but as I studied him I sensed something else.

*There's no plan for release,* I thought suddenly. *It's all for show. Propaganda again. They want to flood the media with letters of apology from American pilots, begging Ho Chi Minh's forgiveness for bombing his country.* It was all very clear to me. No way would I write a letter to Ho Chi Minh, begging his pardon. My resolve to hold out surged even more strongly.

"We'll leave paper and pen here, and you can think about it," Softsoap stated. "You can write something like this." And he laid down a form letter, showing how an amnesty request should be worded. Then he left the room.

*Good. I'll practice my French. I won't think about what will happen when they come back. I won't think about the next step.*

I sat on the stool in the large room and sent my mind back to French vocabulary. Over the past two years since my capture, I had learned to appreciate the brain's computer-like capabilities. I was amazed at the way my brain was able to store and retrieve such a plethora of data. I had alphabetized hundreds of French words, and I was trying to make myself think in French instead of English. I was deep in conjugations and definitions when Softsoap returned several hours later.

"You have not written your letter," he scolded, as if I were a kid who had forgotten his school assignment. "You will have to be punished."

The next morning a guard entered and tied my hands behind me, tied me onto a small, three-legged stool, and then left. Moments later, the door opened just a crack, and a woman peered into the room. My first thought was that she had wandered into the area by mistake; that she had discovered an interesting situation and was curious. I was wrong. She stepped into the room, dressed in full military uniform, and was quickly joined by three other large, heavy female soldiers. On a shouted command, they flung themselves at me and began beating me with their rifles and their fists.

Wood and steel crunched against my skull, and my head reeled. I hunched forward and tried to pull my legs up but I could not protect myself. They threw themselves and their weapons against me with all their strength. I worried that my arm would be broken again, but it was tied behind me, and I could do nothing to keep them from pounding it.

Blow after blow landed on my face, and I remember thinking, *I'm going to be blinded!* I tried to duck my head and protect my eyes, but I was powerless. A steel rifle barrel smashed against my jaw.

*They're going to kill me,* I thought, as another blow landed against my temple.

The women seemed to have a contest going among themselves as to which of them could hit the hardest. Jabbering and shrieking, they slugged me with their fists. My whole body shuddered as their rifles bashed into my shoulders. Finally the stool toppled over. Immediately, the women were on top of me, pounding my stomach, bludgeoning my chest and ribs until I could only gasp for breath. I tried to roll into a ball, but every move I made was countered with another hammering.

*Oh, God let me black out!* I prayed.

I knew if I lost consciousness they would stop beating on me, but merciful blackness would not come.

The guard stepped into the room and pulled the stool upright, and again the women were on me.

*Maybe they won't stop until I'm dead . . .*

My body vibrated with pain. I was rolling under an avalanche of boulders and I could not escape. My eyes blurred, and the women's screeching voices became only a vague, distant animal wail. The pummeling would not stop. Again I prayed for unconsciousness, but it would not come, and I could not will myself into oblivion. I felt the stool topple over again, and the salty taste of blood filled my mouth. Bile churned up into my throat, and I gagged.

The door opened and the guard came in again. He ordered the women to leave and pulled me back up onto the stool with rough hands. In the next moment, Softsoap made his entrance.

"You sit there," he said, as the guard untied me and positioned the stool in front of a small table. "Now, you write," he ordered.

Through bloody lips, I mumbled, "I can't write. You'll have to write for me."

It had worked once before. I would try it again. The commander paused only for a brief second before he agreed. Moments later I read the poorly written document: "To the President of the People's Republic of Vietnam, Ho Chi Minh: I recognize that I have committed crimes against the Vietnamese government, but I have seen the leniency and humane treatment of the Vietnamese people. I request amnesty from the Vietnamese people." I signed my name at the bottom. Softsoap was appeased.

"I will have to take this draft back to my superiors for approval, of course," he told me. "If they approve, you must write it in final form." And he walked out, leaving me alone again in the vile room.

There was no part of my body that did not throb with pain. My face swelled until my eyes were only thin slits in the puffy tissue. My lips and mouth were too badly cut for me to drink. I could draw only tiny, short gasps of air against my bruised ribs. I sat, unmoving, on the concrete floor—it hurt less to sit than to lie down.

*What have I done?* I asked myself over and over again. Salty tears stung the cuts on my face. *I gave in too easily, I should have held out longer . . .*

I chastised myself. But then I argued, *In the end, we all give them something, just to hang on to sanity, to life . . . But it will be nothing of any real value. Anyone who knows me will recognize that letter is garbage.* I rationalized and reasoned with myself, but still it stung. I hated what I had done.

A soft, familiar voice interrupted my chastising thoughts. It was Denton. He was in the torture room two doors down.

"Sam, Sam, it's okay, buddy," he whispered. His voice was like a life-giving tonic to my spirit. Sobs broke from my throat.

"I made them write it, Jerry," I whispered, "but I had to sign it."

"It's okay, Sam. You're okay. Hang on. You did good."

Before we could say more, a guard entered the room and jerked me to my feet. He half-dragged me out the door and then prodded me down a walkway between buildings. I wanted to tell Jerry I was praying for him. I wanted to say something to help him, as he had helped me, but there was no time. The guard pushed me forward toward the dugout cells. I stumbled ahead of him. Every step produced pain that took my breath away. I moved slowly, with my head hanging down, and almost ran into a figure that stepped out into the walkway in front of me.

I looked up just before I bumped into a tall, attractive woman. I was stunned, and so was she. Her dark, almond eyes widened when she saw my bloody face and my filthy clothes. She took a step backward and gasped. For a frozen moment we stood there in the walkway and stared at each other.

"Hello," I mumbled.

"Hello," she answered, in perfect English.

I had the feeling I had stepped into a surreal painting. The faint scent of perfume and soap rose off her and battled the smell of urine and human filth to which my nose was so accustomed. Her skin was clear and honey-colored and soft-looking. She looked more European than Oriental. Her tight sheath dress could have been worn to any American cocktail party, and her short, dark hair could have been styled in any American salon.

Fast-moving thoughts passed through my brain. *Who could she be? What is she doing here?*

I let my eyes travel up and down her. She was almost beautiful. She looked me over too, as if memorizing everything about me.

The guard, awkward with panic, pushed me from behind and again I nearly collided with the tall, mysterious woman. She stepped aside quickly, and the guard's shrill voice commanded, "No stop! No stop!"

He said something to her in Vietnamese, and she walked away from me quickly. I turned to watch her from behind. I couldn't help myself. *Great legs,* I thought, and, *That is one good-looking woman.*

Her appearance, in contrast with that of the other women I had seen in this country, suggested wealth, position, possibly power. I began speculating as I stumbled on down the path whether perhaps her seeing me would prove significant. Had anyone outside our tiny compound been aware of our treatment? Did anyone know we were being tortured? Would she say or do something that might help us in some way? Did she have any authority to question the camp authority?

I doubted it, really. She was a woman, after all, and would receive little respect from the Vietnamese leadership. And though communism preached equality, I had seen none of it in this country. I decided she was probably the wife of an officer, or perhaps a government employee. I learned later that she was Softsoap's wife. She worked for the radio as a news reporter and programmer. I often wondered if she had any of the curiosity, any of the instincts I knew existed in western reporters. Would she ask questions? Would she wonder? She had stumbled on a secret. Now, what would she do? As the days passed, I speculated on several possibilities.

The guard returned me to my cell. Alone in that tight structure, I found myself playing back all the events of those long days in the interrogation room. Could I have done things differently? Could I have held out longer? How much more battering could my body have taken?

I waited every day for Softsoap to send for me again and demand the letter in final form. I tried to ready myself for another beating, because I knew I would resist again. I could not submit without a fight. But the summons never came. I waited and wondered. Had the mystery woman intervened? Had she said or done something to stop Softsoap from coming back for more? I would never know. I could only wonder and thank God that this round was over.

My injuries healed slowly. Cracked and bruised ribs made breathing difficult, and my head throbbed with the pain of a concussion. Dizzy and nauseous, I lay on my bunk for days, but my suffering was more mental than physical. I could not easily rid myself of guilt and sorrow over that letter. The inner turmoil I felt would not be stilled.

*Forgive me, Lord,* I prayed. *I'm sorry, I'm so sorry . . .*

"I'm sorry," I tapped on the wall to Shumaker. "Pass it down to the others."

I knew they did not expect or require an apology from me. We were all "guilty" of the same acts. But somehow their forgiveness and acceptance helped assuage my pain and the sense of guilt I felt at having "apologized" to Ho Chi Minh.

Forgiveness was something we had all come to understand well. Throughout our sojourn in hell, when frustrations mounted and tempers flared, we often had to forgive each other. With practice, it had become easy. We did not find it so easy, however, to forgive ourselves. Ron Storz found it impossible.

Storz knew that, under torture, we had all ultimately yielded to the enemy's advantage. We were puppets in the hands of our captors. But in the midst of this cruel chaos, Storz determined to retain control of one small piece of himself. He steadfastly refused to eat.

He was physically weak and tottering on the brink of emotional collapse when he was taken into the interrogation room. He held out long and hard against the guards' torture, but he finally relented and gave them what they wanted: a signed affidavit, admitting to "crimes against humanity." As a reward for his "cooperation," the guard brought him a razor to shave with. Storz, overwrought at what he perceived as failure, slashed his wrists with the blade.

We heard shouting and the sounds of panicked movements. Rutledge saw guards scurrying toward the other buildings that housed the torture rooms outside the dugout wall. He saw two doctors hurry into the same area.

"What's happened?" Howie hollered at a guard as he ran past his cell.

"Storz dying!" the guard called back as he bolted by.

A couple of days passed before we learned all that had happened— that Storz was alive, that the doctors had been able to save him. Denton asked one of the guards what had happened. "That guard," he pointed toward a uniformed man standing across the yard, "He's Catholic. He gave Storz blood."

It had been a direct transfusion, from the guard's arm into Storz's body. It had saved his life, but there was little that could be done to save his spirit. He continued to leave his meals untouched. We could see that he was becoming wraith-like. Stockdale and Denton, at various times, had both ordered him to eat, but he had given them different excuses, all totaling stubborn refusal. Denton continued to try to get orders to him to eat when he was returned to his room, but Storz continued in his resistance.

In the summer of 1969 we knew we were losing him. Guards found him on the floor of his cell, unconscious. Again the yard flooded with noisy guards who carried Ron up the steps and out of our sight. The camp commander called in a doctor, and they began feeding Storz intravenously.

For weeks, Storz stayed in the room outside the walls. I saw him only through the cracks in my door when he was escorted to the latrines or to the showers. He moved slowly, bent forward was if fighting a strong wind. His skinny, ninety-pound figure was all bones and pallor. As fellow air force officers, Storz and I shared a special bond. My own emotions were dangerously close to crumbling every time I thought about him, but there was nothing I could do. I learned from Denton that he was growing confused and was easily angered. Even Softsoap could see that Storz was losing his grip on reality, and I believe truly pitied him. He gave Storz a deck of cards and tried to teach him to play bridge. A Bible was placed in his cell. But Storz continued to slip away from us.

Hanoi shuddered under the force of a typhoon that summer. For days, torrents of rain swept through the city, and the winds bent trees down to the ground and hurled branches past the window in my cell.

The swollen river, only a few blocks away, spilled over its banks and flooded many of the city's streets. Alcatraz, a dugout dirt bowl, began to fill with water like a dish set under a running faucet. Water poured in under the door of my cell and swirled around my leg irons. By the second or third day of rains, the water rose above the level of the concrete slab I slept on. There was no high ground to retreat to. I stood up on the slab and watched the water as it continued to rise. Outside, in the now swamped yard, a twelve-man air force survival raft bobbed about on two feet of water.

"Are we going to be evacuated?" someone shouted.

I tapped to Jenkins next door, "Will they take us out or use that raft for themselves?"

"It's a twelve-man raft," Harry answered. Tapping was easier than trying to shout over the noise of the storm. "They won't send us out without at least three or four guards, and the raft won't hold us." The guards didn't bother to try to quiet us. They were busy with their own fears.

I watched the water pour into the cell. I was standing on the slab which was about two feet higher than the floor, and already the water was quickly climbing up my legs. *Surely they won't let us drown in here . . .*

I'd never imagined myself drowning. Crashing in a fiery ball, yes— every pilot knows that is a chance he takes. But to stand still and await death . . . I could not believe this was happening to me. Claustrophobia clawed at my throat as the rainwater continued to fill up my tiny cell.

*God, I need you! Save us! Don't let us drown!*

The dark hours passed slowly, but sometime in the night the winds subsided and the rain ceased. The water began to recede from our cells. I stood on my pallet and watched through the bars on the window as the morning dawned with a splendor I was sure God intended just for me. A perfect rainbow sparkled in the sky over rain-washed buildings.

*I see it, Lord . . . Your promise . . .*

A surge of confidence filled me. I would survive. I would go home.

# TEN

# Good Signs

It was 1969. I wanted to believe that, with the election of Richard Milhous Nixon as commander in chief of the American forces, the war would take a distinctly different turn. I didn't know it, but his mysterious plan for winning the war was in full operation. His first step was to try to use China and Russia to pressure North Vietnam into serious, substantive peace talks.

Western diplomats failed to understand a very basic fact about the Vietnamese: they considered themselves superior to their Soviet and Chinese comrades. They gladly accepted material assistance from them, but they would not be influenced into acquiescence at the negotiating table. Again, their fierce independence flared. And so the first objective of Nixon's plan was a failure.

The second objective of his plan, however, was U.S. troop withdrawals. He ordered the first contingent of U.S. troops to begin pulling out of South Vietnam. The South's troops left behind were supposedly strengthened and well trained, able now to finish the war victoriously. It was a plan intended to allow the United States to retain its self-respect and perhaps maintain a measure of credibility in the eyes of the rest of the world. But in order to implement such a plan and protect the South's troops, massive U.S. air strikes would have to be employed. The target: Cambodia.

It was a realistic view, and a militarily sound decision on the part of the new president, but it was met with absolute horror by the antiwar demonstrators and the more liberal politicians in the United States. Congress viewed Nixon's proposal to bomb neutral Cambodia as a violation of trust and refused to approve it. But Nixon saw it as a vital strategic move that would greatly improve the chances of a speedy end to the killing and a definitive victory for South Vietnam. He secretly ordered the bombings to proceed.

In the spring of 1969, news of the forbidden raids leaked out. In Hanoi, we were ecstatic to hear it.

"It's a good sign," I tapped on the wall to Shumaker.

"You think everything is a good sign," he answered back.

I could imagine him grinning on the other side of the concrete wall. I was the company's eternal, if sometimes cockeyed optimist. But a sense of hope did begin to move among us. It was the first we had seen of military strategy and military decisions, rather than State Department diplomacy. I speculated that the war would be over soon now.

"The North has got to be scared that Nixon is going to destroy all their supply routes," I said to Shumaker.

Denton's words came up the line to me. "Calm down, Sam. This thing isn't over yet."

"Maybe not, but Nixon is getting ready to close it down," I answered confidently.

Harry Jenkins, on the opposite wall, said, "Well, I'm not optimistic. It's going to be a long war. This is just one more effort – one more move without the support of the ground troops."

"I still say it's a good sign."

"These are all good signs, Sam," Denton sent up the wall. "But negotiations are slow and the wrap-up may take time."

"One year," I prophesied.

"Probably more like two," Denton answered.

One at a time, we were called in for interrogation and asked what we thought of Nixon's bombing of Cambodia. "Your country is the aggressor. How can you support what they are doing?" Mickey Mouse asked me.

"I hope we take the whole country," I answered.

Mickey Mouse's anger flashed in his eyes. He snapped back, "Your country will never do it." Then, as if disgusted that he had let me irritate him, he gathered calmness around him like a shroud. "The American people are against you," he said confidently. "*They* will cause us to win this war."

Hanoi Hannah enjoyed herself immensely during these troubled days. "Your American president fears his own people," she said. "This should show you the weakness in your own government. There is no support for continued aggression in Vietnam. There will be a military coup in Washington," she predicted. "Nixon will use the military to rid his administration and the Capitol of all those who stand in the way of a complete victory in Vietnam. That is the only way he will be able to carry out his will in this war."

We listened with our mouths open in astonishment. Of course such a thing could never happen in the United States. And yet, we had been so long under the constant barrage of propaganda that we were not certain of anything any more. Still, we allowed ourselves to feel hopeful over the continued reports of the bombings in Cambodia. The air strikes we had so yearned to fly ourselves were finally being employed. There would be good news soon, I was sure.

On Easter morning, the camp radio began playing earlier than usual. At about 9:00 A.M., I heard the cell doors near me opening and closing quickly. I had no time to tap and find out what was happening before my door was opened.

"Come," a guard ordered.

I stepped out onto the walk and saw a table near the door that led out of the compound. It was stacked three feet high with monkey bananas. I couldn't help laughing.

"Camp not authorize you to laugh!" a voice scolded me. It was the camp's second lieutenant in charge of the guards. He tried to sound angry and forceful, but he fell far short of menacing.

I thought for a minute and then said, "Well, I request permission to laugh."

His frown deepened. He studied me. I sensed the wheels turning in his head as he tried to decide what to do. After a long pause, he answered, "Camp authorize you to laugh."

I shook my head and felt the humor inside me melt away. Sadness took its place.

"Take ten bananas and go back to cell," the guard ordered. He pointed his rifle at the table sagging under the weight of the pile of bananas.

Ten bananas. They were small and blackish-colored with a bit of green on them. So this was to be our Easter celebration.

All around the prison compound banana trees grew in abundance. We could see the bananas growing in bunches, hanging from stalks within reach, but never were we allowed to pick them. Today we could have ten. I would have given them all — I would have given *anything* that day — for a letter from Shirley, or for some assurance that she had received the letter the Red Cross had allowed me to write more than two years earlier. Just to know that all was well at home would have been a precious gift.

But there was no knowing. The isolation of Alcatraz was impenetrable. I could only continue to pray and to trust God that He was taking care of my family.

Summer heat arrived and with it came news of events that startled us: men had landed on the moon! The Vietnamese radio reported it to us over crackling air waves.

"The Soviets have now landed on the moon. It is a great day for our Soviet brothers. They have won the race for space. The Americans tried also, of course, but they have failed." Only a year later did we hear the truth and Neil Armstrong's profound statement, "One small step for man, one giant step for mankind."

I learned that my old friend Buzz Aldrin had helped pilot Apollo 11 on that historic journey through space to land near the Sea of Tranquility on the moon's surface. I sat in my cell and recalled the good times Buzz and I had shared during flight school and at various air bases around the country. I remembered driving to Nellis Air Force Base in the early 1960s and meeting up with Buzz on Route 66, near Winslow, Arizona, and racing all the way into Las Vegas. We drove over Hoover Dam at a hundred miles per hour and called it a tie when we reached the Las Vegas city limits. Neither of us could have admitted defeat. We had many losses at the gaming tables, however, while we were stationed together at Nellis. Buzz stood by one night and watched me win two thousand dollars and then lose it all in one bet.

Years later I learned that Buzz had thought of me during his flight into space. He had looked down on Southeast Asia from thousands of miles above the earth's atmosphere and wondered if I was still alive . . . if I would ever make it home again. His first book, *Return To Earth*, dedicated to his wife, included a thought for me as well. My eyes blurred when I saw it for the first time and read the words, "for Sam . . . whose place I took, who took my place . . ."

Talk of release bounced off the thick concrete walls in Alcatraz all that summer. We learned that three POWs had been handed over to the peace envoys in Hanoi and returned to the United States. We were angry yet curious about what seemed to us to be capitulation to the enemy. These men seemed to us to be in direct violation of the BACK U.S. policy implemented earlier for all POWs. Years later we learned the fascinating story of one of those POWs, a young seaman named Doug Hegdahl, who had been swept off his ship, the *Canberra*, in the Gulf of Tonkin in 1967 and captured by North Vietnamese fishermen who turned him over to the military.

Like other POWs, Hegdahl had been imprisoned in Hanoi and tortured and interrogated mercilessly for military information. The prison authority was finally convinced that he was exactly what he said he was: a nineteen-year-old seaman who had spent most of his navy time below deck, a kid who had no military secrets hidden in his psyche. He was not privy to any important military data.

Once he had them convinced of his insignificance, Hegdahl used his status as a sort of American "peasant" to help fend off some of the propaganda assaults. With survival savvy and a tough spirit, he was determined to resist and confound the enemy in any way he could. He worked at keeping the Vietnamese believing he was nothing more than an ignorant farm boy and even convinced them he was a little slow-witted, an ignoramus who had no knowledge or understanding of world affairs.

When word of a possible release spread through the Plantation where Hegdahl was being held, his commander ordered him to ask the Vietnamese to let him be among the POWs sent home. Hegdahl was reluctant at first—he didn't want to violate the POW policy stating that no prisoners should accept an early release unless all prisoners were to be released. When his commander told him he could best serve the cause of the POWs by going home with names and information that the United States could only get from a prisoner, Hegdahl agreed to go.

He was suspicious of the other two prisoners released with him, who had not been cleared for release by the POW command, as he had been. He had no evidence that they, too, were under orders to accept release for the purpose of helping the cause of the POWs left behind. Later conversations with the SRO revealed that their acceptance of early release *was* a direct violation of POW policy. After the general release in 1973, military and State Department edicts forbade us to discuss or disclose that the two had actually betrayed their fellow prisoners by accepting early release.

Hegdahl, as soon as he was handed over to the U.S. military, dropped the guise of a naive, ignorant country boy. He revealed the names of hundreds of U.S. POWs; he documented the brutal and cruel treatment of prisoners in Hanoi; and he gave our new president the proof that would be used later as the basis for a media campaign against the Hanoi regime to counter their lies of "lenient and humane treatment of American prisoners." He delivered vital information that, at that time, could never have exited Hanoi any other way.

Toward the end of the summer of 1969, we in Alcatraz learned that Ho Chi Minh was critically ill. He had been hospitalized with a mysterious illness, but daily radio programs assured the populace that he was being well cared for at the hands of Vietnam's best medical personnel. Updates on his condition played continually.

"The very best medical care is being given to our beloved leader," the radio announced. "All Vietnam's medical expertise is available to him. We are confident of his recovery."

"Yeah, right," I tapped on the wall to Shumaker. "We know what North Vietnam's best medical care is all about."

Shumaker answered, "He's a dead man."

Up and down the walls, we all shared our thoughts on the radio's announcement of Ho's illness. We speculated on his chances of survival. Every one of us had experienced doctoring at the hands of Vietnam's medics. Every one of us had been appalled at the primitive, inept procedures that would have been cause for malpractice suits in the United States. If Ho Chi Minh was truly ill, then his death was probably imminent. We began to feel something akin to anticipation, as if something of profound importance was about to occur.

On September 3, 1969, we awoke to the clanging sound of church bells somewhere in the city. Our guards, moving silently as if in a stupor, entered our cells wearing black arm bands, their faces masks of grief. The deadly pall that hung over the prison told us what the radio news reporter later confirmed. Against scratchy static, the voice solemnly announced, "Our beloved leader, President Ho Chi Minh, has died."

The day of Ho's death was a day of national mourning. Funeral songs, discordant ballads hastily written in praise of Uncle Ho, played on the state radio day and night. The guards in Alcatraz, red-eyed from their crying, moved about in a daze, wearing the angry, uncertain expressions of men whose dreams have suddenly died. The camp radio warned us not to antagonize them during their time of supreme mourning. Some drank until they passed out in a storage room; others moved through the yard and down the walkway like zombies, stoned on some kind of pain-dulling drugs. All day long, outbursts of loud crying and wailing drifted in over the mud and brick walls that surrounded our prison.

For us in prison, Ho's death ushered in a period of great uncertainty. North Vietnam's politics were in disarray, and we could not help but wonder how these things would affect our fate. Questions and conjecture about what would happen to us now dominated our tapped conversations. Some of us were elated, others apprehensive. Two strong, diverse opinions arose as to what we could expect from our captors now. To some, Ho had been viewed as the opponent of harsh treatment, and they were now alarmed, concerned that we would soon move into conditions that would make our earlier tortures seem like child's play. Others, including me, felt that, with Ho's death, the worst was behind us.

For a long time we had been aware of a political rift in Ho's regime. I figured Ho for a hardliner, the one who favored harsh treatment of POWs, rather than more lenient treatment. He was a diehard communist. As a prisoner of the French, he had known harsh treatment and torture. His regime was characterized by hardline policies, and I credited him with being both the innovator and the enforcer of those policies.

In earlier conversations Jim Stockdale had agreed with my views on Ho Chi Minh's position. His years in the navy had afforded him experience and understanding of international politics. I knew him to be a careful thinker and a philosopher. Based on those conversations and my own observations, I felt optimistic. I believed the future could only offer better treatment. Time proved me correct, but at this juncture, I had to concede it was only supposition.

On the day of the funeral people flooded into the city. Gunfire erupted around the Ministry of Defense day and night, and the restless, scurrying sounds of a frightened mob rose up from the nearby streets. Two blocks from Alcatraz, above Hanoi's Red Square, we could see the bright explosions of fireworks in the night sky. Our cells vibrated with the sounds of cannons and multiple twenty-one-gun salutes. The wailing voices of mourners reached a fevered pitch before they finally subsided in the early morning hours.

For more than a week we listened to radio messages declaring, "All the nations of the world send their condolences to the people of Vietnam on the death of their beloved leader." Their beloved leader's death became a media event, one more opportunity for trying to garner international legitimacy and recognition; however, most of this desperately coveted recognition came from the tiny nations that had been brutally carved out of the African continent by Soviet strength — small, new nations with names we had never heard and never read on a map.

We listened carefully to the radio broadcasts and the sympathy messages and tried to collect all the strange new names. To us, it was one more piece of evidence that the world had changed, and we had been unaware of it. But we refused to let it discourage us. Instead, we added a "name the nations of the world" category to our listing game and, in time, we were able to list over 150 countries.

If the Vietnamese people's grief over Ho's death was unfathomable, so were their fears and uncertainties for the future. Who would take Ho Chi Minh's place? Who would lead them on in their quest for unity and the defeat of the western imperialist aggressors?

Ho Chi Minh's forceful persona had been dominant in Southeast Asia for three decades. He had successfully ousted the Japanese "fascists" from his homeland in the early 1940s. Ten years later, he gathered his armies together to drive the French out of Indochina. He had fathered Vietnam's modern nationalistic spirit and fed it with fervor. With his now legendary strength, he had bullied his way into Laos to build trails for the transport of Chinese and Soviet supplies into South Vietnam to further his fight for complete "liberation." Cambodia became a maze of supply systems carrying weapons and equipment to communist forces in the South. Only Thailand held herself rigidly aloof from Ho's reach.

As head of the communist party, Ho meticulously directed the activities of the troops in both the North and the South. His was the strong link with the Soviets and the Chinese. His was the energy and vision behind the fight for unity and "freedom," although South Vietnam, even with its confused and corrupt politics in force, boasted far more freedom than the North would ever offer.

Because every event was an opportunity for diversion for us in Alcatraz, we initiated a contest to name Ho's successor. Jerry Denton and I were declared the winners when the radio announced Le Duan, the party first secretary, as the new leader.

Within days of the funeral, the transfer of power was accomplished, almost too easily, too smoothly, it seemed. I began to wonder if perhaps things were not as they appeared to be. Was it possible that Ho Chi Minh had died earlier in the summer, long before the announcement was made to the population? News of Ho's death could easily have been covered up and its announcement withheld until the regime, reorganized under new leadership, could get a tight grip on the reins of government. It was conjecture only, but knowing the communist manipulation of the media, I wondered if the timing of the events had been contrived.

Nevertheless, Uncle Le sat down in the recently vacated seat of authority and, within weeks, the first breezes of change wafted into Alcatraz. Softsoap came back as camp commander.

"The people of Vietnam cannot release you, of course," he said, during a quiz one day after Hanoi's fevered period of mourning had ceased. "The war will be over soon, but you will remain here. However, the leniency of the Vietnamese people will allow you some special privileges."

Those "privileges" did not appear right away, but I did sense a slight softening in the commander. I didn't understand at that time that there were other factors at work as well, far beyond the walls of Alcatraz and the borders of North Vietnam. I had no knowledge of other goings-on that, combined with the change in the Hanoi regime, had begun to effect change for us.

Softsoap's manner in interrogation was definitely different. We engaged in conversation, *real* conversation that was not directed at propaganda, but was simply the exchange of information and ideas.

"I own a sugar mill, you know," Softsoap told me one day. "The people of Vietnam own everything. It is really much more democratic than your America."

"Where is your sugar mill?"

"In Hanoi." He smiled.

"Have you ever visited this mill?" I asked him.

"No."

"Can you go in and get sugar if you want to?"

"No."

"Can you sell the mill?"

"No," he answered, frowning.

"Do you receive any money from this mill?"

"No." His frown deepened.

"Doesn't sound like you own it, to me." I said. "In America, if I owned a mill I would draw an income from it, and I could sell it for profit when I wanted to and buy another one if I wanted to. In fact, I could give it away. Who says you can't sell it?"

"The government of course, but it belongs to the people," he replied. "Everything belongs to the people!"

"What happens if the sugar mill burns down?" I asked him.

"Then it is lost."

"Does the government insure your property?"

"What is 'insure'?" he asked.

"You insure your property against disaster, like a fire, and you receive money to replace what is lost," I explained.

"Someone gives you money?" he asked. His eyes widened with astonishment.

"Not really. They don't just give it to you. You buy a policy from a company which agrees to pay you to make repairs or rebuild if what you own is destroyed."

"You can buy money to replace things you lose," Softsoap stated. He shook his head, dumbfounded.

"Well, that's sort of how it works," I said.

It was a lame explanation, but how do you explain an intangible like insurance to one who has no concept of economics or capitalism? I was aware again of the wide gulf between communism and capitalism, between a democratic nation and a totalitarian state.

Slowly, over the following weeks, other changes came about.

"You may walk outside today," the guard told me when he came to my cell one morning.

He took off the leg irons and gestured toward the area of the yard where the earthen bomb shelter made a large mound. I stared at him for just a second, and then with long, luxurious strides, I headed out across the walkway toward the mound. I stood and stretched for a moment, and then began walking and swinging my arms, exulting in the sense of freedom to stand and walk about without a guard's rifle in my back, prodding me toward a latrine or a quiz room or the shower.

I was outside! Just for the sake of *being outside!* I breathed deeply and stretched as I walked around the yard. One thing more would have made the morning perfect: if I could have shared it with another Alkie. But that was not allowed. We could be out of our cells, exercise freely in the yard, but not together. However, it was a beginning. We did not want to act too grateful—such humane treatment of prisoners should have been allowed at the time of our capture; international law required it. But we were thankful, and we did not want it to end.

Our new freedom offered us new opportunities for entertainment. Harry Jenkins was the first to take advantage of these. During an exercise period one day, he discovered that the guard's attention was occupied with something outside the yard. Tall, skinny Harry stood on the platform built over the bomb shelter, reached above his head, and disconnected the two sets of electric wires that hung over the barbed wire and the glass-studded walls of Alcatraz. All electric power to the prison compound was immediately cut off. Then, making sure he wasn't being watched, he quickly wrapped the wires around the insulators so that it was impossible to tell that they had been disconnected.

It was nightfall when the lights should have come on before it was discovered that there was no power. We sat in our tiny cells, now black, and listened as the guards scurried around outside, shouting and cursing, trying to find the reason for the power failure. They never looked at the wires above the wall, or if they did, they saw nothing that looked out of place. All night the compound was immersed in darkness, and the next day, during his exercise period, Harry reached up and reconnected the wires when the guard turned his back. The prison authorities never knew what had happened. For days, the Alcatraz gang snickered like kids who had gotten away with a classroom prank. Ah, how good it felt to laugh!

One morning, code flashed across the yard that the guards had built a big fire on the mound that was the bomb shelter, and they were heating a large bucket of water over a crude iron grill. In a little while, as we watched through the cracks in our doors, they ladled hot water into small, round-bottomed basins. I was speechless when, moments later, while I was standing under the shower's dirty, lukewarm trickle, a guard handed me a basin of *hot* water and ordered me to shave with it.

The feel of hot water on my face was an indescribable delight. The crude lye soap offered nothing resembling a lather, but the warmth against my skin produced the closest thing to pure joy I had felt in a long time. The luxury was short-lived, however. The guards quickly tired of the labor of building the fire and dishing up hot water for each of us. They easily convinced the commander that the comfort of American war criminals was not worth their time. A basin of steaming hot water for each man was just too much work. So the luxury faded after that one incident. We returned to the weekly ordeal of shaving in the shower with cold water.

The odd incongruity of Alcatraz struck me almost daily as I made my morning walk around the yard. Beyond the barbed wire and dugout earthen walls throbbed a city of nearly half a million people. Brick buildings, many of them reminiscent of European architecture, loomed against the sky. Trolleys, bicycles, and motor vehicles created a cacophony of modern sounds, while inside Alcatraz noisy, smelly, potbellied pigs, bred for food, wallowed in the mud behind a rickety wood-stake fence, and smoke curled up from an outdoor fire where a caldron of water boiled. Here, within these walls, the forward march of time seemed to be at a standstill.

I prayed every day for a letter from home or for the privilege to write a letter home. Some days, when I thought of Shirley and our children, my chest ached with a real physical pain. We had been apart for more than three years, and I had no knowledge of their lives or their welfare. But I knew my Shirley; I knew she would be carrying on and depending on God, and I was comforted by that knowledge. I prayed constantly for her strength and her courage. I prayed for our release and for strength to endure. Sometimes God's responses to my prayers surprised me.

There was the morning a guard arrived at my cell to remove the leg irons for the day and handed me a large chunk of hot, fresh French bread. The aroma of warm yeast filled my tiny cell. I thought heaven had descended to Hanoi!

"Breakfast?" I exclaimed and quickly got on the wall to send out the news. Immediately word came back to me that every man was getting bread.

After more than three years of only two meals a day, were we now going to get a third? Hunger had haunted my insides for so long that I even dreamed about food. The tiny bowl of rice twice a day, sometimes served with a bowl of sewer greens or almost clear pumpkin soup, was a starvation diet for grown men. We had despaired of ever feeling the comfort of a full stomach.

On many days, the smell of the sewer greens and the sight of the thin, green broth made me retch. Extreme hunger brought on nausea, but I was too hungry to pass up any food. So I waited for the nausea to pass and then ate hungrily. With the exception of Storz, we all believed it was important to eat. We were afraid of growing too weak to resist our captors, or too weak to attempt escape, if the opportunity ever presented itself.

I stared at the crusty, hot bread for only an instant and then devoured it. Afterward, I sat and reveled in the satisfied feeling I had not known for so long. A sense of well-being settled on me, and I whispered, "Thank you, Lord." With an almost-full stomach, I felt my natural optimism swell even larger than usual. All sorts of possibilities came to mind.

"It's a good sign," I tapped to Shumaker. "They are trying to fatten us up for release."

"Do you really think so?" he answered.

"Ask Denton."

"I don't know," Jerry said, "but things are changing. Could be their response to Nixon. Or maybe it's the influence of Le Duan. I just don't know."

Surely those two factors had to be working together to help alter the awful practices that were commonplace in North Vietnam's prison system. But administrative changes were not the major reason for change in Hanoi's game plan. If I had known of the unusual and historic events occurring in my hometown, Dallas, Texas, I would have understood more clearly the reason for our improved conditions. But it would be years before I would understand all that had been done to bring about change for us, and for all the American prisoners of war.

In the meantime, I knew for certain that there was more than political activity responsible for the improved treatment we were receiving. I had seen the hand of God at work too often not to recognize His touch at this time. For me, all these things were more evidence of God's great grace.

For more than two years I had huddled against cold concrete and shivered through months of near-freezing winters wrapped in a single, thin blanket. I shuddered at the thought of enduring a third winter in North Vietnam. Then suddenly one day, quickly following the announcement of three meals per day for every prisoner, a guard entered my cell and tossed me a second blanket.

I could hardly contain my excitement. I bowed my head and praised God. I knew there was a verse somewhere in the Bible that said "every good and perfect gift cometh down from above." I knew this was a gift from Him. I knew that He was ultimately responsible for every small improvement in our conditions. Every gift was, for me, an incentive to continue to trust and remain hopeful. Every gift, however small and seemingly insignificant, was a brief respite from the horror of our captivity.

With less stringent rules in effect in Alcatraz, the guards began to initiate a few changes of their own.

"Sweep!" a guard ordered, opening Jerry Denton's cell and handing him a crude broom made of bundled and tied bamboo shoots. Jerry stared at him a moment. "Sweep!" the guard repeated and pushed Jerry out toward the walkway in front of the line of cells. So Jerry stirred the dirt in the pathway along the cellblock.

The next day a guard hauled Shumaker out of his cell and shoved the broom into his hands with the same command. Shumaker started sweeping, and within minutes I began to discern a pattern in his broom strokes. He was sending coded messages with every swish of the broom. He moved about the yard, talking to everybody in code and carrying information from one end of the cellblock to the other. In a short time, we began to think of Shumaker as our news anchor. Every day, each man gave him the bits of information gleaned in quizzes, and Shumaker passed it all around while he swept.

For some odd reason, Shumaker was the guard's choice for cleanup duty. I assumed my crippled arms kept me off the cleanup duty roster. Denton substituted for Shumaker a few times, but he didn't seem to be able to get the code into broom strokes as easily as Shumaker. The rest of us in our cells cringed when he tried to "talk" to us—he just couldn't do it with Shumaker's smooth nonchalance. We were sure he was going to get caught and be thrown into punishment. We were relieved when the guards decided his work didn't measure up, and gave the job back to Shumaker.

But Jerry was not to be outdone, and he promptly went to work on another communication innovation. We had all noticed that our guards suffered from constant upper respiratory problems and that they coughed, hacked, and spat continually. Denton sent word on the wall that we were going to adapt the tap code to a cough-hack-spit code.

"He's crazy," I tapped to Shumaker and Jenkins.

"He's losing it," they answered.

"It will work," Jerry tapped back. "Line one in the grid is one cough; line two is two coughs; line three is clear throat; line four is 'hauwk'; and line five is spit."

Jerry tried it first from the yard while he was exercising. His loud throat noises carried to every cell, and we all groaned, thinking the guards would catch on and pounce on him with clubs and rifle butts. But Jerry "talked" the entire time he walked about in the yard, and the guards were oblivious to the scheme. As his exercise period ended and the guard motioned for him to leave the yard, he signed off: Cough-cough – pause – cough-cough – pause – cough – pause – cough-cough – pause – hauwk – pause – spit. We all grinned and acknowledged his "GBU" with an answering, "Cough-cough."

Soon all the Alkies were coughing, clearing their throats, and "hauwk-ing" and spitting, but the prison authority never caught on. We assigned every man a code letter for his name (mine was L – clear throat and two coughs), and by beginning a transmission with a single letter, we could direct a specific message to a specific prisoner. After a quiz, we could make instant contact and transmit information to every prionser in Alcatraz without arousing any suspicion. We all felt we had gained a small piece of freedom within the walls of our prison.

In time, we knew for certain that drastic changes had gone into effect at Alcatraz. One particular incident confirmed it for us. Although we had inaugurated other means of communication, tapping was still the best way for me to work on my French vocabulary with Shumaker. We worked together on the wall, one on one, every day. One morning, a guard walked by my cell and heard my soft tapping. He opened my cell door and shouted, "You communicate! No! No communicate!"

I was guilty as charged, but I shrugged and tried to look innocent. The guard stomped away, and I waited to see what would happen next. A quiz and then a thorough beating were the usual penalty for talking to a fellow prisoner, but lately things had been less than usual at Alcatraz. I waited, dread and curiosity an odd mix in my chest. In a little while, Denton sent out the word that Softsoap had declared no more punishment for communication violations.

I breathed a sigh of relief. "It's another good sign," I answered. "They're trying to change our treatment without actually endorsing the Geneva Conventions."

"Maybe," Denton answered. "I'm not sure what to think just yet."

"I think they are getting ready to move us all together. Maybe we are going to go back with the others at Hoa Lo," someone suggested.

Our hopes were high; our expectations uncertain. We talked a lot about living together as a group, as the Geneva Conventions required. We grew bold with our whispered conversations, and when we were caught again and again but not punished, we began to believe we could resist any rules, in any way, and not suffer for it.

"I think we can do anything we want and get away with it now," Denton told us.

We started testing his theory and discovered that, even for the most blatant offenses, we would receive no punishment, only shouted threats accompanied by terse orders to obey the rules. The propaganda assaults and the quizzes continued, perhaps because Softsoap never stopped believing that he might persuade us to accept his way of thinking; or perhaps he felt he had to justify his position within the camp. However, we felt certain that the days of physical abuse were over. The possibility that the war was coming to an end permeated our every thought.

Near Thanksgiving of that year, the guards at Alcatraz decided to observe our American holiday with a "feast." Their special delicacy: dog meat.

I heard yelping and barking out in the yard and went to look through the crack in my door. The small, chow-like dog that the guards had petted and played with for more than six months was howling and crying from down inside a small round bomb shelter that had been dug inside the prison yard. The streets of Hanoi were filled with such shelters— about three feet wide and six feet deep—just large enough for one person to duck into for shelter during the time the United States had carried out bombing missions over the city. Now that a bombing halt had been called, it seemed other practical uses could be found for the holes in the ground.

A guard stood above the shelter and pounded and jabbed the frenzied dog with a large, six-inch diameter bamboo pole. Some time before we had figured out that the Vietnamese believed that agitating the animal before butchering it improved the taste of the meat, but we hated witnessing their cruelty. I turned away from the sight and tried to close out the sounds of the animal's suffering.

For more than two days, they starved the poor beast and pummeled it with rocks and bamboo poles. At the same time, they busied themselves building a crude spit on the dirt mound above the larger bomb shelter. Finally, when they figured the meat had been tenderized long enough, they pulled the dog from the hole in the ground and bashed it into unconsciousness with a large pole.

I stared, appalled, as a guard stretched the dog taut and tied his legs on a pole suspended over small fire. The hair on the dog's body snapped and hissed in the flames, and the young dog again began to yelp and cry in pain. When all the hair had been burned off its body, the guard began to skin the dog. Its final cries died away slowly.

Hours later, when our evening meal was brought to us, small pieces of dark meat lay on the tray. I knew what it was, but ravenous hunger overrode my sense of indignation and revulsion. I knew there was no purpose to be served in refusing to eat. There was little satisfaction in the meal, however—it was dry and bony, a little like roast duck—but it would keep me alive and provide the energy I needed to fight my enemies another day.

Shortly after Thanksgiving, Ron Storz moved back into the cellblock near us, next door to Mulligan. He was emaciated. He had continued to ignore Denton's orders to eat, and now his deathly thin frame was almost frightening. He was all skeleton, and his bony face wore a haunted look. But he was convinced that if he started eating and gained strength, the Vietnamese would begin torturing him again.

"You're all moving out of here," he informed Denton one day. He didn't bother to try and whisper. He spoke out loud wherever and whenever he liked. He had no fear of the guards, and the guards seemed tolerant of his madness. "The guards told me they are sending you out. But I'm not going."

"Of course you're coming with us. We're not letting you stay here by yourself," Denton answered.

One by one, we all tried to convince Storz that his place was with us, that we were in this together. No man would be left behind.

"It will only be worse if I leave," he answered. "Besides, it's all a bluff. It's a trick to try and get me to eat, but I'm on to them. If they do move us, they will never let me be with you. They'll separate us."

"That won't happen, Ron," I told him. "Things have changed some. Can't you feel that it's different now? We'll all be together."

In a conversation with the camp commander, Denton brought up the subject of Ron Storz.

"If we are going to move, you must make Storz go with us," he stated, confident that in this new climate he could make demands and not expect to suffer.

"You are not going to move," Softsoap answered. "No need to worry about it," and he dismissed the subject as unimportant.

A few days later, Denton pressed him for information.

"You may move," Softsoap admitted. "It is not certain. But your Storz may do as he likes."

Denton came back to the cellblock puzzled. We were all a little confused about what the prison authority had in mind for the Alkies. It seemed especially odd that they would suggest that a prisoner could choose his own fate.

As Storz stubbornly continued to refuse the option of leaving Alcatraz, we continued to try to persuade him to come with us. His answer was always the same: an adamant no. We all felt helpless. Except to pray for him, there was nothing we could do.

December came. The camp radio played excerpts from Bible passages, or so they called them. I wondered where they had found a translation that used the words "monopolist" and "capitalist." It was obvious to anyone who had ever read the Bible that what we were hearing was the Bible according to Hanoi Hannah. There was nothing familiar in the readings—no "tidings of great joy," no "peace to men of good will."

The second week of December the order came.

"Roll up."

Guards appeared at each cell door and unfastened the leg irons that had chiseled through the skin of our ankles for two years. After dark, they returned to our cells and blindfolded us for the drive back across Hanoi.

I could feel my senses struggling to identify each man around me. I strained to hear noises that would tell me where we were going. In only about five minutes, I heard the scraping sounds of a gate, then as another gate opened and shut behind us I knew we had returned to Hoa Lo. For this trip the Vietnamese had not bothered to try to confuse us by taking a circuitous route through the city. It seemed it did not matter any more if we knew our whereabouts. A shove out of the back of the truck; a walk across uneven ground; a heavy door thrust open in front of me; a rough push into a cell—I knew immediately I was back in the strip. Las Vegas. The Stardust.

The building hadn't changed in the two years since I had left Hoa Lo. My tiny cell, four feet wide by nine feet long, held two wooden bunks stacked above each other on one wall. It was dark and damp and cold—colder than my cell in Alcatraz had been because the window was uncovered and the concrete walls held in the frigid temperatures like a well-insulated icebox. I shivered, unrolled my mat on the lower bunk, and put my ear to the door. I could hear hoarse whispers coursing through the narrow hallway.

"Johnson," someone whispered loudly from down the hall.

"Down here," I answered, not bothering to whisper.

"Mulligan over here," Jim called out softly.

Up and down the hallway, the Alkies identified themselves.

"Denton in with Mulligan."

"Shumaker and Tanner over here."

I was in the end cell next to the one Jim Lamar and I had shared two years earlier. Tanner and Shumaker had been thrown into the middle room facing the inside courtyard. The camp called it a four-man cell, but there was not enough room for two men to stand or turn in the narrow space between the bunks that hung on opposite walls. Across from Tanner and Shumaker, on the outside wall facing the dry moat and the back wall, were Mulligan and Denton. Jenkins and Rutledge were across from each other in tiny, two-man cells that were too small for even one man to move about in.

"Where are Coker and McKnight?" someone asked.

"They rode over with us from Alcatraz, so they must be here somewhere."

"What about Ron?"

Only Ron Storz was unaccounted for. We shouted his name in hoarse whispers throughout the cellblock, but there was no answer.

Suddenly the door to the Stardust opened, and a guard stomped in, shouting, "Shut up! Shut mouth! No talk!"

He banged his rifle butt on a couple of cell doors, as if for effect, and then charged out of the building. We lowered our voices to whispers, but continued to communicate. Questions bounced off the walls. Why had we been brought back? What would happen to us next?

For hours we continued to whisper and tap in defiance of the prison rules. The rest of the camp lay in silent terror as we boldly communicated among ourselves. We had learned, as the others had yet to learn, that the POWs' position had undergone a change. We had tested and proven our theory that we could resist and even defy the ridiculous rules of the prison camp and not have to pay with our blood.

We had reasoned that the changes were the direct result of Ho Chi Minh's death and the change in Hanoi's leadership. We felt certain that a more lenient hand now held the reins of government, one that was less inclined toward torture and punishment. We figured we could get away with a lot of things now that in earlier days would have been rewarded with the ropes and a severe beating, or worse.

None of us had any idea that there were other forces working to bring about change for us from a most unlikely source. In our greatest delirium, we would never have imagined that relief was soon to speed across the ocean from Dallas, Texas, on a Braniff jet loaded with gifts and letters for all the POWs in North Vietnam. But more important than the plane's cargo would be its powerful media impact. Its roar across continents toward Southeast Asia would fire America's first loud response to Hanoi's propaganda war, and the world would take notice of our plight.

As I lay down on the wooden bunk in my cell that night, emotionally exhausted from the excitement and drained after the long hours of communicating, I breathed a prayer of thanksgiving. I was still an ocean removed from home and Texas, but the grave-like aura of Alcatraz was miles away on the other side of Hanoi. My legs were free of the awful heavy irons. I felt calm and, for the first time in more than three and a half years, I was almost happy. Almost. Only one thought disturbed me: Where was Ron Storz?

A dozen questions plagued my mind. A dozen possibilities responded. If our release was imminent, as I always insisted on believing, Ron's emaciated condition would be seen as an embarrassment to the North Vietnamese, an indictment of their treatment of American prisoners. So what had they done with him? Was he alone in Alcatraz, awaiting death? Would he be cared for? Would he ever go home?

Sleep finally quieted all the questions. It would be two years before they would all be answered.

# ELEVEN

# Groping for Peace

"We are caught in war, wanting peace."

Richard Nixon's inauguration speech had eloquently expressed the dilemma that was felt by the entire country. In the twelve months since the TET offensive, the communist party had entrenched itself in eighty percent of the villages in South Vietnam and now controlled more than sixty percent of the total population.[1]

A second offensive, carried out soon after Nixon took the oath of office, had come like a stinging slap to the new president. American losses were almost equal to those incurred in the first, but enemy losses were one-third those of the earlier assault. Peace talks deadlocked. Quizzes in Alcatraz were dominated by comments like "You will be here the rest of your lives!"

Because all bombing in the North had stopped, we battled the fear that perhaps the North Vietnamese were telling us the truth. It was hard to disbelieve them when we looked at the photos of the disarray and destruction in our own American cities. The upheaval in the United States overwhelmed us. But we didn't dare accept the possibility that Nixon would back away from this fight and leave us to rot in prison in North Vietnam.

With the decision to withdraw American troops from South Vietnam, it became obvious that the administration had finally concluded that a free and sovereign South Vietnam was no longer a viable goal. Four presidents had clung to the belief that a sovereign noncommunist South Vietnam could be won on the battlefield, but Nixon now believed that any dreams of securing a noncommunist South Vietnam were unrealistic and unattainable.[2] He pledged that the United States would extricate itself from South Vietnam while maintaining its honor and credibility with the rest of the nations of the world. He would secure peace and bring home America's sons.

But what of her sons behind bars in Hanoi? What was to become of them?

The military knew for certain that the conditions were abominable. During the Johnson administration, news of our treatment had been deliberately silenced. Only a handful of American civilians knew of the abuses and atrocities being carried out on American prisoners in Hanoi.

One of the awful side effects of the secrecy was that the wives of the POWs had no knowledge of each other, no network of support, and no sense of community support. The military continually advised them to keep quiet about their husbands. As in the beginning, when Shirley was first notified of my capture, all information given to the wives was followed by the admonition, "This is all classified, of course. You must not talk about it."

Jim Stockdale's wife, Sybil, had made contact with wives of MIAs and POWs in California, and a support and awareness organization called the League of Wives of American Vietnam Prisoners of War had come into existence in San Diego in 1967. It had begun pressuring the Pentagon and the oval office to focus national attention on the POW situation and to pressure Hanoi for information about all prisoners. But the rest of the country knew little of the realities of the prisoner of war issue.

One day in Dallas in the summer of 1969, Henry Kissinger contacted Ross Perot, founder of Electronic Data Systems (EDS), to express the administration's interest in the welfare of American POWs in Vietnam, and to suggest a way to address the issue. The national security advisor could offer nothing more than his encouragement. There would be no direct support from the government.

"You'll have to use your own resources," Kissinger told Perot.

For Ross, that was good news and bad. There would be no government restrictions to tie his hands, but neither would there be help from the country's top agencies. It was a sort of "Mission: Impossible" scenario—a case of, "Should you choose to accept this mission, we will disavow any knowledge of your activities . . ."

Ross's response: Let's get involved.

Meanwhile, in a television studio on the other side of Dallas, another man set the stage for what would be the first step toward actually accomplishing change for us in Alcatraz.

Murphy Martin anchored a weekly talk show, "Face To Face," featuring timely news topics and interesting personalities. He brought the mother of an MIA to Dallas to discuss the POW-MIA issue. She told of the waiting, the wondering, and the frustration of being rebuffed at every attempt to find out what was being done to find her son. Viewer response to the program was overwhelming. Letters of support came in to the station in bundles. Murphy knew immediately that he had exposed an issue that stirred Texans' hearts. He too, said, "Let's get involved."

With the support of the station management, Murphy began to formulate a plan to take POW-MIA wives to Paris to confront the North Vietnamese negotiators personally.

"We'll take a full film crew and photograph the women in Paris," he proposed. The trip was scheduled for September, 1969.

Preparations began with a publicity campaign to inform the world that four American women were coming to Paris to try to find out about their husbands who were supposed to be prisoners of the Hanoi regime. Newspapers around the world picked up the human interest aspect of the story. Hanoi was, for the first time, being called to accountability.

The public media blitz did its job. It was a great propaganda tool for the Americans, for a change. Public sentiment moved over onto the side of the American women who only wanted confirmation as to whether their husbands were alive or dead and information on their whereabouts. The requests were reasonable and legal under the terms of international law. The pressure of world opinion bore down on the Vietnamese to do the only honorable, humane thing: meet with the American women.

They arrived in Paris the first week of September. The Vietnamese scheduled a meeting only after agreement was reached that it would be closed to press, military and government representatives. Throughout the day, news reporters and camera crews gathered near the building to await the outcome of this unusual confrontation. The meeting lasted for several hours. The North Vietnamese negotiators served the women tea, exchanged cautious courtesies, and then berated them with the same propaganda being used on their husbands many miles away.

"We are not required to give you any information," they told the women. "Your husbands are war criminals, and the Geneva Conventions do not apply to them. They are not entitled to humane treatment."

The women's cautiously worded requests appeared to make no impact on the North Vietnamese. After several hours of discussions, the men rose to indicate that the interview was over. The women asked if letters and family pictures could be left with the negotiators to be delivered to the American captives in Hanoi's prison system. Shallow promises followed them out of the door.

On the steps of the compound, fifty members of the press met the women. Flashing cameras captured their weary expressions and their story graced newscasts and the front pages of newspapers all around the world.

Murphy and his group returned to Dallas and assembled a documentary titled "Red Tea and Promises." Ross Perot agreed to sponsor its airing. Next, Ross and three associates established United We Stand, an organization with the sole task of working to stimulate national unity and to promote national interest in the issue of POWs and MIAs. Across America a slow awakening began.

In Hanoi, we were oblivious, of course, to all that was transpiring beyond our prison walls. Our captors told us only the things that suited their purposes.

"The Americans have sent their women to do their negotiating for them," Hanoi Hannah sneered into the microphone. I was angered at the inference of American diplomatic weakness, but I felt frustrated as well. We discussed the questions on the wall, but could come up with no explanation of the events in Paris. We had no idea the women were wives of POWs and MIAs. Although we did not know it, the plight of POWs and MIAs began to reach into the heart of the nation.

"It's a shame we can't just send Christmas dinner to every one of those guys," Murphy said.

"Let's do it!" Ross exclaimed.

It was a wild idea, probably impossible.

After four airlines turned down their request to charter a plane into a war zone, Dallas-based Braniff said yes and agreed to supply two planes, not just one. One plane would fly directly to Hanoi, filled with gifts and goods for the prisoners. The other plane would fly to Paris, with letters and gifts from the families.

There was much to be done, and little time to do it all before Christmas. They were surprised that the most difficult task turned out to be locating the families of the POWs. The military's policy of keeping the matter secret and instructing families to remain silent made a major detective project out of tracking the POWs' families. It was a slow, frustrating process. One POW wife in a city knew of another, and that one knew of one more, and so it went, until hundreds of families were contacted. Shirley found out about the plane bound for Hanoi just one day before its scheduled departure. Frantically, she put together a package for me.

Fifty-two POW wives accompanied the flight headed for Paris. The flight to Hanoi, however, met with difficulty before it left the ground.

"Seems there's a little problem of insurance," Murphy told Ross. "We can't get insurance for a plane going into a war zone."

"How much does a plane like that cost?" Ross asked.

"Six or seven million dollars."

Ross responded, "Well, tell them if the plane gets shot down, I'll buy them a new one."

The charter left Dallas uninsured and started on what became a confusing journey to Bangkok, Vientiane, Tokyo, Anchorage, and Copenhagen. Requests to land in Hanoi were denied at every stop. The plane returned to the United States still fully loaded.

Newspapers and news broadcasts around the world carried the story of the civilian jets. Regardless of the fact that the journey's primary objective had failed, the prison authority responded to it by making many of the changes that surprised us in the fall and winter of 1969.

The documentaries made in 1969 about the POWs showed Americans the reality of the North Vietnamese atrocities. For the first time, it was publicized that the regime in Hanoi was a vicious, cruel one. The image of a benevolent Uncle Ho began to blur, and the portrait of a harsh, murdering despot took its place, for those who were willing to see. Propaganda met with propaganda.

It was at that time that we in Alcatraz were first allowed out of our cells for an exercise period after nearly two years of total confinement. The third meal was added shortly thereafter. Hot water, though only a short-lived luxury, came at that same time. My extra pair of socks, an extra blanket, and finally the move from Alcatraz back to Hoa Lo all came in response to the first efforts of American citizens determined to fight the propaganda war of Hanoi with a propaganda war of their own.

At the Dallas headquarters of EDS, Ross continued to fuel the propaganda war. Shirley joined the effort, spending long hours in the EDS workroom and traveling as a spokesperson for United We Stand. In most situations she found sympathy and discovered women who were willing to get involved in the national effort. But on one occasion, she left feeling sure she had failed to make the issues clear. At the end of her brief speech, a woman sitting near the back of the room raised her hand to ask a question.

"I'm so glad to hear somebody is finally concerned about prison conditions," she commented. "Is anybody doing anything about the ones up in Arkansas?"

*Will people never understand?* Shirley wondered.

For Shirley, one of the most galling realities of the war was that all personal letters to POWs from their families had to be sent and received through a group in the United States called the Committee for Liaison. It was an organization sympathetic to the North Vietnamese, and some of the committee's membership, such as Lenny Davis, openly advocated the violent overthrow of the U.S. government. But the wives of the POWs and MIAs had to work with and through the Committee for Liaison if they wanted to have contact with their husbands because Hanoi rejected all communications that came for POWs from any other source and refused to allow any other agencies to deliver mail from the POWs, including the International Committee of the Red Cross.

My first letter to Shirley came to her through the Committee of Liaison in 1969, three and a half years after my capture. Although she was ecstatic to hear from me finally, she was appalled that news of the letter's arrival from Hanoi came to her through a phone call from David Dellinger, a man who had aligned himself with an organization that she believed was traitorous to the U.S. cause in Vietnam; an organization she believed to be communist-backed.

As the POW-MIA issue made headlines, the air force began to change its attitude and its dealings with the families of its missing and captured. For three years Shirley had had to endure terrifying phone calls from a civilian air force employee.

"Mrs. Johnson," he would say, "I have something to tell you about your husband—it is all very secret, of course. I'll be down to see you in a few days."

For days, Shirley would be frantic with worry that the air force had learned I was dead and that they were coming to break the news to her in person. When the representative finally arrived, all he had were bits and pieces of information that had been deciphered from coded letters received from other POWs who were being allowed to write home. There was never any news of me.

"You are scaring me to death," she told him one day. "Just tell me whatever you have, tell me you're coming and that everything is okay, but stop with all this secretive stuff. You're making me a wreck!"

Meanwhile, the letter-writing campaign in the United States was burgeoning. Hundreds of thousands of Americans were writing letters to the Hanoi regime and its representatives in Paris and to the POWs. The letters arrived in Paris only to be bagged and bundled and added to the growing piles filling up the rented warehouse because the North Vietnamese continued to refuse to accept them.

The new year began much as the last one had ended: with peace demonstrations drawing huge crowds and the Nixon administration suffering depressing bouts of frustration over this interminable war that no one seemed to be able to end. The goal of peace with honor had sounded so viable a year ago; it now sounded like a pipe dream. Both honor and peace seemed beyond reach.

The announcement of troop withdrawals from South Vietnam, which had been heralded as a sign of the beginning of the end, created a whole new set of problems that no one had had the foresight to anticipate. It set the army at war against itself.

A phenomenon called "short-timer's fever" erupted within the ranks in South Vietnam. Already battered with uncertainty about their part in this propagandized war, many troops began to wonder why they should risk their lives on one more battle if they were going to be sent home in only a few weeks. They could see no reason to go forward into a battle or a booby trap in the jungle, only to be sent home in a body bag a few days before they would have been able to fly home alive and whole.

Discouragement hovered close as we listened to radio reports on the progress of the peace talks. Even through the communist tripe, we could discern the truth that efforts at peace were going nowhere. The days seemed to drag endlessly.

The administration in Washington, D.C. grew desperate to find a way to break the deadlock on the peace talks in Paris. Nixon announced the escalation of the war into Cambodia, where North Vietnamese communist troops and supplies were being sheltered. The president found himself undone when the North Vietnamese and the Vietcong used the American presence in Cambodia as a reason to boycott peace talks. The war was again at a stalemate.

The quiz room at Hoa Lo became a photo gallery again, plastered with pictures of the violence in the United States. I could not believe what I was seeing. But, of course, there were no pictures of the one hundred thousand demonstrators who marched through the streets of Manhattan on May 20, 1970, in a show of support for President Nixon.

In 1970, Nixon lifted the secrecy that Johnson had laid over the POW-MIA issue. He began to publicize the plight of the POWs and MIAs.

Washington, D.C., became the focus of activity on behalf of the American POWs in North Vietnam. Sybil Stockdale and several other wives, including Shirley, traveled to the capital to form an ad hoc committee changing the League of Wives into a national organization called the League of Families of POW-MIAs in Southeast Asia. In another of many interesting ironies, many of the POW wives who signed the charter were the wives of the men of Alcatraz. They had managed to discover each other, in spite of efforts to keep them apart. They began fighting side by side for our cause, not knowing, of course, that we, too, were fighting side by side for our survival.

Bracelets bearing the names of missing or captured American servicemen found their way into every city and hamlet in the country. Men, women, and children wore the reminders on their wrists. We were no longer the forgotten casualties of the war in Vietnam. We were the focus of national attention.

Murphy took advantage of the renewed surge of media attention to make another try at getting information out of North Vietnam. With a full film crew, he traveled to South Vietnam and filmed all the prison camps where North Vietnamese captives were held. He then contacted Hanoi and asked permission to tour all the prison camps in North Vietnam where American captives were confined.

"Here are your people," he told Hanoi, handing over films of prisoners held in the South. "Now let us go in and film our people," he proposed.

"We don't have any people in South Vietnam," was the official answer.

Neither Murphy nor the Red Cross from a neutral country were allowed to go near the prisoner of war camps in North Vietnam. Only those who would take back the story Hanoi wanted told were allowed to visit certain parts of the prison facilities in Hanoi and to speak with certain POWs who had rehearsed their roles for each encounter—some were prisoners who had been severely tortured to insure their cooperation; others made their statements carefully because of friends held in torture who would suffer if they said anything amiss. A few others were willing participants in the elaborate facade—they had turned their backs on the code of honor and shifted their allegiance to the enemy. And so each American who was allowed to visit Hanoi's prison camps was treated to a carefully constructed theatrical production created to play to a willing audience.

Meanwhile, the U.S. administration continued "groping for peace,"[3] reaching with eager but cautious fingers toward an elusive solution to the fighting and killing in Vietnam. However, the solution would continue to elude them for another three years.

## Notes

1. Samuel Lipsman, Edward Doyle, and Editors of Boston Publishing Co., *The Vietnam Experience—Fighting For Time,* (Boston: Boston Publishing Company, 1983).

2. William Appleman Williams, Thomas McCormick, Lloyd Gardner and Walter LaFeber, editors, *America In Vietnam, A Documentary History* (Garden City: Anchor Press/Doubleday, 1975).

3. Henry Kissinger, *The White House Years* (Boston: Little, Brown, 1979).

# TWELVE

# Bad Nephew

I was awakened suddenly by the sound of doors opening. A harsh voice shouted nearby. I lifted my head slowly and saw the gray light of early morning creeping into my cell. I felt confused and disoriented, as if waking out of a deep dream. And then, streaming in with the dawn, came the memory of last night.

"Hoa Lo," I whispered to myself as I looked at the filth-covered cement walls of my cell in the Stardust block of the Vegas strip.

I shivered. The large, barred window on one wall gaped open, and the cold winds of December swirled in and stirred the two thin blankets that covered me. I wore my two pair of now threadbare socks, but still my feet were numb.

I felt my insides recoil at the sight of the wooden leg stocks built into the end of the bunk where I lay. I drew my feet up quickly, not wanting even to touch them. From my ankles to my shins, my legs were still bare and hairless from two years earlier when I had lain for two months in leg stocks in the Mint.

I had forgotten how cramped these cells were; how each cellblock had been cut into tiny cubicles separated by narrow dark, hallways to prevent communications. It was a foolish and futile effort on the part of the Vietnamese to silence us, and we had overcome it quickly. I had forgotten how the smell of urine had saturated the concrete building and how the sunshine never quite seemed to break through the cold dimness of the hallways. But the memory of Alcatraz was fresh.

Alcatraz, with its tomb-like cells and dugout earthen walls, had seemed a silent, constant death threat. Here, in Hoa Lo, the Hanoi Hilton, the shadow of death did not seem quite so smothering. Emotions I had been too exhausted to examine the night before flooded in like a torrent. Relief mixed with excitement. Finally, I was back among the living! I felt almost giddy!

No doubt, the memory of Hoa Lo's earlier horrors, the torture room and the meat hook, was blunted a little by Alcatraz's more recent horrors. I had only good feelings about being back. My friends were nearby, and together we would make it through whatever lay ahead for us. I worried about only two things: the fate of Ron Storz, and those leg stocks at the end of the bunk.

I had been unable to fall asleep the night before until I had asked Denton, "Do you think they will lock us in the stocks?"

He had tapped back, "I don't think so. I don't think we need to worry about anything like that any more."

And so I had fallen asleep at peace.

Some of the Alkies, however, were not so pleased at discovering they had been returned to the Hilton. Mulligan, in particular, was terribly distraught. He had been certain that when we left Alcatraz we were on our way to release. His disappointment at seeing Hoa Lo was deep and cutting.

Walking outside that first morning, it appeared to me that Hoa Lo hadn't changed much in the two years that I had been buried in Alcatraz. It was as if time had stood still. The same narrow path led to the same smelly bucket-dumping area inside the building that housed the Mint, where I had spent those awful months prior to going to Alcatraz. The showers still consisted of small cubicles built in a row, parallel to the Stardust and the Desert Inn. The water that dribbled from a rusty pipe in each of the tiny shower stalls was the same dirty, tepid, pathetic stream. I shivered as I stepped up to wash myself. The winter morning air was cold against my bare skin. As I stood there rubbing the goosebumps on my arms with the same bar of lye soap that never lathered, I knew suddenly that, while Hoa Lo had stayed the same, I had not.

The water running off my shoulders and chest was filthy, but I felt cleansed. It was an inner kind of cleansing. Alcatraz had done for me what no amount of scrubbing could ever have done. I had a different idea of the things that were truly important. I felt a purity of purpose inside me and a fresh determination to go on and see this ordeal to the end. I was ready to begin fighting again with all the strength that was in me, and I believed I was now stronger than ever. How quickly that strength would fade, however. How quickly I would find my resources exhausted in the continuing fight for survival.

But on that cold morning in December, 1969, I was filled with anticipation, ready to resume action in this war of resistance. Jerry Denton, first in command in the Stardust, ordered us all to make it a priority to locate the rest of our gang. Coker and McKnight were here somewhere, but where?

Within Stardust, communications were fairly easy. The sound of tapping carried throughout the cement corridors; there was only one door to watch, and Jenkins could easily clear for us by lying on the floor and watching through the rat hole in one corner of his cell. We tapped and talked boldly with each other. It was not as easy, however, to make contact with the other cellblocks. No one wanted to talk to us. No one responded to either our tapping or our hand signals, with the exception of Bill Franke and Jim Lamar, who had heard the commotion of our arrival the night before.

Inside their cell in the Desert Inn, Franke and Lamar had stood on each other's shoulders and peered over the high windowsill to see us. The sight of us walking to the showers in the morning light confirmed what they had guessed in the darkness the night before. They were quick to answer our whispered queries as we were herded past their window. But the rest of the camp lay silent.

It seemed things at Hoa Lo were *not* the same. Although the facilities appeared unchanged, many other things had changed greatly. It was a very different Hoa Lo than the one we had left two years earlier.

The commander of Hoa Lo was Cat, our old enemy. Over the years of my captivity, he had appeared at every camp—a see-all, know-all commander in charge of all POW facilities in Hanoi. He had delighted in seeing us squirm under his torture, but now he seemed to be doing a bit of squirming himself. His command was reduced to one camp, Hoa Lo. His demotion had been a result of the change in the Hanoi regime, no doubt, and he looked worn and a little frightened. I wondered if perhaps he had been the scapegoat for the new regime as they implemented their new policy of "leniency" in the POW camps.

We discovered very quickly that the military structure among the POWs was in chaos. Few prisoners were actively communicating—it took us days to locate Coker and McKnight in the Mint—and command among the POWs was in the hands of navy commanders who were not the senior officers.

Where was Jim Stockdale? Cat's comment to Denton that Stockdale was "tranquil" terrified me. What had they done to him since removing him from Alcatraz? What would have made him relinquish command of the camp?

I heard Lamar's whispered voice coming from the shower stall next to me a few days after our arrival in Hoa Lo.

"Stockdale's in the Thunderbird, but he can't talk."

We were all terribly worried about our SRO. After a few more snatched conversations and surreptitious communications during siesta, we learned that the North Vietnamese had given him a roommate who vowed to turn him in to the Vietnamese if he tried to communicate.

An Air Force lieutenant colonel I'll call Harry James (for his family's sake) had survived a crash in an F-51 a few years earlier, but he was left with severe and painful burn scars. He seemed to have his own agenda about fighting the North Vietnamese, and it did not include getting caught in the crossfire when Stockdale resumed his aggressive war of resistance from the Thunderbird. Knowing this, Stockdale was afraid to try to command while sharing a cell with him. He was afraid Harry James's presence could jeopardize the safety of the men under his command.

That was not Stockdale's only fear, however. He had endured so much physical and emotional battering that he worried that, in his weakened state, he might make an unwise decision that would undermine the resistance effort or cause more trouble for the other POWs. He was afraid his thinking might be unclear, and he would inadvertently damage the position of the war effort. For these reasons, he had reluctantly relinquished command to the next in rank—navy commanders Bill Lawrence and Byron Fuller. (Only months later would I learn the extent of the awful tortures Stockdale had suffered.)

The task that faced Lawrence and Fuller was monumental. Morale among the POWs in Hoa Lo had sunk to its lowest point. Over the many months and years of imprisonment, most of the prisoners had begun to suffer from "battle fatigue." They were tired of resisting. The propaganda programs that played hour after hour on the camp radio began to sound possible and plausible to many of them. They began to doubt their reasons for resisting. A few may have given up fighting altogether. It was difficult just to exist under the constant barrage from the Vietnamese telling us we could be in prison forever, or for the rest of our lives.

Even some of our staunchly conservative compatriots had begun to wobble in their resistance of the enemy. That first week back in Hoa Lo, we heard the familiar voices of Jim Lamar and Bill Franke reading communist radio scripts over Radio Hanoi. Jerry Denton, whose rank now made him SRO at Hoa Lo, stepped up to command, "No more tapes for the Vietnamese!"

Neither Lamar nor Franke had considered it "cooperating" with the Vietnamese when they acquiesced and agreed to read on the air. In fact, they deliberately butchered the communist propaganda by mispronouncing words and accenting the wrong syllables to distract from the meaning of the messages. Whenever the word "guerrillas" appeared in the script they dragged the first syllable and made it sound like "go-rillas." Of course, only the American POWs recognized or appreciated the humor.

Because reading on the air gave them access to the entire camp, Lamar and Franke also figured that they might be able to communicate surreptitiously with the rest of the POWs. The opportunity, however, never arose.

To Denton, an American voice on Radio Hanoi only served to give credence to the communists' message and enabled their lies to be delivered in easily understood English. Whether intending to or not, anyone who voluntarily read communist scripts on the radio was aiding the enemy efforts. He ordered it to stop.

Cat proudly showed Denton articles in the propaganda magazines, such as *New Outlook,* that had been written by American POWs. Still other prisoners had written short propaganda pieces parroting the North Vietnamese point of view. The table in the "library," the small building between the Stardust and the Desert Inn, was covered with samples of POWs' writing skills. We who had come from Alcatraz were appalled.

The North Vietnamese had begun to win the propaganda war here. It was obvious that the prisoners were doing whatever they were told to do without having to be pressured or tortured. The BACK U.S. policy that had been implemented earlier was forgotten. Resistance had died a quiet death.

There was a desperate need in Hoa Lo for new hope and fresh courage for resisting. Perhaps the Alkies could supply a generous dose of both. We had figured out that Hanoi was now under the reins of a less stringent regime, one that favored less of a hardline approach to the treatment of POWs. We had proven that we could resist their orders and not be tortured into submission. Instead of pressing harder to gain their ends, the prison authority simply gave up when we refused to obey. Now we had to convince the prisoners at Hoa Lo of these facts—that they could resist without suffering for it; that there was no longer any reason to cooperate with the Vietnamese—that *they* were now the paper tigers, able to snarl and snap at us, but no longer able to destroy us.

There were about eighty prisoners in the Vegas strip, and we were sure that we could get the message out to all of them. A handful of POWs were housed outside the strip, beyond a wall and a complex of offices, in what we had dubbed New Guy Village. But the rest of the camp was empty of prisoners. It would be difficult to get the word to the POWs outside the strip, but we felt in time we would be able to make contact. We would do whatever we could to make sure that every man in Hoa Lo prison learned of the change in Hanoi's philosophy toward the POWs.

Denton's passion was always communication. Immediately upon our return to Hoa Lo, he inaugurated a routine that we all hoped would begin to restore a sense of military order to the camp. It started in the Stardust. We all talked on the wall every day at noon. The danger of being caught was slim because a guard couldn't come in without first being seen, and we didn't believe we were at risk of punishment even if we *were* caught. All but Shumaker were glad of the daily conversations.

Denton's brash communications had always bothered Shumaker, even in Alcatraz. I have to admit that, at first, Denton's "cough-hauwk-spit" stuff had made me a little uneasy too, but with the changes in Hanoi, I felt more comfortable these days. I really believed we could risk defiance of the prison rules without fear of beatings, deprivation, or any of the other sadistic forms of punishment the Vietnamese had employed on us.

Shumaker, however, was worried about attracting attention that might cause the prison authority to scrutinize his other activities. He was one of the few POWs who was allowed to write letters home, and he was a master at encoding his postcard-size letters with POW names and intelligence information such as abbreviated accounts of torture and brutality. His greatest fear was that he would be caught and accused of spying. The thought of jeopardizing our tenuous communication link with the United States horrified him and made him a little less confident about some of the other aggressive communication ideas that were proposed.

During those first early days back at Hoa Lo, Lamar and Franke led the way, and soon POWs in the other Vegas cellblocks began to respond to us. We stood on our bunks in the Stardust and whispered loudly when the coast was clear. We used the few minutes in the shower to tap to the man in the next stall. That was how we learned that Coker and McKnight were stashed in two of the three tiny dark hovels in the Mint. In the third was another prisoner who, like Coker and McKnight, had attempted an escape.

In the spring of 1969, Ed Atterberry and John Dramesi had escaped over the wall of the Zoo. Their escape plan was well thought out, including makeshift costumes that would allow them to blend in with the Vietnamese once they made it into the steets of the city. One rainy night, while the guards were preoccupied with staying dry, they slipped out of the Zoo undetected and made their way toward freedom. A search party found them at first light, no more than about five or six miles from the prison, hiding behind a wall of bushes. They hadn't realized that the Zoo sat right in the middle of a division-size military unit. Their plan had been doomed to failure from the beginning.

Back at the Zoo, both Dramesi and Atterberry were isolated and tortured brutally for more than a month. Dramesi survived. Atterberry did not.

Once we made contact with the Thunderbird, Stockdale sent word for Denton to keep command a little longer while he recouped and figured out how best to deal with the presence of Harry James.

We whispered and tapped in the shower and in our cells; we signaled anyone in sight at any time—we were consumed with the need to get word out: The Vietnamese policy has changed! They won't punish you anymore! Refuse to do anything they ask you to do!

Slowly, over a period of days, fear lessened its grip on the camp. In a kind of semaphore, messages were flashed across the yard from one cellblock to another. Stories of what had gone on in Hoa Lo began to unfold. We were surprised to learn that there were four full colonels here in Hoa Lo with us, living in Desert Inn. But none of them had taken command of the camp. The word was that they had been tortured and pushed to the point where they believed they could not make a move without the Vietnamese dragging them off to quiz or torture.

Our experience had shown that the worst treatment was usually dished out to the highest ranking officers, in the hope that when they caved in, the junior officers would quickly follow suit. No doubt the four colonels had suffered greatly. They had decided, as a group, to step back and do nothing that would cause the Vietnamese to inflict more punishment on them. Together, they made the decision to isolate themselves from the other POWs and to abdicate their authority as senior military officers.

Like Stockdale, they had experienced torture and deprivation; but unlike Stockdale, they had never aligned themselves with the other POWs. They continually refused to communicate, offered no leadership to the prisoners who, much like a loose band of individuals, struggled alone and finally acquiesced under pressure from the enemy. The mystery of Hoa Lo's serious morale problem was at least partially solved for me. I could understand how difficult it must have been to stand strong in resistance when there was no support from the men who were supposed to be in leadership.

Fairness compels me to repeat, however, that I have learned that each person's level of resistance is different. No two have the same threshold of pain. What would cause one to crumple to the floor in agony might be no more than a major discomfort to another. And I know too, from firsthand experience, that the Vietnamese were patient and tenacious in their efforts to find each man's point of final resistance. Who knows what atrocities the Vietnamese inflicted or threatened that drove the four colonels so deeply into themselves that they chose to remain outside the military chain of command?

How thankful I am for the strong support I found in Denton and the others during the severe test of Alcatraz.

The last two weeks of 1969 passed quickly. Christmas came and went with little acknowledgement, except for the carols that played on the radio and the acute attacks of homesickness that always accompanied that season. The new decade, 1970, began with little fanfare.

We learned one morning from Lamar and Franke that the four colonels were being moved out of Desert Inn. Some of the Alkies watched through their windows as the four were marched out. Tapping and whispering at the showers later told us they had been moved in with the handful of POWs in New Guy Village. The Desert Inn now had room for Coker and McKnight, and Dramesi was moved into the tiny cell across the hall from me.

"Johnson," I tapped to identify myself to Dramesi as soon as I was sure the guard had left the building.

No reply.

I tapped again. And again. Still no answering taps.

Later, during siesta, I tried whispering across the hall. Finally, Dramesi answered.

"Why didn't you answer my taps?" I asked him. I knew he could hear me. The sounds reverberated through the concrete walls like thumps on a bongo drum.

"I can't tap," he answered.

"Sure you can."

"No, I never learned."

I couldn't believe it. He had been in prison five years and he hadn't learned the tap code!

"Don't worry," I whispered. "I'll teach you."

For weeks, I tried to get Dramesi on the wall. He made some small progress, but he was terribly slow, and for some reason he was reluctant to clear for guards so that I could tap. Whispering to him was difficult through the tiny, barred window on my door, as well as risky. After getting caught several times, I felt disgusted. Even though we didn't expect the kind of punishment dished out in the past, it was still unnerving to have the door thrown open and an armed guard push me onto the bunk and shout, "No talk! No talk! You be punished!" I finally just gave up trying to teach Dramesi how to tap.

To me, he was an enigma. He had one thing only on his mind: escape. Maybe he believed that learning to communicate in this place was a concession to the reality that he was here for the duration of the war. I never figured it out. The code was complicated, but with practice it could be learned, yet Dramesi wouldn't practice. His inability to communicate further isolated him from the strength and support of his fellow officers. His loneliness must have been intense. I pitied him, but I wasn't sorry when he was soon moved into the Desert Inn with Coker and McKnight. Maybe they could teach him to tap.

In the weeks that followed our return to Hoa Lo, we continued to see evidences that prisoners were still disregarding the code of conduct and ignoring the BACK U.S. policy. It was especially obvious at the noon meal when clusters of prisoners could be seen sitting outside at tables in the center courtyard, eating in the sunshine and visiting freely with each other, while others were still being isolated. It was an unheard-of liberty for most of us. This lack of unity infuriated the Alkies. From his cell window, Shumaker had a clear view of prisoners chatting, enjoying the freedom to eat outside, and he nearly bellowed with rage.

"They're taking special favors," he whispered too loudly across the hall to Denton.

"Even their food is different," Jenkins whispered. "They're getting bananas and fruit while we're getting garbage!" Up and down the wall, our party line echoed our anger and disgust. Every man in the Stardust could hear the conversation.

"They are obviously cooperating with the enemy," Denton said. "We'll get word to them," he vowed. "No one is to take any privileges unless everybody gets them. Don't *anybody* accept privileges!"

It was not an easy task to convince hungry prisoners that they should not accept extra portions of food; that they should return to their cells to eat alone, like the rest of us, instead of eating outside together in the courtyard; that they should return to the hard stance of refusing to give the North Vietnamese any cooperation on any issue. They were not willing or ready to return to torture. They were reluctant to believe us that they could resist and not be punished.

One day, a surprising occurrence within the camp helped finally convince the prisoners in Hoa Lo that Hanoi had indeed changed its thinking toward its prisoners. A guard opened the door on Tanner and Shumaker's cell and escorted them to an interrogation room. They walked into the room expecting to face an officer at his desk, but instead they found a ping-pong table and a small French pool table.

"Go," the guard muttered. He nodded toward the pool table and the cues in the corner and stepped aside to make room for them to play. Tanner and Shumaker shrugged and arranged the balls on the miniature-sized table and played for about half an hour. Then the guard escorted them back to their cell.

Life for the American POWs was indeed changing. A stint in the game room was scheduled for every prisoner; exercise periods continued; and by February, 1970, every prisoner in the Vegas strip was given a roommate. No more solitary confinement—except for one troublesome prisoner who was not yet deserving of this privilege. I alone remained in solitary confinement.

Even Denton, who had been in solitary for all but four months of his captivity, was not alone. He and Mulligan were together in the cell across from me. Every day I wondered when I would be given a roommate.

By now, communications were climbing to a sophisticated level. With all of Vegas participating, we had been able to establish note drops in the game room and in the shower and had made contact with the other cellblocks within the camp. I was in the middle of the communication system, tapping and whispering with the rest of the men, but the long months of living alone were beginning to take a toll on me.

For more than three years now I had been solo. In earlier months, I had been able to draw strength from just knowing my friends were nearby, from hearing their voices and their constant tapping. But suddenly, the knowledge that I was the only one left alone was oppressive. I imagined my buddies playing chess together, talking in the cells without fear and caution; I visualized them eating together and playing pool in the game room. The awfulness of being alone overwhelmed me.

"We'll do something about it, Sam," Denton tapped to me on the wall.

"Hang on, buddy, you'll be all right," Mulligan whispered.

As SRO, Denton spoke to Cat about me and demanded I be given a roommate, like all the other prisoners.

"Ah, Denton, I am your good uncle," Cat answered. "I have good nephews and bad nephews. Johnson is a bad nephew. He will never have roommate."

Jerry gave me the news, but promised, "Don't worry, Sam, We'll think of something."

For prisoners who lived together in pairs, the trip to the shower was a great opportunity for communication with the other men in the Vegas strip. One man could clear while the other man tapped. But I had no one to clear for me, and no way to do it for myself. I couldn't raise myself up to look over the shower stall and see a friendly face because my shoulders were still too weak. The solitary walk to the shower became for me another reminder of how alone I was.

Before, when every man had been in solitary, tapping had been our primary occupation. But now that everyone else in Vegas had a roommate and they could talk freely to each other, the tapping tailed off and the party line was often quiet, except at noon. I grew more and more discouraged.

Weeks passed. My spirits sank even lower. Sometimes I sat silently on the hard bunk in my cramped cell and felt hot tears spill down my cheeks. I tried to pray, but some days the words would not come. Loneliness overwhelmed me.

Spring came, bringing warm days and a reminder of how quickly the hot summer would arrive. I thought about the hordes of droning insects and the intense, damp heat that would soon make my days and nights even more miserable. I could not summon any trace of my usual optimism.

Denton and Mulligan, in the cell across from me, did their best to encourage me, but nothing seemed to help. The visits to the game room, alone, seemed to underline my solitude. The guard stood and watched as I made clumsy gestures at playing French pool by myself. I joked half heartedly about being behind the eight ball, but there was very little humor in me any more. I always returned to my cell more disheartened than before.

A couple of weeks before Easter, the camp radio began to talk about the celebration of that holy day in the States. Thinking about past Easters, with Shirley and the children, brought on an intense bout of homesickness.

On Easter Sunday, a guard showed up at my door and commanded, "Dress up."

Inside the quiz room, the interrogation table was laden with candies, cookies, and fruit, and beside this feast lay an open Bible. A Vietnamese officer and a Vietnamese man wearing clerical clothes stood behind the table.

"Hello," the officer said, smiling broadly and gesturing toward a chair. "Take seat. So, now you visit with evangelical priest. Here, tea."

I sat down and accepted the cup of warm tea. The preacher looked at me intently. Something about him made me believe that he understood everything that was being said, but the officer, no doubt a party member, acted as interpreter for us. His presence in the room with us was required.

"That looks like a Bible," I said to the preacher.

"It is," the officer answered for the preacher, delighted that I had noticed the carefully arranged prop set out to give credibility to this pretense of religious freedom.

"I'd like to read some passages out of it," I ventured.

"No, you may look at it, but no read," the officer answered.

"It probably isn't even a Bible," I taunted him.

The officer picked it up and held it so that I could see the lettering on the black leather cover. The preacher began to speak, and the officer repeated his words in English.

"The Vietnamese people offer you an Easter service, one for all pro-*test*-ants and one for Catholics. The Vietnamese people wish you to share their religious freedom."

"If you allow religious freedom, why won't you allow me to read the Bible?" I asked.

"Is not allowed," he answered, frowning.

"I don't believe it's even a Bible," I told him, and he merely shrugged.

"Take candy, eat!" he gestured to the table covered with food. "Drink tea."

I grabbed a handful of cookies and some fruit and sipped the cup of tea. I couldn't take my eyes off the beauty of that black leather book. I wanted nothing so badly as to hold it and read the words of Jesus or some of David's Psalms. But the Vietnamese government did not allow men to read the Bible. In earlier days, these absurd observations of our national and Christian holidays had been amusing, even entertaining.

I had looked forward to the diversion their strange "celebrations" offered us. But this time it was just terribly depressing. It was all so farcical.

*Just let me out of here,* I thought, angered and frustrated until I remembered the awful emptiness of the cell I would return to. I was suddenly very tired. Back in my cell, I sat alone and thought, *It's too much. I can't go on any longer.*

Over the next weeks, desperation set in. I was hungry, weak, and tired of trying to be strong. I couldn't sleep. I stood and paced the tiny space in my cell until I fell on my bunk in exhaustion. *Why are they doing this to me?* I asked over and over again. And then I answered my own question: *They hate me. They want to break me.*

My body began to pay the price of total despair. It was too much effort to stand up straight. My shoulders felt heavy and slumped. My rolling Texas gait, once so energetic and decisive, was now the pathetic shuffle of an old man. The walk to the shower seemed longer every day. I was worn out by the time I returned to my cell.

For the first time, I recognized that I was close to breaking. I was helpless against this enemy. There was nothing I could do. In the past, I had been able to outwit them. But now, I was weak and empty. I had no strength for fighting anymore. I was suddenly very afraid.

Only once before during my captivity had I felt so close to breaking. I remembered the days I had spent in the Mint when loneliness had been my fiercest enemy; when I had been so hungry that I had been willing to eat water bugs in my cell. I had thought then that I had reached the end of my endurance, but I had survived. I had clung to God, determined to keep on believing that he had not forgotten me. He would not forsake me! I had hung on to Him and the horror had subsided.

At that time, I had come to a place of total release; all that I had and all that I was lay in God's hands, and I knew I trusted Him totally to do with me as He pleased. It was time to return to that place of release again. Sobbing, I cried out to God and gave Him all my fear, my loneliness, my desperation. It was a slow work, but I knew it was the only way I would find solace.

Twenty years later, I listened to a theologian's discourse on the book of Job. With an academician's logic, he criticized the flow of the work, theorizing that the stages of grief were incorrect; that emotions under such circumstances would not follow the order laid out in the chapters of Job. I knew instantly that this man's knowledge was intellectual, not experiential. I knew he had never suffered the awful pain that tore Job's heart.

I knew, because I had lived part of Job's agony—separated from my family, buried alive among cruel enemies, covered from head to foot with awful boils—oh, yes, the progression of grief that Job describes is exactly the way it occurs. From grief to grief, and finally to relief, but only by way of complete release.

Because there was no other way to go, I went down on my knees. Because I could hold on no longer, I let go and felt the everlasting arms of God catch me up in love. I felt myself enfolded by God and comforted as only God can comfort. I will never forget the sense of His presence when I was cut off from all other sources of companionship. In those days of utter desperation, God transformed my awful cell into a shrine of worship. I began to regain my courage, and with it came renewed determination to resist the enemy.

The prison authority's continued refusal to take me out of solitary confinement was a deliberate and blatant violation of the Geneva Conventions. As I discovered new strength, I began to think about the avenues of resistance that were open to me. The only one that presented itself to me was a hunger strike. Like Storz, it was the only area of my life over which I had been able to retain any measure of control. It was the only leverage I had to pry Cat out of his stubborn stance.

If, as we suspected, a release was imminent, the prison authority would not want me to fast for very long. Cat would have to relent soon or be embarrassed when my emaciated appearance contradicted Hanoi's claims of "lenient and humane treatment." I prayed about it, talked to Denton about it, and determined it was worth a try. After all, our positions as POWs obligated us to resist the enemy in every way possible. For me, this was the only route open.

I began eating only about one-fourth of the food on my tray. The Vietnamese noticed right away and began putting larger portions on my plate, but I ate only a few spoonfuls at each meal. One night, after I had sent the evening meal back almost untouched, a guard opened my cell and ordered, "Dress up."

"Where am I going?" I asked, when Cat showed up.

"Ah, Johnson, you have been chosen to go on a visit to our museum," he answered.

"I don't think I want to go," I answered. *It's got to be some kind of propaganda exercise.* I didn't want to risk being filmed outside the prison camp, where my activities might be construed as supportive or accepting of the Vietnamese policies. "I'd like to talk to Denton about this."

"Denton is going too!" Cat beamed.

I was suspicious, but as with all matters in this prison, I had no real choice. A few minutes later I climbed on a bus and found myself in the company of about ten other pajama-clad prisoners. Denton was not among them, nor was there any familiar face.

*Oh, no,* I thought. *This was a real mistake.*

I sat alone up front, separated from the other POWs with a guard beside me, as the bus pulled out of the prison yard and merged into Hanoi's city traffic. In a few minutes, we arrived at a massive, French-built brick building and climbed off the bus to walk, single file, through what I guessed was a history museum. The "glorious history of Vietnam" was illustrated and photographed for us on every wall.

Simple, unsophisticated drawings hung behind glass on the walls. Crumbling, broken pieces of urns and dishes lay on shelves and in glass cases. There was nothing grand or large or impressive. Drab and colorless displays, constructed out of crude materials, stood in every hallway. Some hung crookedly, others drooped, and all of them looked as though school children had put them together. I thought of the Smithsonian Institution back home and realized again how primitive this culture was, compared to our own.

Vietnamese civilians wandered through the wide hallways. They looked as if they had just come from the office or the classroom. They belonged to a different level of society than people I had seen before, and our appearance was obviously strange to them as well. With our gaunt, unshaven faces and our dirty prison-issue pajamas, we were an unusual group. Little clusters of Vietnamese stepped aside and whispered to each other as we paraded through the halls.

I looked around constantly, watching for cameras that might be filming this "field trip" as proof of the Vietnamese "lenient and humane treatment." I never saw any, but I was uncomfortable anyway. Our guards pushed us forward, let us take fruit and cookies from a table set up in one room, as if we had been a visiting delegation, and then walked us back out to the bus again. A guard sat next to me in the front to make sure I had no conversation with any other prisoners.

As we drove away, I thought, *They still haven't given up their goal of changing our view of the war. They still believe they can influence us to come over to their side.*

Back in my cell, I shook my head and wondered at the thinking of this people. Had they really been hopeful that a little field trip to a museum would persuade us to join them in their "glorious revolution"?

There was little change in my life after that. No cellmate, and no reason to believe I would be getting one soon. Denton decided it was time to do something for me. His decision to inaugurate a voluntary fast among all the men in Vegas was met with some resistance. It was still a scary thing to defy blatantly the prison authority or to organize a rebellion within the system. Men had been beaten and thrown in for a session with the ropes for such things. The POWs in Hoa Lo weren't totally convinced that they could get away with such disregard for the prison rules without incurring severe punishment. And they weren't convinced it would do any good.

"Start small, just a few men a time. Eat only half rations. Pass it on," Denton said. "It will move like a spontaneous response, not like an organized rebellion. We've got to try."

For two weeks in early May, the half-fast continued. Cat made some vague promises, the fast ended, and some prisoners were allowed to go from one cellblock to another to visit. But I remained in my cell alone in the Stardust.

I stopped eating altogether. Oh, how hard it was to refuse to eat when I was so hungry all the time. But I soon learned that when hunger reaches a certain point, a sort of stupor sets in. At times, I nibbled on fruit or bread, just enough to keep from keeling over, and I drank every drop of tea and water I received. I was already skinny, and in only a few days I looked near death. My six-foot, two-inch frame weighed only about 125 pounds. But still Cat made no move to give me a cellmate.

I waited each day for noon to arrive when everyone in the Stardust communicated together. During the other long hours of isolation I practiced my French. Shumaker continued to give me words to learn, and I categorized them all alphabetically in my mind and practiced verb conjugations.

That spring, 1970, Cat began letting me write letters home to Shirley for the first time since my capture and imprisonment, perhaps as some sort of compensation for keeping me in solitary. I was thankful for both the emotional consolation and mental stimulation writing gave me, but I discovered it was also a terribly frustrating undertaking.

The limp and paralyzed fingers of my mangled right hand had atrophied. I could not even grip a pencil, much less print a letter on paper. I tried again and again, but every attempt ended with the pen clattering to the floor and my anger erupting in a muffled curse. I had no choice but to learn to write with my left hand. This was no easy task. Awkward and irritated, I practiced the alphabet like a kid with a primer. Every letter to Shirley was a slow, tedious project.

I was slowed down even more by the fact that I was sending coded messages in each letter. Shumaker had taught me how while we were in Alcatraz, and I welcomed this chance to get involved finally in the effort to get the names of POWs out of Hanoi, along with other bits of information valuable to the U.S. military.

Since the guards allowed only a few minutes to write the letter when they brought me the pen and the form to write on, I spent many hours each day planning what I wanted to write. I mentally encoded the message, memorized how it had to be written, and then reviewed it throughout the day until the guards brought the writing materials. Then, while the guard stood and watched, I wrote as quickly as I could (which was quite slow, actually). I signed each letter feeling satisfied, victorious.

Of course, every letter was censored, but it was nothing more than a ridiculous formality.

"You can't write that like that," Cat would say of my letter. "Write it this way . . ."

He didn't really care what I wrote as long as I said the positive propaganda stuff—"the treatment is good, I am well . . ." Hidden and encoded in the generalities were the POW names, and between the lines lay desperate longings for my wife and children.

For four long years Shirley had waited for a letter from me and now, finally, she held one in her hands. But something was terribly wrong. The handwriting was shaky and labored; the letters slanted to the left instead of to the right. Although the unfamiliar scrawling was difficult to decipher, Shirley knew with certainty that I had written it. But with that certainty came a sense of unease. Through a blur of tears, she read the cryptic message I had worked so hard to compose.

*He's all right, I know he's all right . . . ,* she told herself over and over. *There's a good explanation, I know there is. . . .*

Under instructions from the air force, Shirley forwarded my letter to military intelligence to be examined for a coded message. Not only did they decipher the hidden message, but they also secured a handwriting analyst because the writing in the letter was so different from my normal style. The analyst's conclusion gave Shirley more cause for concern.

"Major Johnson wrote this letter with his left hand," an intelligence officer told Shirley.

"That can't be," Shirley argued. "He's right-handed."

"We're quite sure," the officer repeated. "The analysis of his handwriting indicates he has been through a lot, but he has come through with strength. He's okay."

*I don't believe it,* Shirley told herself, trying to suppress her fear. *That would mean he's lost the use of his right hand. No, I won't believe it. It's got to be something else. He's probably using a concrete surface to write on— that's why the writing is so shaky and uneven. It has to be that . . .*

Our oldest son, Bobby, was in his first year of college when my first letter arrived in Texas. Shirley wanted to tell him about the letter in person, not over the phone, so she waited until he came home for a weekend visit, and then she ran into his arms with the news.

"Your dad is alive! He's all right!"

She stood dumbfounded when he answered without much emotion, "I've always known he was alive, Mom. I always knew he was okay." Bobby never stopped believing. Many years later, when I was getting acquainted with the man he had become, I learned that he chose physics as his major at Texas A&M because he thought I would be proud of him.

I was already proud of my son long before I knew of his academic achievements. And of my daughters, Gini and Beverly, as well. Shirley's letters were short and obviously strained after military intelligence rewrote them to accommodate its coded messages, but the love and strength of all my family came through even the most awkwardly worded sentences. They were fighting hard with me and for me. I was immensely proud of their courage and strength. And terribly lonely for each one of them.

As my solitary confinement continued, I grew so starved for human companionship that I counted the hours and then the minutes until it was time for my daily walk to the shower. I always hoped I would catch a glimpse of a friend. One day I saw Lamar go into the stall next to mine. There was little time for conversing because a guard stood in front of the door, but I tapped, "Hi."

"God bless you," he tapped back softly, and I returned to my cell feeling better than I had in days.

Another day, while standing under the shower pipe, I heard a "psst" and looked up to see McKnight's face hanging over the wall grinning at me. The guard nearby looked up and screeched, "No! No!" He rushed into the shower stall and hauled McKnight down. He hollered and stormed and stomped his feet while McKnight pulled on his clothes, and then hurried him back to his cell.

A few days later, I was again in the shower when I heard a soft voice singing, "There are no fighter pilots down in hell . . ." It was McKnight again. He was serenading me, and his off-key voice sounded beautiful. I joined him on the old fighter pilot's chorus, but our concert career was cut short as a guard grabbed McKnight out of the shower and dragged him off again. For days, that old tune hung around my thoughts and brought hot, stinging tears to my eyes.

Day by day, the self-enforced fast continued to reduce my strength. I became so weak that the walk to the game room was almost too much exertion for me. One day, while I stood near the pool table, the room became a gray blur and I felt myself sliding to the floor. The guard found me lying in a heap. I heard his high-pitched voice squealing as if from a great distance. I struggled to pull myself up and lean against the wall until my head cleared. Another guard rushed in and together they half-dragged, half-carried me back to my cell.

A few minutes later, a doctor opened my cell door and put a handful of pills into my hand. I had no idea what they were, but he thrust a cup of water toward me and waited until I swallowed all of the pills. I lay back on the hard bunk and heard the click of the key in the lock as the guard left me alone in my cell.

Denton's tapping roused me out of semiconsciousness.

"Sam, I'm giving you a direct order: Stop the fast. Don't hurt yourself."

It was time to give it up. I had gone as far as I could go in resisting the enemy. I wondered if Cat would relent and give me a cellmate. I wondered if I had starved myself for nothing.

Futility is a ferocious enemy. It attacked unmercifully during those early months of summer, 1970, as we heard reports of the depressing state of the war. Peace negotiations were going nowhere. At home in the United States, the controversy over the war raged across the continent like a brushfire out of control. Radio Hanoi broadcast bloody descriptions of antiwar demonstrations on university campuses. The bitter dissent in our homeland was Hanoi Hannah's favorite topic. Of course, she told us nothing of the activities of United We Stand or the League of Families, or any other positive activities in the United States. We had no knowledge of any efforts being made on our behalf.

In May, the sounds of bombs and gunfire and low-flying planes faded after a last mission which destroyed several North Vietnamese supply dumps. The Defense Department announced that once again there would be a bombing halt. All "large-scale" air raids over the North would cease. The skies over North Vietnam grew silent.

We often wondered what would be our ultimate end. For hundreds of days, thousands of hours, the camp radio had jabbed at us with talk that our country had deserted us. At times I asked myself if it could be true. Would all our resistance be for nothing? Would the United States concede to the noisy, antiwar activists and declare that the war was, in fact, an unjust one? Would they completely withdraw and leave us here without a fight? Would they negotiate our release, or let the communists dispose of us as criminals?

Had I known then of the action of the Senate that summer, June, 1970, my concerns for myself and my fellow POWs would have been even more fearful. The members of the United States Senate voted to repeal the Tonkin Gulf Resolution, withdrawing support for U.S. forces in South Vietnam. It seemed the propagandists we were fighting so painfully here in Hanoi had scored a decisive victory in Washington, D.C.

Only Jerry Denton was able to deliver news that gave me a surge of hope and renewed optimism.

"Sam," he whispered during siesta when the cellblock was empty of guards. "Cat told me you are going to be allowed to visit with Mulligan and me. Try to act surprised when they come to get you or they'll know we've been communicating and they'll call off the visit."

I could hardly contain my excitement. For the next couple of days, I froze every time I heard a sound outside my cell. *Is this the day?* Finally, one morning after breakfast, a guard opened my cell door and said, "Dress up. You're going to visit your friend Denton."

My hands shook as I pulled on my long pants for the walk down the hall to the next room. I had to force myself not to run to Denton and Mulligan's cell. When the door opened, two pairs of skinny arms grabbed me and pulled me into the cell. We hugged and pounded each other on bony backs, and my whole body shook with sobs I had tried to hold back.

They looked much older than men in the prime of their lives. Their faces were thin and haggard. Their shoulders made sharp points under the ragged fabric of their shirts, and Denton's hair was now very gray. But at that moment, they were the most beautiful men alive.

Denton looked at me intently, and tears filled his eyes. He didn't have to say a word to tell me I looked like the walking dead. I had grown so skinny that I could hardly stand, and I too had started to gray. The joy we shared at seeing each other was tainted somewhat by sadness as we saw the evidence of the horrors each had endured.

"Here, have one of these." Mulligan offered me a cigar, and I took it with trembling hands. We all three sat and smoked and laughed and cried. We talked and played cards, and I basked in the wonderful feeling of being with other human beings. I knew it wasn't a permanent arrangement, but it was a change from the awful solitude of my cell. At first, I was terrified the guard would come back for me too soon. Every time I heard a sandal slap against a bare foot in the hallway, my heart lurched in my chest.

When I was allowed to eat my noon meal in the cell with Denton and Mulligan, I thought I would cry again with joy. I intended to eat every bite, but we talked so much that we hardly ate at all. There was so much to say—a thousand things we had wanted to tell each other about our wives and our children!

"Here," Mulligan offered, holding up a pipe. "It came in a package from home. I'll show you how to smoke it."

"For pete's sake, Mulligan, I know how to smoke a pipe," I answered. Let him know I hadn't ever smoked a pipe before? Not a chance.

I watched closely as he stuffed tobacco into the bowl and lit it. It looked easy enough. I fumbled a little, finally got the thing lit, and we sat and puffed together for a while. When the guard returned to take me back to my cell before the evening meal, Mulligan pushed the pipe and a little pouch of tobacco into my hands.

"Take it back to your cell with you," he said. "I've got another one for myself."

My throat ached with the effort to hold back tears as I shook hands with Denton and Mulligan. I couldn't speak to say good night.

The emptiness of my tiny, concrete cublicle was even more oppressive to me after the laughter and fellowship I had enjoyed all day with my two good friends. When the dingy, dust-coated light bulb clicked on at dusk, illuminating the gray solitude of my cell, I reached for the comfort of Mulligan's pipe.

I leaned back against the concrete wall and began stuffing tobacco into the bowl of the pipe. I didn't know I was supposed to pack it down, and so the tobacco lay in a loose pile. I inserted the match deep into the bowl, drew in a long breath, and pulled the flame right into my mouth and down my throat. I screamed and choked, and the pipe clattered onto the concrete floor. I grabbed my teapot and guzzled the little bit of lukewarm tea left in it, but it wasn't enough to put out the fire that seemed to be burning all the way down my esophagus. The next day, when the guard took me to visit my buddies again, I told Mulligan, "Keep your pipe. I'll find something else to keep me busy till I get a roomate." Both Mulligan and Denton enjoyed a good laugh over my pipe-smoking episode.

For the next two days, I spent most of the daylight hours with Denton and Mulligan. We were allowed to go to the game room together, and we challenged each other to pool and ping-pong. I wasn't much of a challenge—it would take me years of practice to become adept at anything as a "lefty"—but I gave it my best effort. We played and talked, and I was buoyed by their companionship. At night, the guards returned me to my cell alone.

Cat was relenting—I was sure of it. But he was going to do it his way, in stages. He didn't want to give the appearance that he had conceded to me in this battle of the wills, but I could smell victory. I began to feel stronger and more hopeful. And a few days later, that hope was rewarded.

"Roll up," the guard in my doorway commanded.

Excited, I quickly rolled my few belongings into the bamboo mat and waited to see what would happen next. The guard motioned me to leave the cell. Moments later I was thrust into the cell that Tanner and Shumaker shared.

The dangling naked light bulb shed just enough light for me to see the two skinny, dirty, unshaven Alkies. In the tiny space between the bunks, we stood and hugged each other. In all the years that he had been teaching me French, I had never had the freedom to speak to Shumaker except in a soft whisper or tap code through a concrete wall. I had never seen either Tanner or Shumaker except in stolen glimpses through a tiny crack in a door or through a rat hole. Now suddenly, I stood in the cell with them, and we could talk to each other without threat of punishment! What I felt at that moment can only be described as pure ecstasy.

My new cell was a four-man cell, though it was hardly sufficient for two. Only slightly larger than the one I had left, it had two bunks on one wall and two more hung on the next. The single high window in the cell was in the third wall to prevent us from being able to stand on a bunk and see outside. But every day Tanner stood on his waste bucket in the corner and cautiously peered over the windowsill to see the goings-on in the courtyard.

Every day at noon, when Vegas communications went into full power, Tanner and I cleared while Shumaker tapped on the wall. Communicating was much easier now, with three men—one to watch the door, one at the window, and another on the wall. Getting caught was no longer a major concern.

It was great to be back in the system again! I felt like part of a news team on network television with Shumaker as the anchor. He reported to Denton everything Tanner had observed out of our window that day, and Denton responded in code. Then Shumaker relayed the news to Tanner and me.

One day, without explanation, Shumaker refused to tap during the noon communications.

"I'm just not going to do it," he said.

"What's wrong, Shu?" I asked him.

"It's just not right today. I don't know what it is, but something's not right. It feels dangerous, I don't know . . ."

Tanner looked at me and shrugged his shoulders.

"It's an order from Denton, Shu," I told him. "We're not going to start disobeying orders *now*, are we?"

"I'm not going to do it, and I don't think you guys ought to either. There's nothing important to talk about today anyway, and I don't think we should risk it."

I was uncomfortable. Denton was in command. If he said communicate at noon, we would communicate at noon. I knew what I had to do.

"Look, Shu, I'm the senior officer in this cell, and I'm going to have to override you on this. We are going to communicate."

Tanner cleared for me, and I tapped on the wall to Denton. It would have been safer for us to have two men clearing and one man tapping, as usual, but Shumaker just sat on his bunk and looked miserable. For the next few days, he spoke only when he had to, and Tanner and I stayed out of his way as much as the cramped space in our cell would allow.

I felt I knew Shumaker well, after all we had been through together over the years. I could only guess, but I figured he was struck with a sudden anxiety attack over the possibility of losing some of the freedoms we had worked and suffered so hard to gain. Maybe he thought if we pushed too hard the Vietnamese would retaliate and the days of horror would return to Hoa Lo. He never said. In a few days he returned to his old self. As a trio, we went to the game room together and took turns playing French pool and ping-pong. In our cell, we played chess and talked and resumed our communications on the wall every day at noon without any further conflicts. In the company of my friends, I began to regain some of the weight I had lost during the fast. And with the return of my strength, my optimistic outlook returned as well.

For Shirley, twelve thousand miles away in Texas, the outlook was grim. That summer was filled with one domestic crisis after another. Gini, our middle daughter, finished driver's education and was driving into the garage when she shoved her foot down onto the accelerator instead of the brake. Shirley screamed and Gini panicked as the car smashed into the wall of the house.

A grease fire erupted in the kitchen that summer, and smoke damaged the entire house. Gini's cat, Charlie, crawled into the clothes dryer and spun around on permanent press until Shirley got suspicious of the odd clunking sound. Shirley opened the dryer door and stared as Charlie crawled out and staggered across the laundry room floor. The poor cat was never the same after that. He started using the fireplace as a litter box, even when there was a fire burning. The smell of singed cat fur mingled with the smoke smells that lingered after the insurance company painted and replaced cabinets, carpet, drapes, and floors.

Although her sense of humor remained strong, Shirley's energies began to wane. Raising three teenagers active in the drill team and sports while maintaining a full schedule of traveling and speaking was a costly drain on her physically and emotionally. She and many other POW-MIA wives were stretched to the limit of their endurance with all the responsibilities that faced them. They simply had to have help. Dallas Cares was formed.

An organization composed friends of the POW-MIA families in the Dallas area, Dallas Cares offered a network of moral support. Members accompanied Shirley and other wives to speaking engagements and often accepted some of the invitations for them. They set up booths at the Texas State Fair and continued the POW-MIA media barrage already in operation. For women like Shirley who were already on overload, they eased the daily burdens, and their voices strengthened the American cry demanding our release and improved treatment.

Throughout the summer of 1970, we continued to see Hanoi's response to that cry. One by one, we were all impacted by the Americans' loud demands that North Vietnam follow the Geneva Conventions; we all experienced improved conditions as a result of the groups working for our cause—it just took a little longer for some to gain those benefits than for others.

It was late in July when Denton tapped on the wall, "Stockdale's going to be moved. Someone talked to him in the shower and he said he asked Cat to move him."

"Where's he going?" Shu tapped back.

Don't know yet," Denton answered. "We'll let you know whatever we find out."

As it turned out, I was the first to learn of Stockdale's new accommodations. It was July and very hot. Mosquitos and flies divebombed around my head, and I could feel myself on the edge of irritability. Tanner and Shumaker were miserable too. We all lay on our bunks trying to avoid any motion that would make us sweat more. I frowned at the sound of a key in our cell door. It wasn't time for a meal or for a shower, and we had already been to the game room. When the guard ordered me to roll up, I felt myself go cold all over.

*Back to solitary! I can't do that again,* I thought. My hands shook as I rolled up my belongings in my bamboo mat. *Please, Lord,* I prayed, *I did forty-two months solo . . . please, no more . . .*

Tanner and Shumaker shook my hand and hugged me. The guard pushed them aside and muttered, "Quickee, quickee!" He led me a few steps down the narrow dingy corridor and around the corner. He opened a nearby door and thrust me into a tiny cell.

I couldn't believe this was happening. Solitary again! I dropped my roll of belongings on the narrow bunk and slumped against the cement wall. In the next instant, the guard reappeared and prodded me toward the tiny cell across the hall. He unlocked the door and pushed me inside where a startled Jim Stockdale stared at me. I gasped and threw myself at him. He met me with a huge bearhug. For many long minutes we stood and cried in each other's arms while the guard locked us in together.

Stockdale looked twenty years older than his age. His skin was sallow and his face gaunt. His lusterless eyes had lost their intensity, and when he sat down on the edge of the bunk, his hands fidgeted. The serene strength that had characterized him when I first met him was gone. In its place was fear and such absolute sadness that it was almost a physical presence in the cell.

The guard didn't bother us for several hours. I guessed that this was supposed to be an all-day visit. When the noon communications on the wall began that day, I sent the message, "Stockdale's here in the Stardust."

Denton sent back the question, "Does Stockdale want to take command?"

I looked at Stockdale. His white head hung low, and he answered softly, "No, I'm not on my feet yet . . ."

I tapped the answer back to Denton, "Remain in command for a while yet."

I felt real physical pain when I looked at my commander. He jumped every time he heard sounds in the hallway. His eyes, with their deep, dark circles, had a haunted look to them. But the thing that gave me the greatest pain was the way his conversation was confused and halting, as if he couldn't remember what he wanted to say or quite how to say it.

Since first meeting Jim Stockdale, I had reveled in listening to him talk. His brilliance in the fields of philosophy, military history, classical literature, and almost any other topic could hold one spellbound. But now, his thoughts were disjointed. He tried to tell me about his experiences since leaving Alcatraz, but his thoughts trailed off unfinished, and he often sat and stared as if lost somewhere in a confusing maze of memories.

I tried to control the terror and anguish I felt.

*He'll get better*, I told myself. *All he needs is a little time . . . I'll help him understand that the horrors of the old days are behind us. He'll get over this . . . Oh, Lord Jesus, please let him get better!*

I told him softly, "Jim, since Ho Chi Minh's death, things have changed. You don't have to worry about torture any more. The Vietnamese are under new orders now. They can't pressure you into relenting if you refuse to cooperate with them. We can resist without being punished."

Jim shook his head. He just couldn't believe it was true.

"Watch. I'm going to prove it to you. When the guard comes around, you let me do the talking. You'll see."

The opportunity came soon. That afternoon, Cat called us in to quiz together. I stepped forward a little, to stand in front of Jim, as if my presence could shield him from the unpleasantness of this encounter. Cat sat at his desk, eyeing us carefully, as if not sure what he should expect. His lips quivered. He seemed reluctant to say what he had to say, afraid almost.

"Ah, Song, you and Stockdale together again. But you must be good. You will obey the rules. If you don't, you will not be allowed visits. If you continue in disobedience, we will punish you."

It was vague talk. I knew when the Vietnamese talked like this it was nothing more than dribble. I waited to see what he would ask of us.

Cat shoved a piece of paper across the desk toward us. I picked it up and looked at it. It was propaganda gibberish.

"If you are truly repentant, you will write this. You will agree to obey all the camp rules."

I could sense Stockdale's alarm. I could almost smell the fear coming off of him. He had been through so much; he was terrified it would all begin again. He knew he had to resist them, but he was afraid he wouldn't be able to hold out for very long.

I clutched his wrist and answered quickly for both of us. "No, we're not going to write that."

I heard Jim's sharply inhaled breath. He stood still and waited while Cat responded as I knew he would. He blustered and blew and made a few threats and sent us back to our cell. A few minutes after the door had shut behind us, the guard returned and gave us a deck of playing cards.

Over the next few days, Jim and I visited together in his cell during the daylight hours. We played cards together and went to the game room together, and he began to talk to me. In halting, slow words, he told me of the months spent in isolation in a tiny, hot box of a cell called Calcutta. The worst that the enemy could conceive of had been inflicted on him. He had survived the ropes, deprivation, beatings, and every sort of inhumane treatment. He had defeated the North Vietnamese at their own game, but the cost had been great.

On one occasion, he was ordered to face a film crew to make a propaganda message. Stockdale was too weak to resist him now, the camp commander mistakenly believed; the recent barrage of torture had taken the resistance out of him. But no, this time Stockdale had his own game plan. He deliberately smashed his face against anything he could find in his cell until his eyes swelled, purple bruises covered his cheeks and chin, and blood seeped from jagged cuts. The Vietnamese swore when they saw him. It would not do to set him in front of a camera in this condition. It would take weeks for the cuts to heal and the bruises to fade. Jim's film career was put on hold.

It was a major victory for him, but like the rest of us, there were other times when he had had no such options available. After emotional and physical batterings that left him nearly dead, he had done what all of us had done—he had written propaganda garbage in order to preserve his life and limbs. And he had lost confidence that he would ever be able to resist the enemy again. He felt he was too beaten down to ever be able to win against this enemy again. When finally placed in a cell, he had been further demoralized by the presence of Harry James, who vowed to report all Jim's actions to the North Vietnamese. Stockdale feared there was no one he could trust.

When tapped communications came into the cell while we were together, he let me do all the tapping. He just sat quietly and sadly on his bunk, saying little and looking bruised and broken.

After about two weeks in the Stardust with the Alkies, I noticed Jim squaring his shoulders when he walked out of the cell toward the shower or the game room. The crisp, solid commander's stance that had once characterized him returned. My attempts to draw him into conversation were rewarded with his profound observations. His thoughts were again cohesive and powerful. He took his place on the wall and began tapping his own communications to the rest of the cellblock. The only thing that bothered me was that he resumed his old habit of consistently beating me at chess.

By the end of the summer, Stockdale was ready to take command again. Fire lit his eyes, and the intensity of old radiated from him. Denton graciously conceded to the senior ranking officer, and a feeling of joy swept through Vegas. Things were back as they should be. I felt a personal sense of victory.

In October, 1970, Stockdale and I were allowed to visit Tanner and Shumaker for a few hours each day. Tanner, from his position at the window, was still the lookout for the Stardust, and every day he reported on the routine of the four silent colonels as they made their daily trip to the showers in Vegas. The men walked in single file, with the guard at the rear, so it was possible for the man in front to respond, if only he would.

"Try writing a note," Shu suggested. "Just hold it up in the window when they walk by. Maybe we can get them to write one back."

The next day there were five, nor four, colonels brought past our window. Tanner whispered, "Pssst! Psst!" One of the colonels looked up. It was Robbie Risner. His whole face lit up with excitement as he saw a message crudely written on brown, rough toilet paper.

"Write note," the message read.

The next day, Tanner held up another note that read, "Pool room under right table leg."

The next day, when our foursome went to the game room, we found our first note from New Guy Village, and we left one of our own for them. Finally! A link was established with the next compound.

We established secret note drops throughout the compound: in the showers under a brick; in the game room in the light fixture—wherever we thought we could hide a tiny scrap of paper. It was always a little risky, of course, because we never knew who would find the notes first—a POW or a guard. But it gave us a great feeling of unity to be connected with nearly all the prisoners in the camp. Only the Thunderbird remained outside the chain.

Harry James's presence was the broken link. Communications with the Thunderbird had to be limited to notes left in the shower or latrine in specially planned places for the T-bird guys. We couldn't sent any tapped messages over to them. No one trusted James not to relay everything he heard back to the North Vietnamese.

Now that communications had been established with the colonels, Stockdale sent word to Risner to take over as senior ranking officer. Robbie took command of Hoa Lo.

Over the next few weeks, the command passed to Air Force Colonel Vernon Ligon, and then a few days later to Colonel John Flynn as they joined the ranks of POWs in Hoa Lo. The camp was finally beginning to function like a military unit, in spite of Cat's greatest efforts to prevent it. Hope began to replace despair at Hoa Lo. News of the war was still discouraging, but the sense of unity and discipline invigorated us all.

Had we but known the events that were being planned for a location only a few miles from us, we would not have been able to contain our excitement. As we were building for ourselves a strong military structure in Hanoi, military strategists and intelligence officers in Florida were building a scale model of a POW camp twenty-three miles from Hoa Lo and planning the most daring rescue ever attempted by the American military.

If we had only known!

# THIRTEEN

# Prisoners of Hope

After four and a half years of captivity in Hanoi, I was accustomed to the night sounds of the city. An occasional shrill voice would rise up from otherwise quiet streets and drop over the walls into Hoa Lo. A single, coughing truck would wheeze past the thick, outer walls of the prison on some late-night expedition. Sometimes I heard the grating of the huge gates that held me prisoner as they opened and closed behind a visiting or departing camp official. Some nights I slept deeply and heard nothing. But on the night of November 20, 1970, I leaped from my bunk and stood close to the window to listen to sounds in the distance.

The sounds of aircraft and flak! And then the answering sounds of antiaircraft guns. The skies over Hanoi had been silent for more than two years, but I knew the sound of air-to-ground warfare. I guessed the target to be within about thirty miles of Hanoi. As quickly as it had begun, the air raid ended.

The next day I was anxious to find out if anyone else had heard it. Stockdale had slept through it, but Tanner and several others had heard the distant ruckus. Questions echoed on the cell walls.

That night, less than a hundred men in North Vietnam were privy to the highly classified operation that took place in a little town twenty-three miles from Hanoi. By the next morning, most of the world would know that the United States had attempted to rescue seventy prisoners of war believed to be held in a camp in Son Tay. It would be months before we in Hoa Lo would know the details of the operation codenamed Ivory Coast.

Air Force Brigadier General Leroy J. Manor commanded the mission. Ground command was assigned to Special Forces Colonel "Bull" Simons, a man whose expertise in unconventional warfare and whose exploits in World War II and in Vietnam had earned him legend status among the Green Berets. He sent word to Fort Bragg, to the JFK Special Warfare Center, for volunteers for a special mission, and more than five hundred men volunteered. Of those, he selected fifty-five to begin training with him.

The mission of the special operation was unknown to all the volunteers. They gathered on Eglin Air Force Base in Florida in August, 1970, to begin training on the remote acreage of the base where a scale replica of the prison camp was built.

For months, they practiced the assault, creating and acting out every eventuality that could arise during the actual raid. They knew they would be raiding a prison camp, but its location was top secret. It could have been anywhere in Southeast Asia – South Vietnam, Laos, Cambodia, or North Vietnam. The exact location would be revealed only hours before the mission was carried out.

The strategy called for one helicopter gunship to fly into the camp in Son Tay and fire rockets to take out the guard towers on the walls. Two more helicopters would land outside and blow open the walls. The rest of the raiders would then join the assault team on the inside where they would release the prisoners, load them into the helicopters, and fly out as they had come in. The whole operation was rehearsed in minute detail until every man in the unit could do his job without mistake.

While the special forces trained and practiced, diversionary attacks on specific Hanoi targets were planned, but the targets and the location of the prison camp remained a secret to all but the highest officials in military intelligence and in the White House.

On November 20, Bull Simons gathered his men together in a room at Udorn Air Force Base in Thailand, where they had flown to await the "ready" signal. In a few hours they would execute the plan that had been devised six months earlier. It was time for Simons to tell them where they were going.

Many years later, in a restaurant in San Francisco, I listened to Bull tell the story of the last few minutes before the operation began.

"We are going into North Vietnam, about twenty-three miles outside of Hanoi, to a town called Son Tay," Bull told his men. "There are about seventy POWs there and we're going to get them out." The room was silent for a second, and then thunderous applause erupted. "No one has ever tried this before, but we are going to do it," Bull continued when the clapping finally quieted. "We could get caught in a firefight and never come back. If there is anybody who doesn't want to go, get out now!"

Not one man left the room.

Bull briefed his men on the details that had been saved for the last moments. Each man knew his job, but it would be different in the real environment. Even though the reconnaissance drones and satellite photos had given them an almost perfect picture of the camp, it was always possible that they would arrive to find things changed. Guards might not be where they were expected to be: additional forces could be inside the camp. Anything could go wrong.

"What if the helicopters that are supposed to come in and get us are shot down? What if they can't get back in to take us out?" Someone asked the question that was on every man's mind.

"We will form a line along the river and shoot as many of them as we can until they kill all of us," Bull answered.

There were no other questions.

A short while later, Colonel Simons and his assault team boarded the helicopters that carried them low over Laos and across the border into North Vietnam. While they were en route to Son Tay, the navy sent a hundred fighters to Haiphong harbor to carry out the diversionary attacks that would enable Simons's helicopters to evade Hanoi's radar. U.S. battleships lying ten miles off the coast of North Vietnam blasted the waters near the coastline and drew the enemy farther off guard.

The diversionary tactics succeeded. Simons's helicopters flew into Son Tay without any conflict with North Vietnam's air defenses. The only difficulty arose when the chopper containing Simons veered off course and, instead of landing outside near the walls of the prison, landed several hundred yards beyond its target in the middle of a Chinese encampment!

"We realized where we were," Bull said, shaking his large gray head and grinning as he told me the story. I thought he looked cramped and uncomfortable, too large for the small table where we sat. His huge, square frame was better suited to a football field than a quiet restaurant. His booming voice carried as he finished his tale.

"There was only one thing we could do — we had to shoot it out with them and cut off their communication lines so they couldn't alert the rest of North Vietnam that we were on the ground near Hanoi. We killed them all and then met up with the rest of our men."

Only then did Simons find out that the POW camp at Son Tay was empty of all but the North Vietnamese guards. The gunship successfully took out the towers and exchanged fire with the guards, killing many of them. The assault team spread out in every direction, but they found no sign of American prisoners. They quickly ran to every corner of the prison, checked every locked door and every cell before finally giving up. Heartsick, they boarded the helicopters and left before the Vietnamese discovered their presence near Hanoi.

For years, the question has begged answering: Why didn't intelligence know that the camp was empty? Was it a terrible intelligence blunder? Is it possible intelligence knew the camp had been emptied but was ordered to carry out the mission anyway, using the operation as a politically expedient tool to build support for an unpopular president?

In Colonel Simons's mind, there was no doubt that military intelligence believed there *were* POWs in Son Tay. The aerial reconnaissance photos of the camp showed guards on daily duty inside the walls. Their clothing and weapons were discernible in the photos. Even their routine within the camp was charted. There was every reason to believe the camp held POWs locked away, out of sight of reconnaissance planes.

Later intelligence reports revealed that the POWs in Son Tay had been moved about thirty days earlier so the camp could be remodeled after the fashion of the Vegas complex at Hoa Lo; however, the guards had remained in the camp and continued to operate on the same schedule, as if there were prisoners inside. Intelligence in and out of North Vietnam traveled slowly; there were hints that things might have changed since the rescue plot had been conceived, but no concrete evidence – not enough to make them believe they should cancel the operation. The raid was history when they learned the whereabouts of the POWs. Operation Ivory Coast was publicly renounced as a failure.

In many ways, however, the raid on Son Tay was a huge success. Americans rallied together to cheer the brave efforts of Bull Simons and his raiders. The families of POWs and MIAs were thrilled over the dramatic and daring effort made for their captive sons and husbands and brothers. Their confidence in American diplomats at the peace talks revived. They no longer feared that the United States would give away its sons to gain peace. President Nixon had demonstrated his commitment to the prisoners of war.

The Son Tay raiders, as they came to be called, returned to the United States. Not one of their number had been lost in the assault on Son Tay. Of the fifty-five men, only one was wounded in the exchange of gunfire, and another broke an ankle while jumping from the helicopter when it landed inside the camp. But every man involved in Operation Ivory Coast brought home a broken heart. The raid had failed to free American prisoners. Their disappointment was deep.

The odd comments we heard on Radio Hanoi in the days following November 20, 1970, made us wonder if perhaps the United States had actually attempted to rescue some POWs, but Hanoi Hannah offered us no details. Of course, the Vietnamese still wanted us to believe that our country had forgotten its prisoners of war. Jim Stockdale, however, felt sure a raid had occurred. Oh, how badly I wanted to believe it!

When the camp suddenly gained additional guards and construction sounds echoed around the yard, we became convinced that the United States had *indeed* tried to execute a bold and daring rescue of American POWs in North Vietnam. We were even more certain of it as the camp began to fill up with more prisoners. I figured the Vietnamese were afraid of another rescue attempt, and they were putting all their prisoners together in the main facility so as to protect them all better. There could be no other explanation for the sudden influx of POWs from the more remote prison camps in the region.

A feeling of anticipation settled across the camp. Some of the Alkies grew restless. Jenkins took up a pastime he had enjoyed back in Alcatraz. He had figured out how to tamper with the wiring in his radio speaker and turn it into a transmitter for sending messages to the other POWs in the camp. By interfering with the regular radio transmission at intervals, like Morse code, he simulated a camp-wide telegraph system from his cell. After a while the guards caught on to what was happening, but they couldn't figure out where it was being done. They placed men at every window and outside nearly every cell until they identified Jenkins as the culprit. But by then, someone on the other side of the camp had picked up on the game to replace Jenkins on the air.

In spite of their paranoia over communication between prisoners, I thought there were indications that the prison authority was softening slightly toward some articles of the Geneva Conventions. Their offer of dental care certainly was a good sign.

"So. Today will have dentist in camp to fix teeth," Cat announced on the radio one morning.

*Finally,* I thought with relief. For months I had been complaining about breaking my teeth on rocks and other foreign objects that showed up in our food. When Denton came back from his "appointment" less than enthusiastic with the treatment, my relief turned to trepidation. When I walked into the makeshift dental laboratory trepidation became horror.

Grimy draperies hung from steel frames separating the room into several tiny stalls. I stepped into one and then stepped back, appalled. Beside the dentist's chair was a bicycle contraption where an aide sat awaiting the signal to begin pedaling to power the drill that lay on a tray next to the chair. The spit sink was a metal bowl fed by a pipe attached to a foot pump under the chair.

"Sit," a guard ordered.

I sat. *I'll let him look, but that's all,* I told myself as the dentist leaned over me. I opened my mouth and let him peer at my teeth. His white coat triggered memories of earlier "medical" care, and I suddenly felt like jumping up and running out. He picked up a metal instrument and began probing in my mouth. I flinched. He stepped back, nodded at the aide who began pedaling as fast he his legs could pedal, and picked up a hypodermic needle that looked as long as my arm.

"Oh no!" I blurted. "Don't touch my teeth!"

The dentist glared at me in confusion and sent for an English-speaking guard.

"You don't want teeth fixed?" he asked.

"No, thanks," I answered and tried to get up out of the chair. The guard's hand stopped me.

"But the Vietnamese people want to take care of you. The Vietnamese people love you," he said, making the word "love" sound like "l-aah-v." I felt like throwing up.

"There's nothing wrong with my teeth," I said, clinching them.

"You have complained," he said, frowning. "You need filling."

"I'll get it taken care of when I get home," I answered, standing up.

"You never go home!"

"You're wrong," I answered, looking down on the guard's five-foot frame from my six feet and two inches. He glared at me and barked, "Go back to room!"

*Gladly,* I thought, *You don't know how gladly!*

Christmas in 1970 was a more joyful occasion than it had been in other years. With all the Alkies together now in the Stardust, I gave thanks for the presence of friends, and we all admitted to growing feelings of hope. I received my first package from home. I was delighted! I was even more pleased to see that the Vietnamese let me keep all that Shirley had sent me. A pharmaceutical representative had given her vitamins for me—potent prenatal vitamins for pregnant women. My body got a sudden surge of the essentials it was starved for. And there was toothpaste, along with a large coffee can filled with gumdrops and jawbreakers.

Every gumdrop had been chopped up into little pieces, as was everything edible that came to us from the United States. The Vietnamese were paranoid about the possibility of things being hidden in packages, particularly in our food. Even my vitamins were chopped up into tiny pieces. They wouldn't let me keep the bottle with me in my cell, but every day without fail, a guard showed up at my door to deliver a crumbled, broken vitamin.

On New Year's Eve, just after the evening meal, we heard the familiar command. "Roll up!" I grabbed my can of gumdrops and stuffed my rolled mat under my arm. Up and down the hallway, doors opened and closed. Out in the courtyard, I could hear voices and the shuffling sounds of a crowd.

Shu, Tanner, Stockdale, and I walked out of the Stardust together and, in moments, we stood in line with several other POWs in a room in the Desert Inn. An inspection line, made up of officers, faced us.

"Take off clothes," an officer commanded.

Shu and I looked at each other, asking silently, *What is this?* The camp commander had never ordered a body search en masse before. In unison, we all dropped our clothes and submitted to the meticulous probings of the guards. Every crevice on our bodies was examined with searching fingers.

I groaned. *They have to be looking for something,* I thought, clenching my teeth and holding my breath as the guard peered at me, down my throat, into my ears, and even pinched my skin. He scoured me from head to foot and every inch in between.

When the search was finally over a guard led us out of Vegas, through Heartbreak Hotel, and across a courtyard in the western section of Hoa Lo to a part of the prison I had never been in before. It was an odd-shaped, four-sided compound, built around a courtyard with eight large rooms opening off of it. Eight-foot bamboo fences stood in front of each large room, encircling a small yard that held a concrete washing trough fed by a thin round pipe.

The sounds of construction we had heard days before must have been these hastily constructed bamboo walls going up. I gathered that the Vietnamese were still concerned about prisoners seeing each other when they went outside. How foolish that seemed to me when they opened a door on Room Seven and I found myself surrounded by dozens of American POWs!

I walked in and stared, incredulous, at the oddly built facility. In the center of the room, surrounded by a five-foot-wide walkway, was a raised, sloping concrete platform, about two feet high. Nearly fifty men had already laid their bedrolls out on it, head to head in long rows. I supposed that the design was intended to keep us above ground level when the heavy rains came in the spring.

In one corner of the room was a latrine. This was a first for us. No more rusty buckets to be carried daily to a community sewage dump! It was primitive and crude, but we had some small sense of privacy. Enclosed by a concrete wall, it was nothing more than a long cement platform which sat above two steps. The platform housed two large, round holes which drained down into a sewer that ran outside into an open ditch. The concrete was cold, damp, and filthy. My nostrils burned from the smell that rose up from the holes and flowed out into the room where the bamboo mats were laid for sleeping.

It was a new day for American POWs in North Vietnam. No longer separated and isolated in tiny cubicles like wild and dangerous animals, we were being allowed to live together in large groups! I drew a deep breath and discerned the faint sweet smell of freedom mingling with the familiar prison odors of urine, human sweat, and mildew.

I looked around the room and saw that I was with my closest friends: the three I had walked over with plus Coker, McKnight, Denton, Mulligan, Rutledge, and Jenkins. The Alkies, except for Ron Storz, were together again. After all the years and all the horrors we had shared, some of us had never seen each other face to face.

I moved about the room with all the others, hugging and shaking hands and studying the faces of men I had heard and spoken with on the wall, in the showers, and through crude notes written with mud-ink on coarse brown toilet paper. All around me I could hear the sound of conversation, not whispered and cautious, but loud and free. Some guys sat down together in small groups on the concrete platform, and others continued to mill about the room, finding old buddies and talking and slapping one another on the back. Emotions ran like an out-of-control roller coaster. At one moment I was laughing, at the next I was wiping away tears.

"Hey, where's Ron Storz?" An air force POW asked the question no one could answer.

"He stayed behind when we left Alcatraz," Denton replied. "He had refused to eat so long he was in pretty bad shape."

A sudden pall fell on us all.

"Hey, it's still practically Christmas," Jerry Denton said, looking around the room at the ragtag band of skinny, haggard men. "Why don't we have a church service? Rutledge, help me out here."

It was nearly 10:00 P.M. The move to "Camp Unity," as it came to be called, had taken hours, but the POWs in Room Seven were not ready for sleeping. Denton's idea met with instant approval.

"Coker and I can quote some Bible passages," Robbie Risner offered.

"And Sam will sing, won't you, Sam?" Jerry asked me.

"You're kidding! I can't sing," I laughed.

"Sure you can. Just sing a carol."

"Shirley won't even let me sing in church when there are other voices to cover me up!" I protested.

"It doesn't matter, just sing a Christmas carol."

I stood up in the walkway, and the rest of the men found places to sit on the concrete platform. All talking ceased, and the room grew silent. *Oh. Lord,* I prayed, suddenly nervous, *Help me, please!*

> "Si-lent night, Ho-ly night,
> All is calm, all is bright . . ."

My voice cracked. *I'm not going to make it through this,* I thought, as emotions pressed against my chest and threatened to choke me. Midway throught the first stanza, the rest of the men joined in.

Risner and Coker shared scripture passages, and Rutledge closed in prayer. The final "amen" was still on our lips when about ten guards pushed open the door and rushed in.

"No authorize! No authorize! Be quiet!"

Rifles jabbed between us to push us apart. A guard shoved Coker and Risner back into the crowd.

"Not allowed!" an officer barked, and ordered us all to be quiet and disband. Mumbling protests, we broke up and turned in for the night, sleeping head to head in long rows on the hard, sloping concrete platform.

The guards' intrusion was not wholly unexpected, of course. We had felt their eyes on us throughout the service, since the first notes of "Silent Night." The only surprise was that they had waited until we were finished to rush in. We had been prisoners of the communists long enough to learn that, to the communist mind, unauthorized group gatherings mean only one thing: insurrection.

The paranoia of the totalitarian regime interprets any spontaneous assembly as a direct threat to the party's control. Could we resist this, as we had so many of the other inane camp rules? To what extreme would they go to punish us if we persisted in holding worship services? We had no way of knowing, but lately we had pushed them with our demands, and they had relented without inflicting much suffering. We determined to plan a church service for the next Sunday. We would pay whatever it cost.

Most of the men in Room Seven were in favor of continuing the church services, so with Risner in command, we made plans for the coming Sunday. We organized our church service, put together a choir, sang harmony, and even worked out a threefold amen to close with, thanks to a marine who had sung with the Mormon Tabernacle Choir.

Sunday arrived. Risner and Coker spoke on Bible passages, the choir sang, and the service closed with a benediction. The guards watched from the window, and as soon as the service ended, they again rushed in and ordered us to break up. Week after week, we planned our services and worshiped together, and the guards continued to harass us each Sunday, barging in and stomping about, pushing us apart and shouting, "Be quiet! No authorize!"

Then one Sunday in February, they interrupted the service and dragged Robbie Risner and two others out of the room. They locked him down in leg stocks and threatened to come back the next week and haul out more men if we persisted in gathering for worship.

We would not be intimidated. We had come so far since the early days of leg irons, rope torture, and total deprivation and beatings. But our task was not yet finished. We were still prisoners of war, and our sworn duty was to fight on until release. We would continue to resist the foolish edicts of the North Vietnamese, and our services would not be canceled.

The next week, services began as usual. We opened with prayer, sang, and listened to a message by Rutledge. Before the benediction could begin, guards rushed in with rifles and clubs, grabbed twenty men — all the navy commanders and lieutenant colonels (Denton and Stockdale included) — shoved them out of Room Seven and trudged them across the courtyard. The dust was still swirling from their footsteps when someone in the room leaned out the window and began singing loudly:

> Mine eyes have seen the glory
> Of the coming of the Lord,
> He is trampling out the vintage
> Where the grapes of wrath are stored.

Soon, everyone in the room joined in.

> Glory, glory hallelujah,
> Glory, glory hallelujah . . .

Like a brushfire, the music spread swiftly throughout Camp Unity. Voices from every room in the compound joined in the singing.

> His truth is marching on!

As the last note of the "Battle Hymn" died, we moved into the chorus of "God Bless America" without missing a beat. The sound of men's voices filled the prison like a huge, unpracticed glee club as more than three hundred men hung their heads out the windows of Camp Unity and bellowed. It was more noise than music, but to me it was beautiful.

*They wanted a demonstration,* I thought as we sang song after song without pausing for breath. *So we'll give them a demonstration!*

We were singing the last phrase of "The Star-Spangled Banner" when guards in full combat garb flooded into the compound with tear gas canisters, rifles, gas masks, and helmets, ready to quell a riot that didn't exist. They ran toward each room, shouting and screeching in panic.

"No authorize! No authorize! Quiet! No singing! Down! Get down! No window!"

I dropped down from my place on the windowsill. It was almost comical to see the confusion and fear in the eyes of the guards as they swarmed in the courtyard, circling us as if we were armed and dangerous. Our singing had terrified them!

I felt a surge of victory inside. The American spirit had not been crushed. Years of captivity, torture, and starvation had not destroyed the souls of the nearly 350 American POWs in Camp Unity. Our bodies might be mangled and scarred, but our spirits remained intact.

The guards milled about in the courtyard, confused and disgruntled, tightly gripping their rifles. For days, guards in combat readiness stood stationed around Camp Unity, as if expecting our violent overthrow of the prison at any minute. Cat sent word that all the POWs in Room Seven would be punished as the instigators of the "riot."

"No wash," he pronounced crisply on the camp radio. We would not be allowed to go outside to the trough to wash for one day.

"Big deal," I said, and laughed at the "severity" of our punishment. Our senior officers were not dealt with so lightly, however. We learned that the men removed from us were placed in Room Zero — "Rawhide" — and locked in leg stocks, as punishment for violating the communists' sacred rule against assembly.

The next day, Cat's voice announced over the camp radio, "Camp authorize church service on Sunday for fifteen minutes. Can have choir and sing, but for fifteen minutes — no more!"

*This is Your hand, Lord,* I thought. I bowed my head and prayed silently, *We're prisoners in a hostile land, raising a ruckus and pushing for our demands — they could take us all out and shoot us if they wanted to. But You've intervened again. Thank you, Lord.*

In June, 1971, Hanoi Hannah told us that the North Vietnamese had offered peace to the United States, but that the U.S. had rejected their offer. The nine-point peace plan came out of secret meetings in Paris between Le Duc Tho and Henry Kissinger, but its offerings were unacceptable. U.S. troops in South Vietnam continued to dwindle until, by summer's end, South Vietnam was, for all practical purposes, on its own against the North in the defense of the areas just south of the DMZ. "Vietnamization" was proceeding as planned.

It was a long, miserable spring for the senior officers, but finally their stocks were removed. Along with the four senior Alkies, five other senior officers were placed in Room Eight, which became the command center for Camp Unity. Here too, Cat believed he could effectively cut them off from communicating with the rest of the POWs by leaving a vacant room between them and the next room. He ordered a tall bamboo fence built around their courtyard, blocking their windows and making it impossible for them to send or receive visual signals.

Room Eight became a prison within a prison. There was no reason for any of its residents ever to leave their private little compound. There was no opportunity for them to see or be seen by other POWs. Cat was smug. He was certain he had finally cut a link in our communication chain. But he failed to anticipate the ingenuity of a Thai POW, Chai Charn Harnnavee, and a South Vietnamese POW, who broke through all the barriers Cat tried to erect.

The camp authority gave these two Asians run of the camp and assigned them the tasks of sweeping the courtyard. They never expected the two would befriend the American officers in Room Eight. The SROs (we came to call them "the colonels") made contact with them and began dropping notes along the fence area. Chai, ever cautious and aware of the presence of the guards, nonchalantly swept the scraps of paper over to us and left them at the base of the bamboo fence around our room. Shumaker and I, sharing responsibility as the communications officers for Room Seven collected the notes.

We read the messages from the command center and then informed the men in Room Seven of policies, plans, and orders from the SRO. We tapped communications to the other rooms and received their replies and passed them on. We did most of our communicating from inside the enclosed latrine area where we didn't have to worry about being seen by guards.

Escape possibilities were a constant topic of discussion among the men in each room and in the communications between rooms. It was uppermost in many men's minds. Could it be done? Should we try to escape? And with the questions came concerns for security.

Not every man in Camp Unity could be trusted. The few men who had actively cooperated with the North Vietnamese lived in a room by themselves across the courtyard from us. We had to be sure all tapping communications bypassed their room. There were others of questionable status among us—men such as Harry James, whose presence in Room Seven made for some awkward and uncomfortable moments.

Harry James objected to our church services; he had refused to sing in our demonstration and generally made things uneasy in the room. His fear of losing our new freedoms may have been the reason, but he also objected to our communicating with the other rooms in Camp Unity. We tried to ignore him, but he was a constant irritation. Others like him in other rooms made it necessary for all communications to be controlled so that sensitive information did not find its way into the wrong hands to be volunteered to the enemy.

And of course in the backs of our minds was the thought that the camp authority could revert to its animalistic tortures at any time. If they did, they would stop at nothing to gain the information they sought. The protection of both the plan and the men was another reason for security precautions.

All transmitted messages fell into one of three categories:

Unclassified—for all POWs: general information, names of POWs recently added to our number; world events we learned from each other and from new shootdowns;

Classified—for SRO in each room: policy changes, requests for senior officers' approval;

Top secret – for specially cleared officers in only certain rooms in camp: information that came in coded letters, and escape plans.

The tap code that transmitted top secret messages was scrambled and changed every day. In Room Seven, only Shu and I knew what each day's code would be. Only he and I received and tapped and relayed each day's messages and then informed the rest of the POWs of the unclassified information.

Because of men like Harry James, we could not let the entire camp know that the United States had been sending parts of a shortwave radio in packages to POWs. A radio was the one missing essential for a successful escape. We waited impatiently as one by one, the parts arrived in toothpaste tubes in packages from the States. If we could communicate with the United States to coordinate pick-up points, it just might be possible to plan an escape. The unit was completely assembled, needing only a power source, when a guard discovered it during a routine search.

Years later, U.S. Congressman Robert Dornan (R-California), who had served in military intelligence and as a news correspondent in Vietnam, told me that a peace envoy from the United States had learned about the radio parts being smuggled to us and gave the information to North Vietnamese officials.

When the radio was confiscated, we ached with disappointment, but we did not give up all hope of executing an escape. Harry James, on the other hand, was furious that we would even consider making an escape.

"I don't think we should be trying to plan an escape," he said one day after a room meeting to inform the POWs of the instructions from the command post in Room Eight. The room was immediately noisy with the question: Do we want to try or not?

I spoke up. "It's part of the code of conduct of POWs. Always try to escape."

"We're being treated better now," Harry James argued. "If we try to escape they'll come down harder on everybody. If a few try, we'll all pay for it."

Differing opinions bounced off the walls.

"I say we go for it!"

"Yeah!"

"It's too risky!"

Coker and McKnight's botched escape effort in 1967 had proved that everyone associated with an attempt was made to suffer. Atterberry and Dramesi's experience in 1969 proved the same. Still, it was hard to give up the idea. Most of us, military to the core, struggled against the thought of accepting our fate and waiting out the war behind these thick, concrete walls.

Several plans circulated through the camp, from digging out under the wall to dressing up like Vietnamese and walking out. But none struck me as really feasible. Where would we go once out of the prison? Could a man disappear silently in a city like Hanoi? Could 350 men?

In every escape plan concocted, the missing element was a place to hide out until a pick-up could be arranged. There was no "safe house." In downtown Hanoi, as well as in the surrounding areas, there was no place an American could go to await contact without being detected. In the river, in the streets, even immersed in a mudbank, not one POW had been able to hide from the North Vietnamese. I was convinced we had to have outside aid to make an escape. But how? This was the question that plagued me.

Larry Guarino, however, was plagued by just *talk* about an escape. He thought we should completely dismiss the topic and wait for release. His stance on escape was probably based on the fact that the risks were great and the chances of success minute, and I couldn't fault him for that. He was responsible for all the men in the room. Every man in Room Seven had strong feelings on the subject, but only Harry James promised flat-out betrayal.

"I'll tell the Vietnamese about any escape plan you come up with!" he vowed one day while standing in the walkway, his scarred face a furious red. Shouting erupted, fists swung, and the guards rushed in to separate angry POWs. None of us was sorry when they moved James out of Room Seven.

Our lives in Camp Unity fell into a routine that wasn't altogether miserable, with Sunday church services being the highlight of each week. Those of us who liked to sing decided to schedule a regular choir practice to get our songs ready for the services. As soon as the guards heard us singing they rushed in, shouting. "No sing! Shut mouth!"

"You gotta be kidding," I said. "These guys think we're gonna take over the camp just 'cause we're singing."

The big, bad American pilots were threatening to riot again, or so the communist mentality reasoned.

"I say we push 'em on this," Coker said.

"I agree," Shu added.

"Everybody in on this?" I asked the choir.

"Let's do it!"

And so we continued to practice anyway. We sent word to Cat that we wanted to be allowed two choir practices per week to prepare our songs for Sunday. He finally relented. Twice a week guards escorted the choir down to a little guard shack where we were allowed to sing our hearts out without harassment. It was one more small victory for us, and we savored it.

The prophet Zechariah once described the people of Israel as "prisoners of hope." How well that describes my state of mind during the months in Camp Unity. All my actions, all my movements were energized by hope. The hope of release constrained me when I would have flung myself against the walls in a futile effort to break free. Hope dominated my thoughts, controlling me in that concrete environment, until the day the trap would be sprung open. Truly, I was a prisoner of hope.

Most of the time, camaraderie among the POWs flowed at a comfortable pace, and we grew used to each other's little personality quirks. We shared just about everything with each other, including some of the goods we received from home. I was tight, however, with my gumdrops. I allowed myself only one small piece of candy each day, to make my stash from Christmas last as long as possible. Several months after the holidays, I still had some broken pieces rattling around in the large can Shirley had sent me.

One day in late summer, 1971, during the peace of the afternoon siesta, I plopped one in my mouth and sucked on it. I felt something stiff, like a tiny plastic sliver, stick against the roof of my mouth behind a front tooth. I tried to work it loose with my tongue, but I couldn't dislodge it. When I picked it out with my fingers, I found it to be a tiny brown speck, about the size of a pinhead, I rubbed it between my thumb and forefinger, and it began to unfold. Amazed, I rubbed some more. In seconds, it had opened to the width of 16 mm film.

"Shu," I whispered. "Look at this!"

Shumaker leaned over and let out a low whistle. Then he looked around quickly. "Hold on," he said. "Get somebody on the window to watch for the guard!"

With one man at the window as a lookout and a cluster of POWs gathered around me, I rubbed and "squeegeed" the film until it unrolled to a length of about twelve feet.

"It's the front page of the *New York Times*," I exclaimed. The print was tiny, and my eyesight had grown extremely poor, but I could just make out the headlines declaring the daring rescue attempt at Son Tay.

"Here," I said, as I handed it to Coker. "My eyes are too bad. Read it out loud for us. Start with the date."

"November 21, 1970."

For what seemed like hours, we sat and listened while Coker read aloud every word of the front page of the newspaper. It was like food, like ambrosia! To starving men! The report confirmed our suspicions of many months before when we had awakened to the sound of distant gunfire. There *had* been a midnight raid. And here were the details—

at least as much as the military was willing to make public. For us in Hoa Lo, it was enough. We were ecstatic. How hard it was to keep from leaping in the air and whooping with joy!

"Tell 'em to come on in and try it again!" someone shouted.

"Yeah, send 'em in to Hanoi this time. We'll be ready!"

Our country had not forgotten us! People had risked death and capture to come in and rescue us. Regardless of the American press's perception of the raid as a failure, we in Camp Unity declared it a victory. That one act of courage did much for our determination to hang on and hang tough. It renewed us and gave us fresh hope. Oh, how desperately we needed to know our country loved us, and the Son Tay raiders assured us it did.

The front page of the *New York Times* was a dangerous thing to be caught with in a Hanoi prison camp. We assigned a couple of POWs to memorize it, and then we used a cigarette to burn it and then dropped the ashes down a hole in the latrine. We learned later that a couple of men in other rooms in the camp had also received the same microfilm in packages from home. We figured the United States had used a shotgun approach, sending out several in different packages in the hope that at least one would get through to us.

Throughout autumn, 1971, we indulged in fanciful thoughts of release and even occasionally dreamed of rescue as we listened to the sounds of reconnaissance drones overhead. They were small, remote-controlled planes, about twelve to twenty feet long, launched out of a C-130 orbiting out over the South China Sea. Under radio control, they flew over and photographed the camp, appearing overhead at about the same time—midmorning—every day. Any guys who happened to be in the yard when the planes flew over waved and shouted loudly, "Come on in! We're ready to go!"

Of course, the guards ran about hysterically, shouting and pushing us out of sight into our rooms. They fired their rifles up into the air at the small planes but never seemed to be able to hit them, although the drones took no evasive action. Even fire from the antiaircraft guns stationed around the camp missed these small radio-operated planes that flew their courses, regardless of the explosions all around them. I always found this good for a laugh.

I guess none of us really believed that the drones were scouting for a rescue attempt, though we might have enjoyed fantasizing about it. Such an attempt in downtown Hanoi was not at all realistic. Son Tay, with its remote location, had offered cover, close access to the mountains and the border, and the possibility of evading radar detection. A bold landing in the middle of Vietnam's capital city, however, was a different thing altogether. I dismissed all thoughts of a daring rescue and focused instead on the state of the war and possibility of an imminent release.

Hanoi Hannah broadcast news of the continual withdrawal of troops in South Vietnam. "Your president knows he has lost. There is no reason to fight any longer. The Vietnamese people have driven the Americans out. You will be left here to die!" If I had not been convinced by the Son Tay raiders that the American POWs were a high priority, I might have succumbed to discouragement.

That fall, Nixon was trying desperately to save his Vietnamization program. His assault into Laos months earlier had ended with little success. Air support for the ground troops engaged in the bitter fighting had resulted in large numbers of Americans being shot down. The Ho Chi Minh trails continued to operate, carrying war materiel into the South, and the North Vietnamese sanctuaries in Laos continued to provide safe havens for the communist troops.

We all knew the dangers inherent in bombing missions over Laos. I remembered flying some of those missions myself and breathing a sigh of relief when I left Laotian airspace. Pilots shot down over Laos were seldom taken prisoner. They were more often murdered at the time of capture.

I chafed at the thought of those futile and risky missions; flying low over targets you couldn't see—targets that could be easily moved and hidden under dense forests. I had seen it all from the ground four years earlier at my own capture. The trucks on the roads pull off and wait until the plane is gone, and then they drive on until the next plane is heard in the distance. Or until their intelligence communication tells them to expect a plane overhead.

The marvel of technology had little effect against the enemy's primitive structures—the truck parks were built of canvas and sticks that the Vietnamese could fold up and drive out of harm's way before the aircraft appeared in the sky. They were difficult to find, even using flares and infrared cameras, yet the military continuously ordered night strikes on these phantom targets.

We just never seemed to get the idea of jungle warfare. Our sophistication was, in a way, an additional enemy to contend with. It was foolish to try to interdict in the jungle with precision hits. Against a mobile, primitive army, it was useless and ineffective. Yet, over Laos, 550 pilots were shot down flying futile sorties, and of that number, only nine came home.

One of those shootdowns was Ernie Brace. Somehow, Ernie ended up in Hoa Lo, and one day he got close enough to Jerry Denton to tell him he knew of many MIAs in Cambodia. They had all been imprisoned together for a while, he said, under the charge of Laotian officers. The Laotians told them that when a release was announced, all those POWs captured in Laos would be separated and detained. They would not be released with the rest of the POWs. I never learned how Bernie had come to be in Hoa Lo, but I know he considered himself one of the lucky ones.

Many days, I was reminded of what a lucky man I was. It wasn't really luck, of course, and I knew that. It was grace—that gift of God's love that He showers on His children even though they have done nothing to earn it. I was continually aware of how fortunate I was to be out of solitary, living among my good friends, and able to move about without irons or leg stocks. I tried each day to focus on the good things and to plan for the day when I would be released.

One day, McKnight decided everybody in Room Seven should learn how to dance. We were all going home someday, right? And there would be dancing in the streets. It was time to get ready for the celebration.

During the noon hour, we cleared off the center platform and turned it into a dance floor. McKnight demonstrated the jitterbug, waltz steps, the Twist, even the Charleston. We caught the curious eyes of the guards peering in from the window, watching our awkward, clumsy steps. They didn't know whether to laugh at the silly sight of grown men dancing with each other on a sloping concrete platform, or to report our behavior to the camp commander. They must have decided we were harmless, if a little crazy. After a few minutes, they walked away shaking their heads.

"Hey, Sam," someone said one day, "Tell us about flying with the Thunderbirds."

"What do you want to know?" I answered, thinking of the all the stories I could tell.

"How about telling us how to do a four-point roll?"

Pretty soon, I was surrounded by a dozen pilots, all listening to the technical details and asking questions. For the next few days, we spent hours talking about flying maneuvers. For a while I lived on the good feelings that came out of reliving the exhilaration of flying. But those good feelings were shattered suddenly when a tapped communication came over the common wall we shared with Heartbreak Hotel.

The prison commander had put all the men in poor health together in Heartbreak. We had spoken with them often on the wall, but on this day there was new information. Two new men had come into the room. They had just come over from Alcatraz. As we talked, it became clear that after they moved us out, the prison authority had used Alcatraz as a holding place for all the men who had "special" problems. Men like Ron Storz, who refused to eat.

"Did you know Ron Storz?" I tapped to the men in Heartbreak.

"Sure," came the answer.

"How is he?" I asked. My heart pounded while I waited for the tapped reply.

"He was pretty bad when we left."

"How bad?" I pressed them.

"Near death."

"Was he moved when you moved?" I asked.

"No."

There were no more questions to be asked. Ron Storz was dead, I could feel it.

*If only he could have held on . . .* I thought. *We're going to get out of here, I know it! He just couldn't wait. Ron, why didn't you hold on a little longer?*

Much of the time, Camp Unity lived up to its name, except for those few occasions when individual tempers flared and personality differences erupted in discord. Perhaps the worst conflict arose over the presence of the handful of turncoats who lived in the room across the courtyard from us. It was hard to forget that they had deliberately cooperated with the enemy in return for special favors.

The colonels in the command post had sent word earlier that we should try to convince them to begin following the code of conduct, regardless of what they had done in the past. "Tell them to stop cooperating, align themselves with us now, and we will forgive and forget," was the message.

For months we had worked on turning them around and bringing them back to the fold. We had tapped to them often, sending the message from room to room until it came to the room shared by the turncoats. We all knew these men had done almost anything the enemy had asked of them, willingly and without argument. They had received better food, better treatment, and had enjoyed freedom to walk about the courtyard without the company of a guard in return for writing letters, making films, and endorsing the North Vietnamese propaganda effort.

These were the POWs the peace envoys had met with. They were the ones whose comments and appearance had allowed the North Vietnamese to continue deceiving the world with the lie that they were a "lenient and humane people" while hundreds of other POWs in Hoa Lo, Alcatraz, the Zoo, Briarpatch, and the Plantation languished in leg stocks, irons, or solitary confinement, suffering severe torture and abuses.

Forgiveness would not come easy.

"Tell them to come on back home," the colonels had commanded us.

In the fall, 1971, one man decided to come home. For the sake of his family's dignity, I'll just call him Bill. Bill began telling Cat "no!" when he was asked to write, or speak, or cooperate in any way. He began refusing the favors and the little extra freedoms he had enjoyed. After a few weeks, he found himself pushed through the doorway of Room Seven, to live among the rest of the intransigents.

It was early evening, and the hum of after-dinner chatter was noisy in the room. At the sight of Bill in the doorway, every man was silent.

Bill stood quietly and stared about the room, meeting hostile eyes in every corner. Finally, I couldn't stand it any longer, I walked toward him, stretched out my hand to shake his, and said, "Sam Johnson, Air Force. Welcome to Room Seven."

I could feel the hostility shift over to me. No one moved. It seemed as if we stood there for hours, stabbed by angry eyes, but finally, another man walked up and offered his hand; then another, and then another. Bill shook hands and nodded in response. He said very little that night as he made his way around the platform to find an empty place to roll out his mat.

Bill's presence was met with muted resistance until the day of our release, but our commander had ordered us to accept him. I believed it was the Lord's command as well. I felt in my heart that I had done the right thing, but it had certainly not been the easy thing.

Accepting Bill was further complicated by the fact that his rank as a navy commander made him the senior officer in our room, immediately outranking Guarino. An outcry rose from the majority, and we turned to the command post for instructions. The order came back: Let him command. The one most upset was Guarino, of course, but the order stood. As for Shumaker and me, we carried on as the communications officers for the room, mutually agreeing that none of the top secret messages would reach Bill.

Bill had not been in command in Room Seven long when the guards decided to shuffle all the POWs in the camp. I rolled up my bamboo mat and walked across the courtyard to Room Two with another Texan, Norlan Daughtrey, who had become one of my good friends. I said goodbye to the rest of the Alkies who were scattered to other rooms in the camp.

The closing months of 1971 saw continued U.S. troop withdrawals in the south. In October, the U.S. ground troops participated in the last major ground operation.[1] Thieu was reelected to the presidency in South Vietnam, and secret talks between Kissinger and the North's Le Duc Tho continued, with a new twist: the U.S. plan demanded the release of all American POWs. Again, the talks produced no settlement and the United States resumed its bombing of military targets in the North.

With the arrival of 1972 came more freedoms for us in Camp Unity. The Vietnamese took down the bamboo fences around each room. They began allowing us to go outside at the same time as men from other rooms were in the courtyard. For the first time, we could mingle freely with other POWs, except for the senior officers in Room Eight. Cat continued to keep them isolated from the rest of the POWs in their self-contained prison.

One of our new freedoms allowed us to help with food preparation in the open-air kitchen built in the center of the courtyard. This sounded great, at first. Then the questions came. Would we be cooperating with the enemy if we worked with them? Could our actions be misconstrued? We discussed it at great length and finally agreed that because we were cooking only for ourselves, not for the North Vietnamese, it would be all right to work in the kitchen.

We scrutinized every new freedom the enemy offered us. When they put up a up volleyball net in the courtyard, we were suspicious of being photographed "having fun" and "enjoying the lenient and humane treatment of the Vietnamese people." The SRO put out the word: Stop play if they come out with cameras. Of course, they could have been photographing us without our knowledge, but we decided to go ahead and play unless we saw cameras. My crippled arms kept me from joining in, but I often stood on the sidelines and watched the games.

Norlan and I spent a lot of time together, and I discovered he was fluent in Spanish. He took me through a review course of my high school Spanish and introduced me to an air force captain who had studied French at the Sorbonne. I practiced and memorized and began assembling a French-English-Spanish dictionary in my head. I had already alphabetized over four thousand French words in my brain-dictionary. At night, when I lay awake, restless with thoughts of Shirley, I carried on long conversations in my mind and translated from one language to another.

In Room Two, I met Navy Lieutenant Commander "Red" McDaniel. I had heard about his resistance and the creative communications he had practiced during his stint in the Zoo. The stories of his long and grim torture were less entertaining. He was among the diehard types, and I was proud to get to know him.

Another, Jim Kasler, became a good buddy of mine. I had known Jim years earlier at Nellis Air Force Base. A jet ace in Korea, he was a legend. The courage that had distinguished him in an earlier war saw him through the horror of the Cuban experiment at the Zoo in Vietnam. He was one of the dozen men who had survived the seasons of terror under Fidel.

Red, Norlan, Jim, and I had many long conversations about the state of the war and Hanoi Hannah's version of world events. When her voice came on the radio in March, 1972, telling us that the peace talks had again broken off, we wondered what would be Nixon's next move.

"The United States refuses to negotiate," she said. "Your president has broken off talks. He knows it is over. He can never win."

A few weeks later, North Vietnamese forces took advantage of the lapse in the peace talks and initiated the fiercest offensive into the South since the TET of 1968. The Eastertide offensive in March, 1972 gave the North a strong grip on some of the South's important provinces. Nixon responded to North Vietnam's assault by ordering U.S. bombers to attack Hanoi and Haiphong harbor. And American peace activists answered Nixon's actions with their own brand of fury. Across the country, antiwar demonstrations erupted and spread like an epidemic. Nixon's "silent majority" was again silent, in contrast to the noisy voices of the peace activists.

"People of the United States are opposed to this dirty war," Hannah spewed at us. Speeches by Dr. Benjamin Spock and other celebrity peace activists played on the radio by the hour. We couldn't believe our ears.

"South Vietnam is weak," Hannah said. "We will be able run over country. American troops are almost gone. South Vietnam and North Vietnam will be unite."

"That's garbage," I said to Norlan and Red.

"The United States is going to have to get tough," they agreed.

"Yes, but *will* they?" Jim asked, knowing no one knew the answer.

In May, North Vietnam surged into the South again, claiming Quang Tri, the northernmost province of South Vietnam as its own. President Thieu and the U.S. negotiators called a halt to all peace talks, indefinitely.[2] There would be no negotiations while the North was blatantly engaged in attacks on the South. Again, peace was delayed.

"We have claimed eighty percent of South Vietnam," Hannah reported. "United States is now pulling out. It is over." (Hannah never bothered to tell us a few months later when the South's forces routed the North and reclaimed the wealthy Quang Tri province.)

The North's assault into Quang Tri had been a sort of land grab. In anticipation of a cease-fire which would freeze all holdings until a settlement was signed, the North ferociously attacked, grabbing whatever lands it could hold. Again the United States answered fire with fire. Nixon ordered the mining of Haiphong harbor and the bombing of both civilian and military targets in Hanoi. Operation Linebacker I was in force.

We heard the sounds of gunfire and heavy artillery. Explosions in nearby areas shook the ground under our feet as bombs found their targets. Antiaircraft guns fired all around us, and we listened with complete and utter joy. Nixon was not about to pull out, as Hannah had said.

After all these years, why did we allow ourselves to listen to her lies? The president of the United States was sending a message to Hanoi, one that could not be misunderstood: We are not yet finished in South-east Asia! At least, that was the way we in Hoa Lo interpreted the sounds of battle. We were elated. But in our tightly controlled environment, where all truth was sifted and replaced with propaganda lies, we knew very little of the acutal events of that spring, 1972. We knew nothing of the intricate negotiations that were, at that moment, under way.

While striking hard with one hand, Nixon reached out with the other. He offered to withdraw all U.S. troops from South Vietnam within four months after North Vietnam released all American prisoners of war and after an internationally supervised cease-fire had been established.

The fate of the American POWs, included as an element of the peace proposals a few months earlier, was no longer just an add-on for consideration. Nixon's new proposal made us the primary focus, the hinge on which the door to peace would swing open. *When* American POWs were released, he said, *then* all U.S. troops would withdraw from the South, if a cease-fire were in effect.[3]

Nixon and Kissinger had finally come to the conclusion that the only way out of the war in Vietnam was unilateral withdrawal. They had to get American troops out. Whether or not Saigon and Hanoi had finished with their war, the United States was about to finish its part. Nixon would have preferred to leave knowing that the South was strong and capable of holding off the North, and able to build itself into a healthy democracy; but he was no longer committed to staying on indefinitely and at any cost to guarantee that for them. Nor was the majority of the rest of the country.

Polls in the earlier years of the war had indicated that the majority of Americans supported efforts to secure a noncommunist government in South Vietnam. By the middle of 1972, most Americans just wanted to see the war end. The ultimate fate of the Saigon government was no longer a primary concern. The main concern in most American minds was the fate of the American POWs in North Vietnam.

If only we had known this! We were comforted by the knowledge of the Son Tay raid, of course, but we still knew nothing of the steady, aggressive actions of the POW-MIA organizations back home, fighting for our release and for adherence to the Geneva Conventions. I tried, as always, to remain optimistic, but at times I struggled with discouragement, especially that summer as I began the sixth year of my captivity in North Vietnam.

I had to force myself not to become morose. I thought of my children and the years I had missed with them. Bobby, my oldest, would be graduating from college soon. When I left, he had been in high school—a shy teenager with a dry sense of humor that was sometimes startling. Over the past six years, he had grown to manhood. My daughters, Gini and Beverly, were now teenagers. Gini was eighteen and I had already missed the firsts that are so important to a young girl – her first date, her first prom, her first corsage. Would I be home in time to be a part of Beverly's giggling teenage years? Was there a chance I would be there for her first date? Her first lead in the school play? I wondered if there was any way the gaps in their lives could be filled. Could the gaps in my own life ever be filled?

What of Shirley and me? Could we capture the years that had been lost to us? I thanked God again for my wife. Her love was a constant in my life. I knew some prisoners worried about their wives, about their marriages, especially those who had been married only a short time before their capture, but that was one worry that did not trouble me. I had no fears that Shirley would get tired of waiting for me and give up. But many wives of American POWs did just that, and the Vietnamese delighted in delivering such bad news from home to already suffering prisoners. They censored all mail from the States, and they seemed to find perverse pleasure in handing a man a letter from his wife, knowing that he would read that she was divorcing him, that she was not going to wait for him to return.

Shirley's commitment to our marriage would remain strong, this I knew with certainty, no matter how long I remained locked away from her. But how hard it was to think of her without pain. Sometimes loneliness hung on me like a dark, heavy blanket that threatened to pull me into black despair.

Bridge became one of my favorite pastimes. Always too competitive, of course, I played seriously, determined to win. Norlan and I organized duplicate bridge tournaments for our room, and even gave some bridge lessons. Every day during siesta we played for two or three hours. At first we made our own cards out of toilet paper. When the guards were finally authorized to give us cards, we used them until they were too thin and fragile to shuffle. We had to lay them face down on a mat and stir them gently before dealing them.

Kasler was a master chess player. We played for hours on a chessboard made of toilet paper until the guards finally gave us a real chessboard. I knew I would lose each time I played him, but I wouldn't quit. My level of play rose a few notches when we found a guy in our room who spoke Russian. He read and interpreted the articles about chess that we found in the Soviet magazines the guards gave us each week. I made a few world class moves, beat a few of the guys, but I never could beat Jim Kasler. Daughtrey was the only one who could give him a good game.

There were other games we wanted to play, like "acey-deucey," the navy's version of backgammon, but we had no dice. The guards wouldn't give us any, so we came up with a way to make our own. We dampened little pieces of bread and, while they were soft, shaped them into cubes. After they had dried and hardened overnight, we painted them with ink-mud. Voilá! Perfect bread-dough art.

One night, I went to sleep with some bread dice drying on the mat next to me, close to my head under the mosquito net. I was almost asleep when I heard a rustling noise. I opened my eyes to stare into shiny black eyes that belonged to the largest rat I had ever seen. He was after my dice.

*How am I going to get this guy?* I thought, holding my breath and trying not to move.

I turned my head slowly, getting ready to pull up the net and slap at him, but he bolted away and scurried off the edge of the platform. I swung anyway and slugged Kasler in the back of the head.

"What's going on?" Kasler turned over and glared at me.

"It was a rat — staring me in the face," I said. "He was after my dice!"

"Where'd he go?"

"He ran off," I nodded toward the other end of the room.

"Let's go get him!"

We crept down the walkway to where a couple of sawhorses held a board that doubled as a table. I peeked behind the table and, sure enough, the rat huddled there against the wall.

"He's there," I whispered to Kasler.

"Let's squash him! Run and hit that board with both feet!"

We backed down the walkway, about half the length of the room to get a running start, and then we ran as fast as we could and hurled ourselves into the air, slamming our feet against the board. The board hit the wall with a loud "Whack!"

Four dozen groggy POWs awoke and bellowed, "What's going on?"

Kasler and I pulled the board away from the wall, and Jim dangled the crushed rat by its tail for everybody to see. A few applauded, the rest swore, and Kasler and I went back to bed. We lay awake a while, chuckling and congratulating ourselves on having rid Hoa Lo of one more filthy rodent.

A package arrived from home not long after that, and the contents gave us almost as much to laugh about as the retelling of the rat incident. Packed nicely in a box from Shirley was a pair of turquoise paisley boxer shorts. I couldn't believe my eyes when I saw them. Shirley knew I never wore anything but blah, basic white. This was so out of character that I shook my head and wondered if she had had some kind of breakdown. Or maybe she was trying to give me something to laugh about. Or maybe the shorts hid a message somewhere. . . .

For weeks, we pored over those paisley turquoise boxers, looking for something—we had no idea what. We were convinced that military intelligence had sent them, not Shirley. And we were sure we would find something on them somewhere. The shorts passed from one pair of hands to another, each man convinced he would find the hidden message in a hem, under the elastic, in the paisley. We never found anything, and I never did put those boxer shorts on, even though they were a break from the noncolors of prison life. I just sat and stared at them from time to time, baffled. Years later, an intelligence officer told me the stitching in the waistband was done in Morse code. Out of prison, the message seemed trite and easily forgettable.

That summer, the United States continued its troop withdrawals from the South, and peace talks resumed. In Camp Unity, the hot months dragged by with little or no further changes. Once a month, a guard came to each room and led us out in groups of two or three to sit at a table in the yard and write our letters home.

I continued as communications officer and kept up steady tapping to the rooms on either side and sent messages with hand signals from the window. Now that the bamboo fences were down, we could see each other across the yard and "talk" to each other from nearly every room. Oddly, we were still not allowed to communicate with neighboring rooms from inside, but we were allowed to congregate and visit outside together each day.

I should have been accustomed to these crazy inconsistencies of the North Vietnamese by now—I had lived with them for more than six years. But they still managed to surprise me sometimes. And they never ceased to disgust me. I continued to be amazed that the North Vietnamese still steadily went about the business of trying to brainwash their POWs. They continued to operate as though we were going to suddenly say, "Okay, you're right. Democracy is bad, communism is good." One day, they announced that some POWs were going to be taken downtown to view war displays in a museum.

The colonels in the command post were the first to be told to go. They simply refused to make the trip. A few other prisoners were asked to go, but all of them answered no. We all watched with interest to see how the camp commander would react to outright defiance. He did nothing. We concluded that he no longer had the authority to punish prisoners, but there was no way we could be sure of that.

So many years of torture and punishment had conditioned us to wonder how far we could go in our resistance. Even though there had been many changes, we could never have said we were certain that things would not regress to the days of horror. Each new opportunity for resistance was, in a way, an experiment, and each brought with it an occasion for momentary fear.

That summer, the voice of Jane Fonda hung in the air over Camp Unity. Our camp guards and the commander were overjoyed to have a celebrity of her status come over and align herself with their "humane cause." I'll never forget seeing a picture of her seated on an antiaircraft gun, much like the one that had shot my plane out of the air and given seven years of my life to the North Vietnamese prison system. I stood in front of her photograph in a quiz room and stared in disbelief until the twisting in my gut made me turn away.

Jane Fonda's visit met with approval by some of the POWs, however. The number of turncoats among us had dwindled as several, like Bill, had come back to our side, but there were still a few in Camp Unity who would not "come home." Two senior officers, a marine lieutenant colonel and a navy commander, had not only convinced themselves that their collaboration was all right, but they had also led some of the junior officers into betrayal. They had decided that it was okay to cooperate with the requests of the North Vietnamese, and they gladly met with peace delegates, like Jane Fonda, feeding her the lies she was so ready and willing to swallow and reinforcing her already twisted view of the war.

It has always puzzled me that someone like Jane Fonda, lauded as brilliant and gifted, could be so fooled by the obvious set-up that the communist regime placed before her. For an actress, accustomed to sets, rehearsed scenes, and memorized dialogue, it was especially strange that she could not see that she was actually on a carefully built film set. She did not see, or refused to see, the facade in front of her. It seemed she, of all the peace delegates, should have observed the props so often used in her trade to create an illusion of truth.

Meanwhile, North and South Vietnam continued to quarrel over the peace proposals; the South would not accept any compromise, and the North would not give up its intent to own and govern South Vietnam.

In the fall of 1972, another secret meeting between Kissinger and Le Duc Tho yielded a draft of a nine-point peace agreement, but again complications arose. Now that the issue of POWs dominated the peace proposals, Hanoi countered with a proposal of its own. Hanoi decided that President Thieu should release all communist (Vietcong) prisoners held in the South, if Hanoi was required to release all American POWs held in the North. For years, the Hanoi regime had refused to admit or acknowledge that it *had* any troops in the South. Now, suddenly, it was balking at signing a peace proposal that did not make the release of all Vietcong POWs held in South Vietnam a condition for the release of all American POWs held in the North.

The fate of American POWs was, for years, an unknown and little cared about issue, except to our families and close friends. But now, near the end of 1972, it was the primary issue in the mind of President Nixon as he sent Kissinger back into secret talks with Le Duc Tho.

In October, the talks appeared to have produced proposals that would lead to a final peace settlement, and Hanoi Hannah declared, "United States and North Vietnam have reached agreement." America heard the announcement, "Peace is at hand." Our hearts rose and fell with each declaration. I lay awake at night and considered all the pieces of information we had, sparse and one-sided though they were.

"This is it, Norlan," I said. "It's going to happen this time. It's almost over."

I had to draw long, deep breaths to steady the loud pounding in my chest.

"Maybe," Norlan answered. Maybe he was afraid to be too sure. "Maybe, Sam. . . ."

A few days later, President Thieu backed away from the plan, and Hanoi reported, "United States refuses to sign peace proposal."

President Nixon, thousands of miles away, called in his regotiators. He had studied the peace plans, the counter plans, and the latest responses of both North and South. He had grown tired of the word games with the North and the South's unwillingness to compromise. His message: I don't care what you give away, just get the POWs out of North Vietnam.[4]

What irony! During the closing months of 1972, the fate of American prisoners of war became one of the most volatile issues of the peace talks. We had come full circle. Since the first shootdown in 1964, the American POWs had been danced across the world's stage as puppets, unwillingly telling the story of North Vietnam's "lenient and humane treatment." We were the reluctant, tortured spokesmen for the Hanoi regime, forced into repeating its lies in exchange for our lives, our limbs, and our sanity. We were used and abused to help Hanoi find its place of "honor" among nations. And now, in the closing months of the war, we found ourselves once again on center stage, dangling from the hands of politicians in pursuit of peace.

## Notes

1. Harry G. Summers, Jr., *Vietnam War Almanac* (New York: Facts On File 1985).

2. Ibid.

3. Henry Kissinger, *The White House Years* (Boston: Little, Brown, 1979).

4. Ibid.

# FOURTEEN

# The Taste of Freedom

The winter sky over Hanoi was gray – the same color as the dirty concrete walls in Room Two. Everything I looked at was gray, from my dingy pajama-like clothes to the smoke-filled air I breathed.

Around me a dozen or more cigarettes glowed. I held one in my own hand and looked at it with distaste.

*I don't even smoke, for Pete's sake!*

I flicked it to the floor in disgust.

I always took the cigarettes the guards offered so I could give them to the smokers, but lately I'd begun smoking a few myself. I was nervous, very nervous. Maybe I thought the nicotine would soothe me. But instead of feeling calmed, I only grew more disturbed. Something was about to happen. I knew it! Nothing could quiet my inner restlessness.

I got up and moved about the room. *Conversation. That's what I need,* I thought. But lately, talk always turned to politics and peace talks and the presidential elections in the United States. I was sick to death of it all. I just wanted to go home.

I sat down next to Norlan. "So, what's it going to be?" he asked me, looking up from the Spanish-English dictionary he was trying to write on scraps of toilet paper. "Nixon or McGovern?"

"Geez, Norlan, I can't stand this much more. Can't you think of anything better to talk about?"

Perhaps Hanoi Hannah had done her job too well. Perhaps I had come to believe that she was right – that the American people were so fed up with this war that they might give up on Richard Nixon and replace him with George McGovern. Hannah loved to tell us that the peace demonstrations made it very clear whom the American people wanted. George McGovern obviously represented the masses and would win. According to Radio Hanoi, the doves were stronger than the hawks.

"The people have already chosen," Hannah said. "Your people hate their president. He will not be reelected."

And so I wondered. And I worried. And I grew angry. American prisoners of war had recently become a bargaining tool. Would a new president trade away our lives?

I could have cried with relief when Hannah reported the results of the presidential elections in November. Richard Nixon was the easy victor.

"So much for the silent majority," I said to Red and Norlan, "It seems to me they've spoken loud and clear."

"Yeah," Norlan answered. "There may be lots of peace demonstrations saying one thing in the streets, but the ballots are saying something else." It was true. The American people had spoken. There could be no doubt that they wanted Richard Nixon to remain in the White House.

Nixon knew he had the support of the American people, but what he needed even more was the support of a congress that was growing impatient with this war. Legislators who had been hawks during earlier administrations had gradually evolved into doves as the war dragged on. More and more, the Congress was being dominated by liberals who would oppose him in everything unless he could bring this war to a satisfactory end. He instructed Henry Kissinger to bring him a peace settlement that all parties could sign before his inauguration in January, 1973.

Kissinger returned to Paris to negotiate with Le Duc Tho. After eight grueling sessions, he came back to Washington, charging the North Vietnamese with procrastinating. Hanoi countered by accusing the United States of forcing it to recognize the sovereignty of South Vietnam, and the talks stalled again.

Richard Nixon faced the most formidable test of his presidency. What was it worth to him to get the peace settlement he wanted? And what of the congress that wanted to tie his hands in every matter that pertained to this war? Could he risk angering them by going after Hanoi with full force and fury? One thing was certain: unless Hanoi agreed to return to negotiations, there could be no peace settlement. He decided to drive Hanoi to the bargaining table with military might.

It was exactly one week before Christmas. I was half-asleep, cold and uncomfortable under my thin blanket, when I heard sounds in the distance. *That's not thunder* . . . I was suddenly wide awake. *Aircraft! B-52s!*

I shook Kasler awake. "Listen!"

"It's an air raid," he answered, groggy from sleep.

"No, those are B-52s!"

"It can't be B-52s, Sam. They'd never use 'em up here. Go back to sleep," Jim grumbled.

I turned over, but I couldn't go back to sleep. Something of major magnitude was happening somewhere near Hanoi. But what?

The next night, around midnight, explosions again erupted in the silence.

"Listen!" I shouted, jumping to my feet. "I'm telling you, those are B-52s!"

"Shh," Keslar hissed at me as he went over to stand by the window and listen. A huge smile spread across his face. "I never thought the United States would do it!" he said, now as excited as I was. "Nixon is really getting with it!"

Soon everyone in the room wakened to the glorious sounds of battle in the night. We were incredulous. For a long time we listened to the shattering and exploding sounds of gunfire, bombs, and antiaircraft artillery and missile fire all around us. It was still in the distance, but it sounded closer than the night before. Maybe Haiphong harbor? We tried to pinpoint the targets. We couldn't be sure, but we were excited and filled with new hope.

The next morning, the guards, testy and nervous, entered Camp Unity and rounded up about fifty POWs. We watched with concern as they left the yard. Was it possible they intended to retaliate against the U.S. bombing by executing American prisoners? We had no way of knowing. The North Vietnamese were capable of anything. There were no guarantees in this ignoble society.

Those of us left in Camp Unity listened each night as the bombing worked its way from Haiphong to the city, coming closer each night. The noise of the night battles rose to a deafening crescendo as the assault on North Vietnam marched across the sky. After about a week, bombs began to fall on Hanoi. The attack began in the middle of the night. Buildings in Camp Unity shook as the first bombs landed on their targets in the city. I awoke and sat upright. The window framed a fiery red- and yellow-streaked sky. A haze of smoke hung in the air.

*This is it!* I thought, as the room reverberated with the force of the explosions. Instinctively, everyone in the room dropped to the floor. *Hanoi is under attack!*

The sky was filled with dozens of B-52s, each carrying a capacity load of more than a hundred bombs. The sounds of the bombs hurtling through the air sounded like hordes of geese in flight, and as they hit the ground and began to explode one by one across the city, we covered our ears and dove against the walls in search of some kind of shelter. The roar was unrelenting. It was as if every gun and every missile in the city were firing simultaneously with the explosions of the American bombs.

*They know where we are,* I told myself, trying to assure myself that our countrymen wouldn't blow us away. *They'll flatten everything but this prison, if they have to. It's all over but the shouting!*

Other POWs in Camp Unity were not so sure that the bombs would not land on Hoa Lo. The buildings trembled and the ground shuddered as if a huge chasm were about to open in the earth beneath our feet.

Powdery chunks of concrete and plaster fell around us, and the huge steel ceiling beams overhead swayed from side to side. I heard shouted exclamations of terror.

"We'll all be killed!" someone screamed.

"Not a chance," another answered, echoing the feelings of a bunch of us who got up off the floor and scrambled to the large windows, crowding and pushing to get a view of the battle that we hoped and prayed would be the end of this war, the end of each man's private war with Hanoi. A loud chorus of cheers rose up spontaneously, and a crowd of guards rushed through the smoke in the yard, screaming and cursing.

"Shut up! No talk!" they cried, their faces wearing terror.

Later Shirley told me that many wives of POWs were also terrified that their husbands would be killed by the bombs falling on Hanoi. Shirley, however, was not one of them. She was delighted. She had lived with a fighter pilot long enough to understand precision strikes and bombers' missions. She knew the military was able to avoid endangering our lives while carrying out its mission against Hanoi. She might have been a little unnerved, however, if she had known that one bomb did land inside Hoa Lo, slightly injuring one prisoner.

The next night, when the bombing resumed, we watched our guards jump into the little round holes dug in the courtyard to escape the destruction of the falling bombs. The buildings shuddered and the booming sounds of explosions drowned out all other noises. We huddled against the concrete platform in Room Two and waited out the long moments of warfare that raged over our heads. I felt as though I was in the center of a battle scene reminiscent of World War II. My throat filled with smoke and dust, and the roaring bursts of explosions left my ears ringing.

The following night, as the bombs began to fall again, we lost all electricity in the camp when one landed on a nearby power plant. Over the next few days, we ran short of both water and food. There was no more rice, no tea, and no tiny portions of pigfat. Instead guards handed us little chocolate candy bars—Soviet rations, I figured—some of the best tasting food we had had since our capture.

The next day, the entire town of Hanoi was evacuated. Some prisoners had made tiny holes in the walls that faced the back moat and had lined up more holes with those in the back wall. They could see out into the city streets that suddenly grew silent. They watched all the military movement through the city and then watched as families and school age children ran from the city to safer ground in anticipation of another night of horror.

From Haiphong harbor to the coastal territories and on into the city of Hanoi, the navy and the air force's B-52s continued their assault. I counted at least three missile sites situated around the prison defending the city. We could hear the missiles fired in volleys of three from each different location.

During the first few days of battle, we listened to the loud "pop" of solid-propellant missiles as they flew into the air toward the American bombers. As the battle dragged on, the loud "pop" became a "hiss," like the sound of Roman candles on the fourth of July. I knew then that the enemy was floundering. They had depleted their supply of the so-phisticated, modern defenses sent down from their Chinese and Soviet allies and were now digging into their storehouses for the older, out-dated liquid-propellant missiles.

During one intense battle over Hanoi, I watched a B-52 take a direct hit from a missile. The plane broke in half and exploded in the air. The tail gunner appeared to parachute out safely, but I couldn't be sure until a few days later when he joined us as a prisoner in Camp Unity.

The guards in Camp Unity became obsessive about keeping us inside and out of sight as the battle continued over Hanoi. They chased us away from the windows if we tried to look outside. I thought it was because there was an increase in the number of drones overhead during the day—we could hear their engines as they passed over—as if they were searching, anxious for reassurance that we were okay. When I was finally able to sneak a look into the courtyard, I discovered just what it was that the Vietnamese didn't want us to see. The ground, the build-ings, and all the trees in sight were draped with chaff.

The foil-like debris that could confuse and stifle radar detection was strewn all over the yard and hanging off the roofs of the prison build-ings. Our fighters were doing a good job of messing up the enemy's de-fenses, and the North Vietnamese didn't want us to know it.

Each day, Hanoi Hannah gave us her version of the battle raging over Hanoi. "The American aggressors have mined and bombed Haiphong harbor, even with B-52s. But the people of North Vietnam will never give in. We will fight to the last man to ensure the sovereignty of the Vietnamese people." On about the third day, Hannah's voice was silenced when bombs scored a hit on the radio tower.

In Room Two, we speculated on how long the bombing would con-tinue. "How long do you think it will take them to capitulate?" I asked Norlan. No one knew the answer, but I didn't think they could hold out long against the American forces.

The guards told us repeatedly that everything had been moved to hills, underground. "We can fight forever," one told me arrogantly. "Our munitions are all underground. We are in no danger from American ag-gressors. We will not be defeated!"

North Vietnam insisted that the bombing stop before talks could be resumed. Nixon wanted a firm date set for the talks before he would stop the bombing. It seemed there might be yet another stalemate. On December 28, 1972, Hanoi had had enough of the American bombs. They sent word that they were ready to begin "technical talks" and would meet with Mr. Kissinger. Agreement was reached. There would be a time limit on the talks, and no new issues could be introduced that had not been addressed in the October proposals. On December 29, Operation Linebacker II ended. All bombing north of the twentieth parallel ceased. Henry Kissinger returned to the negotiating table with instructions from President Nixon to do whatever it took to get a peace agreement. Give away anything—except the American prisoners of war.

A few days later, Hanoi Hannah was back on the air. "American aggressors finally stop their pirate acts," she reported. "Obviously, North Vietnamese have won the skirmish. The bombs have not done major damage to North Vietnam. We are able to repair quickly. This has been a futile effort on the part of America."

Was it the truth or more of Hannah's fiction? There was only one way to find out. We had to make contact with some of the B-52 pilots who had been shot down over the last few days while flying the bombing mission over Hanoi. We knew some of them had been brought into Hoa Lo, but could we reach them? In a few days, a POW broke through to the tail gunner I had seen jumping out of the exploding B-52, Sergeant Roy Madden. Roy told us all the city's rail yards and all the bridges across the Red River had been destroyed.

I began to feel truly hopeful that the war was almost over. The bombing had stopped; whatever had hindered the signing of a peace settlement could be resolved. It must be nearly over. I could feel it.

Over the next several days, I grew more and more restless. I paced in the small walkway around the sleeping platform. I smoked more cigarettes. I stood and stared out of the window and watched for more signs, *any* signs that would reinforce my certainty that I would soon be going home.

One morning, I watched from the window as several guards dressed in white coats led Roy, our newest prisoner, the B-52 tail gunner, across the courtyard and out of Camp Unity into New Guy Village. Later he told us he had been the "guest of honor" at a staged press conference. The room was filled with journalists and photographers representing the communist countries of the world.

"The prisoner is injured," a spokesman told the press corps. "But the lenient and humane people of North Vietnam have cared for him. His leg is saved."

The gunner sat in silence, ordered not to say a word. His injured leg, wrapped in gauze and plaster, lay propped up in front of him as a showy display for the cameras. The half-dozen guards dressed in white appeared to be an attentive medical entourage for this lone injured American. It was all very impressive, but nothing more than another elaborate facade. Roy's wound was already turning gangrenous.

On January 2, 1973, President Nixon got what he had so desperately wanted: technical talks to work out the peace agreement began in Paris. It was one day before Congress was due to resume. Nixon won his race against time. Five days later, Kissinger and Le Duc Tho met secretly to resolve the two remaining issues standing in the way of a final peace agreement: The DMZ and the dilemma of the actual *signing* of an agreement.

The proposed agreement included a place for the signature of a representative of the Vietcong. South Vietnam's President Thieu had stubbornly refused to acknowledge the valid political presence of the Vietcong, and he had no intention of signing a peace agreement that recognized their presence in South Vietnam. A compromise solution, after much haggling, was offered to the South which would allow the Vietcong representatives to sign on the same page with the North Vietnamese representatives without being specifically named as a party to the agreement. Then Saigon would sign on the same page with the U.S. representatives. Thus, all four parties to the conflict could sign and be fully represented, but Saigon would not technically have to recognize its political nemesis as part of the peace settlement.[1]

While haggles over the technicalities of the signing continued, Radio Hanoi reported that the "obstinate Americans are still refusing to negotiate on a nine-point plan." In fact, the opposite was true. The United States was ready to sign. South Vietnam's President Thieu was the only one still reluctant to agree to the final peace settlement. President Nixon grew increasingly impatient with Thieu's delays. He sent Thieu a terse message which said, in essence, we are going to make our own peace with North Vietnam, with or without your assent. We are going to get out and make sure we get our POWs out. The United States would seek its own interests and sign a peace settlement with the North, with or without Thieu's approval.

Thieu's frequent delays may have been nothing more than one man's desperate, last-ditch efforts to stall his country's ultimate fate: its fall to the communists in the North. However, Nixon's ultimatum stopped the clock, and Thieu ran out of time. He had no choice but to sign the agreement. His long-fought battle against a coalition government was finally lost. The door gaped open for the Vietcong to step firmly into South Vietnam's political future.

On January 15, 1973, President Nixon ordered all U.S. offensive action against North Vietnam to cease.[2] The next day in Hoa Lo, guards entered each room and ordered all prisoners into the yard. I was certain something momentous was about to occur. For nearly seven years I had been a prisoner of the North Vietnamese, and this was the first time all prisoners had been allowed to be together in the same place at the same time.

Cat stepped in front of us. In a quivering voice, he read the peace agreement to us in Vietnamese, and another officer interpreted. I heard the words "release in thirty days" . . . "beginning with longest held POWs . . ." I felt the heat of tears burning in my eyes. My heart pounded until I was sure it would explode. I couldn't move, yet I couldn't just stand there! I wanted to jump and scream and dance!

*He just told us we're going home, and yet here we all stand, like statues . . .*

Cat's voice droned on. He read us only the portions pertaining to prisoners and release, but it seemed we stood in that courtyard for hours. Finally, when I thought I couldn't stand any longer, he folded the paper and spoke in a voice that was shrill with intensity.

"As you know, the United States will violate this treaty and we will keep you here for the rest of your lives."

*Liar!* The word screamed in my brain. *Give it up! We're going home and you know it! You can't keep us here any longer!*

Seconds later guards dispersed us and we ran to each other, hugging and crying and whooping with joy. Nothing Cat could say could dampen the fire of our excitement. We were going home! Guards tried to direct us back to our respective rooms, but we stepped around them and shook hands and laughed and slapped each other on the back until we were finally forced to separate and go to our own rooms.

Back in Room Two, the celebration continued. Red and Norlan and Kasler and I sat together on the concrete platform and contemplated our families, our homes, and the reunions that awaited us. For most of us, it was a long night filled with wonderful anticipation. Sleep was the farthest thing from our minds.

A few days later, the POWs who had been removed from Camp Unity during the Christmas bombing climbed out of rusting, coughing trucks and made their way across the courtyard and back into rooms in Camp Unity. They looked awful, as if they had been ill and mistreated, as we all had in former days. We learned that they had been hauled north to a primitive prison facility near the farthest border of North Vietnam, near China. It seemed the North Vietnamese thought they could use American POWs to guarantee that at least one border route into China would not be bombed. It was a smart tactical move on the part of our enemies, but a deadly one for one of the fifty Americans.

In the dismal, primitive facility, the POWs found themselves worse off than ever before. It was bitterly cold, and the guards were poorly trained. They knew little and cared not at all for the routine care of prisoners. In a short time, most of the prisoners became ill. One contracted malaria and died shortly before the others were returned to Hoa Lo.

The nights and days following Cat's reading of the peace settlement are a blur of anticipation and excitement in my memory. I slept little, smoked a lot, and paced until I had to sit down out of sheer exhaustion.

The formal peace pact was finally signed in Paris on January 27, 1973. The next day, Secretary of Defense Melvin Laird announced an end to the military draft in the United States.[3] It was a deft political stroke, neatly placed at the end of a war directed and dominated by political expediency—a fitting punctuation mark at the end of a long, unpopular war.

I felt the full impact of our pending release when our captors began grouping us together in rooms by date of shootdown to be released together. Once again I found myself in with all the Alkies, except Ron Storz. It seemed fitting, somehow, after all we had shared, that we be together for this final victory. Yet my heart ached with thoughts of Ron. If only he could have hung on a little longer. If only . . .

"Sam, you gotta listen to this!" Jerry Denton's face wore an expression of disbelief. He had just returned from one of the last quizzes Cat would demand of him.

"What is it, Jerry?" I was smoking and pacing and fighting to control the feelings of claustrophobia that threatened to overwhelm me now that I knew my release was imminent.

"Cat says that the B-52 bombings just about wiped them out! Once the bombing started they figured it was all over. They fully expected Nixon to send in ground troops. They were waiting for a full scale invasion, and they knew they couldn't win!"

"What are you saying, Jerry?"

"Nixon stopped just short of a complete victory! I don't know what all he gave away to get the peace settlement he got, but if he had continued the bombing a few days longer and followed up with ground troops, he could have had his peace and not had to give up anything!"

Puzzlement must have shown on my face.

"Don't you see? Nixon got mad, threw out a little punishment with the bombers, and then said, said, 'Okay, that's enough—the war's over.' It's like he didn't know how much damage the bombing did. We didn't win the war, Sam, we just quit!"

The Christmas bombing, Linebacker II, effectively shut down the Hanoi war machine. The North no longer had sufficient resources to continue a full-scale war of aggression against South Vietnam, but that fact was never used at the bargaining table when the final peace agreement was drafted. U.S. negotiators traded and bartered as if they were dealing with a military equal rather than with a defeated nation whose capacity for war had been depleted.

While we waited out the last days before release, the prison authority made one last "benevolent" gesture toward us. They gave us the letters from our families that had been accumulating for us for years, but which they had witheld for some unfathomable reason. For days, I sat and read and reread the thirty-some letters from Shirley and the children and my parents, many with dates as far back as four years. Packages they had witheld from us found their way into our hands as well, and we feasted on chocolates, tea, and coffee.

The cigarettes so carefully rationed by the guards were suddenly abundant, and I began taking as many as I could get. I grew more and more restless and nervous, and I smoked every cigarette down to the smallest butt.

One night after dinner, word passed through our communication link that Robbie Risner was being escorted to each room to talk with all the POWs. He would be giving us the particulars about our release. He wasn't the highest ranking officer among us, but he was one of the longest held POWs, and so the privilege fell to him. He arrived at our room about nine-thirty.

"There will be nine bus loads of POWs released first. These will be the earliest shootdowns, the injured and sick, and of course the turncoat," Robbie's voice delivered the information like a newscaster reporting the facts, but I knew inside he was jumping with ecstasy, as I was.

"We're going to be allowed to shower and shave," Robbie continued. "And they will give us new clothes to wear home. We can take our letters and gifts from home out with us, but we aren't to take anything that belongs to the Vietnamese people."

We listened quietly as Robbie gave us instructions, but as soon as he left the room buzzed with conversations about smuggling techniques. How could we get some of this Vietnamese stuff out with us? No one was ever going to believe Vietnamese soap unless we took some home with us. And Vietnamese toothpaste – it defied description. The only souvenir I wanted from North Vietnam was my drinking cup. For me, it symbolized our war of resistance for seven long years. It had been a means of communication and, as such, a means of survival. It was all I wanted to take home from Hanoi's prison system. I vowed I'd find a way.

It was nearly midnight that night when guards began escorting us to the showers. There was an almost party-like atmosphere as we all lathered up our gaunt faces and shaved for the trip home. Sometime during the early morning hours I finally lay down on my bamboo mat for the last time, but sleep never came.

The next morning, February 12, 1973, everything happened just as
Robbie had said it would. About 4:00 A.M. a guard came in with a pile
of clean clothes. We exchanged our dirty prison garb for pants, a shirt,
and a windbreaker.

"Hurry, hurry!" One of the young, English-speaking guards pushed
a duffel bag into my hands. There was some sort of schedule being enforced here, and we were obviously running behind. I reached quickly
for my drinking cup and stuffed it into my bag when the officer turned
his head. With awkward movements I tried to pack my letters in around
it so it wouldn't be detected if the prison authority ordered one final
inspection before our departure.

About six o'clock, when we were all dressed and ready to go, guards
sent us out into the courtyard where they lined us up to wait. I could
feel myself growing tense as the moments passed and no bus arrived.

"There is delay. All sit down. You will wait."

*How long?* I thought. *I need a cigarette . . .*

"Pssst!"

*We are still whispering! We're going home today, and we still have to
whisper at each other . . .*

"There's a woman in that room!"

The message traveled through our group seated in the courtyard like
a small brushfire.

"Where?"

"In that room, there . . . somebody's talking to her through a crack
in the wall."

She was German, a nurse captured in Danang. The Vietcong had
sent her up to Hanoi, and she had been imprisoned in Hoa Lo with
us, but we had never seen her or learned of her presence among us until
that last day in prison.

"Is she okay?" someone asked.

More whispering, and then someone answered, "Yeah, she's okay. She'll
be released with the next group of POWs."

We sat and waited in the courtyard for more than an hour. My insides
were taut with fear that this whole thing was going to fall apart. That
we wouldn't be able to leave today. I didn't think I could walk back into
a prison room again.

*Please, Lord, let the buses come,* I prayed.

As if in immediate answer, the guards ordered us to our feet and motioned us through a gate and into another courtyard where nine small
buses and three ambulances waited with their engines idling. The highest ranking officers among the POWs rode in the first bus, the sick and
injured were placed on the ambulances, and the rest of us, about fifteen

to a bus, climbed on wherever the guards motioned us. I sat down in a front seat on the seventh bus. A strange silence fell over us as the buses drove out into the streets of Hanoi toward Gia Lam Airport.

I chuckled as I remembered bits of a conversation from the night before.

"So, who's going to sit with the turncoat on the bus?"

"I want to sit by him on the plane. How 'bout we open the door at thirty thousand feet and throw him out?"

Denton and Stockdale's more professional demeanor prevailed, as always.

"We'll just leave him alone," they said, leaving no room for argument.

"Okay then," I said, "Let's grab Rabbit and take *him* along and throw *him* out at thirty thousand feet!"

Everyone in the room cheered.

The convoy of buses wound through Hanoi on streets that had not changed since the French occupation two decades earlier. The huge steel bridge that had spanned the Red River now lay twisted and half-buried in the mud and water of the river, destroyed by American bombs dropped by B-52s. We had to cross the river on a flimsy, primitive pontoon bridge to get to the airport.

Near the runway, we sat outside an administration building to await the arrival of the planes that would carry us out of Hanoi. Nearby, military forces appeared to be standing in readiness. MiGs on alert sat on the runway.

In a little while, an officer boarded the bus and said the hated words, "Must wait!" He nodded toward the building. We picked up our duffel bags and followed him inside.

It was midafternoon. Our day had begun before sunup, and still there was no sign of an American plane. I began to wonder again. I lit up a cigarette.

"American planes are not coming."

I heard the words, but I couldn't believe them.

"Back on bus—everyone! Back on bus!"

Like sheep, dumb with apprehension, we climbed back on the buses. The convoy drove through the airport past what appeared to be a terminal building. From the side, I could see the devastating effects of the American bombers. The building was almost totally destroyed.

The buses stopped in a line and waited another half hour. Finally, the first American C-141 landed on the airfield. Every man on the buses rushed to a window to join his voice with the chorus of cheers and whoops of joy. We watched as the huge plane touched down on the runway and then turned toward a ramp far too small for its mammoth dimensions.

The first three buses and the ambulances drove off the road and up to the ramp, and the first planeload of prisoners of war were on their way home.

A short while later, the second plane arrived, and cheers and applause rang across the tarmac. The second trio of buses drove up to the ramp, and the next load of POWs were off. Only the last three buses remained on the runway. Time suddenly stood still.

Hours later, those of us in the last group were sitting, sweating on buses parked in an isolated area off to the side of the airport. A Vietnamese officer climbed on board and announced in stiff, accented English, "Americans violate peace treaty. You not going home. You stay in Vietnam the rest of your life."

A loud, angry roar shook the bus. I could feel terror trying to rip me apart inside, but I couldn't let that happen. These people were liars – they had been lying to us since the day of our capture. Why should we believe them now?

I was the senior officer among this group of POWs, and I knew it was up to me to do something quickly before panic and confusion wrought havoc on this bus. I stood up next to my seat at the front of the bus and shouted, "You guys just have faith. I know the U.S. Air Force, and they may have had weather delays or mechanical delays, but I know they've got fifteen or twenty planes *extra* standing by, and they will be here. I promise you. *They will be here!*"

Another hour passed, and I began to question my own brave words. Had the Vietnamese been telling us the truth? But they had not moved the bus away from the airport . . . We still sat in readiness for a plane that had promised to come for us.

*They'll be here,* I said again. *They'll be here . . .*

Just then, in the early evening mist above the runway, the silver wings of a C-141 caught the glint of the setting sun. I stood and leaned out the window and watched through a blur of tears as its wheels touched down on the runway.

The men on bus number seven were strangely silent as the plane turned and headed toward the boarding ramp. There were no shouts of welcome, no cheering or whoops of joy. We were overwhelmed with relief and at the same time exhausted from the awful hours of apprehension. We had neither heart nor energy for celebration, and so the only sounds that emanated from us were the sounds of long-held breaths finally exhaled along with a few soft, almost muffled sobs.

The bus engine sparked into life and drove to the front of the terminal building we had passed earlier in the day. The view from the bus window made me catch my breath in astonishment. From the side, the building had been nothing more than piles of brick and rubble, but the front of the building still stood. It had been freshly painted; a canopy had been erected over the front walk, and two or three long tables had been set out on the ramp for processing the prisoners.

*Another facade,* I thought. *The building is demolished, nothing but crumbling brick, but if they only let you see it from one angle, you'd think it was perfect.*

Photographers grouped around us, held at bay by a few guards who kept them in front, where the building could be viewed intact. My surprise and disgust must have registered on my face because a Vietnamese officer interrupted my thoughts and spoke to me in excellent English.

"It does not matter what you have seen," he said, "or if you tell your people that American bombs really destroyed this building." He seemed to be waiting for me to respond, and when I didn't, he went on. "The cameras will photograph only the front, so that only the standing walls are seen in the pictures. You may tell American aggressors that the terminal building at Gia Lam Airport was demolished by your bombs, but it will not matter. These pictures will be shown only in communist countries, and the people will believe whatever they are told to believe."

We walked up to the long, cloth-covered tables set up on the ramp. There, hoping to look important and formidable, sat Rabbit. To me, he seemed only stiff and uncomfortable in his freshly pressed khaki uniform and his hat bearing the red star. I pitied him suddenly. I was leaving this country. He had to stay.

I listened as our names were called and checked off a list. One by one we stepped up to the next table, which was manned by Americans. Our names were called and checked off again. I moved through the process like a machine, unfeeling, unthinking, my eyes welded to that C-141 waiting at the ramp.

At the end of the last table stood Air Force Colonel Jim Dennett. As I caught sight of him, the numbness that had crept over me fell away. *Jim!* I had flown with him and known him all the years of my military career. He knew my wife and my children . . . I walked up to him and saluted him with all the military ceremony I could muster. He returned my salute and in the next instant we were hugging and back-slapping, and I was wiping my face with my sleeve.

The sheer joy of being alive and in the presence of Americans finally overcame me. Great, huge sobs I had tried to hold back broke loose. Jim put his arm around my sloping shoulder, grasped my crooked arm, and motioned for an airman to pick up my duffel bag. Together we walked toward the plane.

At the top of the stairs into the plane stood a nurse—the first American woman I had seen for nearly seven years. To me, to *all of us,* she was beautiful. When she hugged me, I thought I had never smelled anything so sweet.

As soon as I was seated in the plane, another nurse brought me hot, fresh American coffee. I sat for just a moment, warming my cold hands on the cup and letting myself savor the rich aroma. In a few moments, a State Department representative sat down beside me, and together we pored over a list of POWs, matching names I had memorized with those the department had received. While the remaining POWs finished being checked off at the tables, I verified names on the list from the hundreds I had mentally stored in my memory bank.

"Do you show Ron Storz on your list?" I asked him. *Of course, he is dead,* I told myself. And then I argued, *But no one saw him die, only the Vietnamese know for certain . . . maybe there's a chance he recovered at Alcatraz after we left. . . maybe he'll be coming out on another plane.*

The representative opened his folder and let me read the official record for myself: Ron Storz, U.S.A.F., died in captivity.

I dropped my head. Anger, like a huge fiery ball, beat against my ribcage. *Why, Ron, why? Why couldn't you hold on just a little bit longer?* I looked out the window at the darkening sky and the crumbling buildings around the airport. Sadness flooded me and washed away my anger. *We made it out, buddy! We made it!*

As the powerful engines of the plane ignited, its passengers grew quiet. We sat in taut silence as the plane taxied down the narrow runway. When we felt the wheels lift from the ground and retract into the belly of the plane, we all gave a loud cheer and the tears started spilling again.

We were headed for the Philippines. It was a short flight. The official from the State Department visited with each man, comparing his list with the names that had been memorized. The nurses served us more coffee, asked about our condition, and readied us for our arrival at Clark Air Force Base.

As we made our final approach for landing, an air force officer came and sat down by me. "Colonel Johnson, you're the senior ranking officer in this group. You're going to have to make a statement to the press." I was a full colonel now, promoted during my captivity, and it was up to me to greet the waiting crowd at Clark AFB. I wondered what I would say, how I would say it without breaking down.

Another cheer rose up as we felt the wheels of the plane touch down. We were safely out of reach of the North Vietnamese prison authority. They could never touch us again. The first leg of our journey home was completed.

The commander of the Pacific Fleet stood on the tarmac to greet us as, one by one, we exited the plane. The press, with full camera crews for live televising back to the States, the entire personnel of the air base, even some men from the naval base stood by to welcome us home. I remember coming down the stairs quickly—Shirley told me later that she watched me on television and I moved so fast that she caught only a fleeting glimpse of me. The speech I had composed in my mind to deliver to the press was never used. Jim Mulligan was the first off the plane and made some fitting remarks for the press.

It was nearly 10 P.M. With the change in time zones and the delays getting out of Hanoi, we were much later than expected, but still the crowd had waited to welcome us like celebrities—no, like heroes! I felt overwhelmed. Banners made by school children hung everywhere. Voices in the crowd called out, "We love you!" and "Welcome home!" I could feel tears streaming down my face again, but there was nothing I could do to stop them.

Camera crews crowded around us as we boarded buses that would take us to the base hospital. Shirley got a good look at me on television when a camera caught me leaning out a window to wave good-bye to the people who cheered us as we drove away from the airfield. I learned later that military intelligence had neither issued a final list of all the POWs being released nor made contact with the families of the men until the very last moment before release. She had spent days wondering if I would be among the first group of men returning home. My release was confirmed only hours before I left Hoa Lo. When she saw my face on television, Shirley knew for certain I was on my way home.

### Notes

1. Henry Kissinger, *The White House Years* (Boston: Little, Brown, 1979).
2. Harry G. Summers, Jr., *Vietnam War Almanac* (New York: Facts On File, 1985).
3. Ibid.

# FIFTEEN

# A Texas Homecoming

At the hospital, I walked into a room and found Roy Madden, along with three other POWs already there. Madden's injured leg was elevated and swathed in bandages, and he looked uncomfortable. He had seen a doctor earlier, but there were more appointments scheduled for the next morning. Even at that time of night, as weary as we were, all of us who had just arrived had to see a doctor. But all we really wanted to do was eat!

After a cursory exam, the doctor's next words sent a shock of horror through me. "We'll have to restrict your diet," he said. "Just until we get you on your feet, of course."

"You gotta be kidding!" I moaned. There had been nothing but juice and hot coffee on the plane. I was ravenous, and for the first time in more than six years and ten months I was out of range of Vietnamese pigfat. I simply would not accept the idea of jello and a poached egg.

"Let me eat!" I roared. "There's nothing wrong with my system!"

The doctor grinned. "What do you want?"

"I want steak and ice cream."

"That's too rich for you right now."

"That's what I want."

"I can't let you have that yet," he answered, shaking his head.

"I'm telling you, I can eat anything."

The doctor walked out and returned a little while later with a signed form allowing me to go into the hospital cafeteria and order anything I wanted. I felt like a kid who had just licked the schoolyard bully. I walked down the hall toward the cafeteria clutching my little slip of paper, daring anyone to get in my way.

A suite near the cafeteria had been set up just to serve POWs, and as I walked inside the smell of steaks cooking on a grill filled my nostrils. Behind a long table set with steaming food dishes and cutlery stood a young man waiting to serve.

"What'll you have, sir?"

Without blinking, I answered, "A banana split."

Every man in line shouted, "I'll have the same!"

I ate my banana split while I walked through the line to order the main course—a huge T-bone steak.

"How do you want it?" the chef asked.

"Medium rare."

"You can have eggs if you'd rather," he offered.

"Give me both," I answered. I ate it all and went back for another bowl of ice cream.

I met my escort officer a little later, and again I found myself in tears. He was Jim Howerton, a man I had known all the years I had been in the air force. We found a quiet place to sit and talk, and he filled me in on some air force gossip and brought me up to date on my family.

It was the escort officer's task to inform each POW of family changes—deaths that had occurred, crises he would have to face when he returned home. The only sadness he shared with me was the death of my favorite aunt. Gently, Jim told me that she died while I was imprisoned. Other POWs, however, had to face agonizing personal tragedies upon their release. Many men learned from their escort officers that their wives had divorced them, or a child had been killed or injured, or an elderly parent was seriously ill. My heart ached for the excruciating pain so many men had to face at home after the horror of their prison experience in Hanoi. For so many, the suffering was not yet over. Perhaps it would never be over.

The Red Cross had rigged a telephone link to the United States and every POW waited his turn to make a call home. The line stretched down the hall and, to me, looked endless. I was restless and anxious to talk to Shirley and the kids, and the waiting seemed interminable. Jim grabbed a big pot of coffee and took me into the lounge to continue our visit while I waited for the line to shorten.

For hours we talked. He told me about Shirley and her involvement with the POW-MIA organization, about Bobby and his college activities, about what was going on in my daughters' lives. We talked about old flying buddies and more about the air force; it was only when we saw shafts of sunlight shine into the room that we realized we had talked all night.

"I've got to call Shirley," I said, suddenly appalled that I hadn't made my call home yet.

"There's still quite a wait. Why don't we get breakfast first?" Jim suggested.

While I sat and drank coffee and ate six eggs, poor Shirley, thousands of miles away in Plano, Texas, paced the kitchen floor, waiting for the call she had been told to expect from me. All day, her closest friends had kept her company while she waited out the endless hours of February 12. They had all gone home around supper time, and another group had arrived to keep watch with her until I called. It was 10:00 P.M., Texas time, before we finally spoke.

It was hard to talk. My voice kept clogging with tears. Shirley too was struggling to talk. I tried talking to the girls, and we cried some more. I knew we would have to do our serious communicating in person. For now, it was enough to hear each others' voices. The only person missing was Bobby, who was away at school.

"What took you so long to call?" Shirley asked me, and I felt a little embarrassed.

"Jim Howerton and I sat up all night talking," I told her, explaining the lines waiting for the telephones and apologizing for being so late.

She forgave me instantly and then asked, "Is your hair gray?"

I looked across the room at Jim where he sat waiting for me. He'd told me to expect that question. Shirley's luscious brunette hair had turned nearly white over the past seven years, and she was worried about how I would react. That was her one fear about seeing me. Would I think she looked old and unattractive?

"Not really, Shirl," I answered her.

"Oh . . . oh, well, mine is pretty gray . . ."

"I don't care what color your hair is, honey . . ."

We were supposed to talk only about five minutes, but because almost everyone else had already used the phones, we were able to talk a lot longer. There was so much to say, but it was impossible to say it all.

In Dallas at the Channel 8 newsroom, Murphy Martin had kept a continual vigil, interrupting evening broadcasts since after news at 6:00 P.M. to tell viewers to stay tuned for an exclusive interview with the family of POW Colonel Johnson who had just been released from prison in Hanoi. He had called Shirley repeatedly during the evening to find out if she had heard from me. The plan was for Shirley and the girls to go down to the newsroom as soon as I had called. Of course, by the time we finished our conversation the evening news had begun. Shirley called to tell Murphy she wouldn't be coming down.

"There is still time for you to get here. Come on down," Murphy insisted. "We're not closing this program until we've heard all about Sam's phone call."

Shirley and the girls sat at the news desk with Murphy, and the cameras focused in on them. Shirley whispered to Murphy, "Don't ask the girls to say anything. They can't talk about their dad without crying. Especially don't ask Gini."

At the end of the interview, Murphy turned in his chair and asked Gini, "What do you think you're going to do when your dad gets home?"

Shirley cringed and then listened with surprise when Gini answered in a clear voice, "Just love him."

There wasn't a dry eye in the newsroom. Even the cameramen reached for their handkerchiefs.

Back in my hospital room, I discovered that I was scheduled for dental appointments, medical exams, and a psychiatric examination. The day passed quickly as I moved from one examining room to the other. The medical team at Clark decided to leave all treatment on my hand and arm and shoulders until I got home. Roy Madden, however, needed immediate attention. His leg was amputated that day.

The end of our first full day of freedom arrived and except for Roy, who was heavily sedated, most of the POWs on the hospital floor were restless and looking for something to do. We begged the nurses to let us have a party.

"We don't want any rowdiness on this floor," the nurse in charge told us sternly.

We began to plot an escape. We had friends and acquaintances who lived on the base — we'd go to one of the houses and celebrate our freedom. The floor nurses on the night shift were our willing accomplices.

The whole fourth floor was in on the break-out. It wouldn't be easy. There were guards everywhere. We couldn't even get on an elevator without our escorts or someone to give us permission unless we were going to the cafeteria or the lounge on the first floor. But if we could get to the first floor without arousing suspicion we could make our escape.

Three or four at a time, we rode the elevator to the first floor, headed toward the cafeteria, and then as soon as we were out of sight of the guard on duty we made a quick right turn and ducked into a room that opened onto a delivery loading dock. Thanks to compassionate nurses, cars arrived at the dock at five-minute intervals and drove us to a house on the base where we ate, exchanged stories and laughed together all night. It was our first successful escape. It wasn't until dawn that we realized we hadn't worked out a plan to get back into the hospital.

We had to get back in a hurry. Probably the staff and military were already looking for us.

"Let's just walk in the front door, get in the elevator, go back up to our rooms, and get into our beds," I suggested, too tired to wrangle with the problem.

We can't do that!" McKnight shouted.

"That's the only thing I can think of. Come on, George, what are they going to do to us anyway—throw us in jail?"

We piled into cars and drove to the hospital.

"Just don't stop," I told everyone as we walked toward the guard at the front desk. "Just keep going . . ."

We walked in the door, still wearing our hospital pajamas, and past the startled guard at the desk who stared for a long second and then finally hollered and hurried after us. We stepped onto the elevator and watched the doors close on the guard's confused expression. Up on the fourth floor, we all crawled into our beds and dozed before the nurses arrived to check on us. Not a word was ever said about our escape.

Our stay at Clark AFB was supposed to be four days, but we were impatient to get home, and we began lobbying to get out of there sooner. After only two days they began moving us out.

During the short stop at Travis AFB, an officer boarded the plane and told me I had a phone call from General Chappie James at the Pentagon.

"I just wanted to tell you welcome home, and thanks for the job you did over there, Colonel," he said. I knew he was referring to the coded messages I had sent home in my letters. He continued, "It would be best if you didn't mention anything about the tortures and treatment that you suffered from the North Vietnamese—for now. We want to get all the POWs out, and we don't want Hanoi to come up with any reason to stop the releases."

I wasn't sure I understood. Don't tell about the treatment? I didn't want to jeopardize any further releases, but based on Cat's comments and the way we understood our release, that information would have no impact on the release. Was that really the reason for the gag order?

"You'll no doubt be asked to make speeches and talk to various groups now that you're home, but the air force does not want you to mention the torture and abuse you experienced in prison. Please make this clear to the rest of the men on the plane with you."

He thanked me for my wife's contribution to the POW-MIA cause, and then he asked me not to talk about turncoats either. *Present a united front*, I thought. *No dissension among the returning POWs . . . all are heroes, brave and true.*

I hung up the phone feeling puzzled. On the plane during the last leg of the journey home to Texas, we talked about General James's command. I learned later that the men on the earlier flights home had been given the same order: Don't tell about the Vietnamese torture of American POWs, and don't make any references to the men who did not live up to the military code of honor.

These things bothered me. Perhaps the military really did fear that the Vietnamese would stop the release if we smeared them with stories of their awful violations of the Geneva Conventions. I could understand how the United States might be cautious about antagonizing them before all the POWs were released. But the men who had cooperated with

Letter from Sam to Shirley, 1972. Form provided by the Committee of Liaison for prisoners to write home on

File picture from Air Force, 1963, that sat framed on Shirley's dresser throughout Sam's seven-year imprisonment

Family picture, 1972, that Shirley sent Sam while he was in prison. *From left:* Shirley, Beverly, Bob, and Gini

American POWs at Hanoi's Gia Lam Airport, awaiting flights for
home, Feb. 13, 1973. Sam is fifth in line, head bowed, directly above
Vietnamese wearing hat

Sam acknowledging press and crowd at Sheppard Air Force Base,
Wichita Falls, Texas, February 17, 1973. U.S. Air Force photo

Sam greeting his family on the tarmac at Sheppard Air Force Base.
U.S. Air Force photo

Sam and Shirley together, after seven years apart, Sheppard Air Force Base. U.S. Air Force photo

Shirley speaking at press conference, Sheppard Air Force Base, February 27, 1973. U.S. Air Force photo

Col. Sam Johnson – back home, back in flight suit, back in the air.
Homestead Air Force Base, Florida, 1976

Sam and Shirley, 1978, at Homestead Air Force Base, where he was
wing commander

Sam with prison mug

Alcatraz Gang reunion aboard the U.S.S. *Yorktown,* 1981. *From left:* Pam and George Coker, Suzanne and George McKnight, Shirley and Sam Johnson, Louise and Jim Mulligan, Jim Stockdale, Jane and Jeremiah Denton

Sam Johnson with his family, 1991. *From left, back row:* Beverly Johnson, Jim Mulligan holding Susan Mulligan, Gini Johnson Mulligan
holding Jason Mulligan, Sam Johnson, Shirley Johnson, Bob Johnson, Cindy Johnson. *Front row:* Shannon Mulligan, Karen Mulligan,
Bobby Johnson, John Mulligan, Robyn Mulligan, and Beth Johnson.

the enemy—why should the rest of us cover for them and let them get away with their crimes?

I decided there would be time to deal with these concerns later. Right now I just wanted to savor the fact that I was in the air over Texas, approaching San Antonio where I would board an air-evac plane for the last leg of my trip to Wichita Falls where Shirley was waiting for me.

It was a short flight. I was nervous and excited. I lit up a cigarette and then decided not to smoke it. I crushed it out and never lit another one.

"Colonel Johnson, we'd like you to say something to the press," an officer asked as we made our final approach.

"It ought to be Robbie Risner; he's the senior officer," I answered.

"We'd like it to be a Texan, Sir."

I was back home in Texas, all right. I grinned and said, "I'd be proud to."

I tried to to gather my thoughts. I could see crowds waiting, held back by a line of security officers, but all I wanted to see was Shirley. I wiped my sweating hands on the pants of the new dress uniforms they had given us at Clark and tried to swallow the huge lump that was lodged in the back of my throat. *Would I be able to say anything?* I wondered.

I stepped off the plane into falling snow that lay three inches deep on the ground, and saluted the commander of the base. I looked out at the crowd and saw Shirley and the girls amid the masses of smiling faces. Someone thrust a microphone up close to my mouth, and with hot tears burning my cheeks, I said, "It's the greatest feeling in the world to be back on Texas soil. I want to thank God."

Suddenly all I could see were cameras. Voices from the press corps shouted at me from every direction.

"How to you feel, Colonel Johnson?"

"What's it like to be home after nearly seven years?"

"What are your plans for the future, Colonel Johnson?"

The security police strained to hold back the families for this short, formal press appearance. I was impatient too and finally swatted at a microphone that kept pressing toward my face.

The public relations officer spoke loudly: "I think we have had enough of this for now."

The press was slow to back away. Film crews pushed forward and cameras filled my vision. Finally Murphy Martin, standing by with the Channel 8 team, began bellowing and giving orders like a drill sergeant so that we could make our way through the melee to our families. The security line split wide open and the families spilled onto the tarmac. The first to reach me was my son, Bobby. In the next instant, the girls hurled themselves at me, and then Shirley was in my arms.

There were no words.

I stood and wept in the circle of my family. I clung to each of them as if letting go would bring down the world.

For a month, Shirley stayed with me in Wichita Falls while I underwent medical evaluation and treatment, but the children had to return to their respective schools. Doctors performed surgeries, one on my hand and one on my arm to try and straighten the arm and find the nerve that had been buried under the damaged bone. It was a futile search. They were able to do some reconstructive work; a tendon transfer gave me some limited use of one finger and thumb on my right hand, and a third operation later would restore some flexibility to my index finger. But there was nothing they could do that would allow me to be right-handed again.

I spent a week in intensive debriefing and interrogation by air force intelligence, listing all the names of POWs I had stored and giving them every scrap of information I had collected through the years in Hanoi. Probably the funniest session was the one with the base psychiatrist. The air force decided we all needed extensive counseling.

The doctor came into the room and asked in his most professional voice, "Can we talk?"

"Sure," I answered, and leaned my head against the back of the chair. In a few minutes I was fast asleep. The doctor was more than a little disturbed when he told Shirley I had fallen asleep while he was talking to me.

"He's exhausted." Shirley told him. "What he needs is rest, not counseling."

The next day, when the doctor returned, the same thing happened again. I felt a hand shaking my shoulder and awoke to see the distraught face of the psychiatrist peering down at me.

"Colonel Johnson, you keep falling asleep when I try to talk to you. Can you think of any reason for that?" he asked, pencil poised over his note pad.

"Your questions aren't stimulating enough, I guess."

The doctor walked out of the room. Later that day, another psychiatrist talked with me for a while and told the rest of the staff to stop bothering me.

The day I was finally allowed to go home to Plano was unlike any day I have ever experienced. The entire town turned out to welcome me. Brightly colored banners declaring love and welcome hung above the streets and along the storefronts; high school bands played along a parade route as I rode through the city. Everywhere I looked there were people shouting and cheering. It was a hero's welcome, and I was overcome by it.

The front yard of our home was filled with flowers and banners, and as soon as I climbed out of the car the neighborhood children ran toward me from every direction. Inside the house, there were more flowers and more banners draped over the doors, across the tops of windows, and above the fireplace mantel. The children tried to follow me in, but someone formed them into a line and guided them in the front door and then out at the back after they had greeted me. For hours, it seemed, I hugged and greeted children. We laughed and said we didn't think there were that many kids in the whole town. And then we realized they were running back around to the front to get in line again!

It was late at night before the house finally quieted and everyone went home. I dropped down on our old brown sofa in the living room and looked around at the familiar things that sat in their familiar places— Texas landscapes on the walls, family pictures here and there, along with other knickknacks and memorabilia Shirley and I had collected together through the years. In some ways, it was as if time had stood still in Plano, Texas.

I breathed deeply and looked across the room at Shirley. Her eyes filled with tears. I crossed the room quickly to take her in my arms. Out of the corner of my eye I caught sight of the huge, red rose arrangement made in the shape of Texas standing in the dining room. I was home! Whatever the world might be doing outside these walls, nothing could touch me here. The war was over.

# The Alcatraz Gang

George "Cagney" Coker married and remained in the navy for several years after his release. After his retirement, he moved to Virginia and accepted a position in government intelligence.

Jeremiah Denton served as the commandant of Armed Forces Staff College after his release. After retiring from the navy, he was elected to the United States Senate from his home state, Alabama. Now retired from public life, Jerry lives in Mobile, where he enjoys fishing and golf.

Harry "Ichabod" Jenkins retired in San Diego after a command tour in the navy. He still loves flying and is at work on his own experimental airplane.

Sam Johnson retired from the air force and returned to Texas in 1979 after graduating from the National War College and serving as wing commander in Florida and air division commander in New Mexico. From 1984 until 1991 he served as a representative in the Texas State House of Representatives. In 1991 he was elected to the United States Congress.

George McKnight married an air force nurse and served as air attaché in Canada for two years. He retired and now lives in Florida, where he flies for a cargo airline.

Jim Mulligan lives in Virginia Beach, Virginia, where he operates a business with his family. Though retired, he maintains close ties with the navy. In 1982, his son, Jim, married Colonel Johnson's daughter, Gini.

Nels Tanner now lives in Covington, Tennessee. He served a tour in Pensacola, Florida, before his retirement from the navy. He now flies for United Parcel Service.

Howie Rutledge retired from the navy and moved to Oklahoma where he entered the political arena. He was defeated by a small margin in his bid for the U.S. Congress. He died of cancer in 1985.

Bob Shumaker stayed in the navy to command Monterey Naval Station, the naval language school. After an assignment at the Pentagon, he retired and moved to North Dakota where he served as associate dean of the Center for Aerospace Sciences at the University of North Dakota. He is now a retired country gentleman living in Virginia.

Jim Stockdale served as commandant of the Naval War College after his release. He was later assigned to the position of commandant of the Citadel in Charleston, South Carolina. He returned to California to accept a post as a senior research fellow at the Hoover Institute on War, Revolution and Peace at Stanford University. He resides in Coronado, California.

*Captive Warriors* was composed into type on a Compugraphic digital phototypesetter in ten and one half point Plantin with one and one half points of spacing between the lines. Plantin was also selected for display. The book was designed by Cameron Poulter, typeset by Metricomp, Inc., printed offset by Thomson-Shore, Inc., and bound by John H. Dekker & Sons, Inc. The paper on which this book is printed carries acid-free characteristics for an effective life of at least three hundred years.

TEXAS A&M UNIVERSITY PRESS : COLLEGE STATION